Praise for

WE REFUSE

Named a best book of the year by *Smithsonian* * *Kirkus Reviews* * *Chicago Review of Books* * *The Emancipator* * *Ms.*

Winner of the Organization of American Historians' Darlene Clark Hine Award

Winner of the Massachusetts Book Award for Nonfiction

Winner of the Association of Black Women Historians' Letitia Woods Brown Book Prize

Finalist for the African American Intellectual History Society's Pauli Murray Book Prize

"Compelling and often counterintuitive." —*New York Times*

"Eye-opening." —Gayle King, *CBS Mornings*

"Illuminating, informative, and ultimately, hopeful." —*Minneapolis Star-Tribune*

"Kellie Carter Jackson has outdone herself with this masterfully researched and endlessly readable exploration—and celebration—of Black refusal to racism and oppression." —*Ms.*

"Enthralling.... A fascinating array of histories that highlight the ingeniousness, efficacy, and relatability of Black political maneuvering across several centuries of oppression....By astutely delineating how Black resistance strategies have always existed on a spectrum between the binary of nonviolence vs. violence, Carter Jackson demolishes an unnecessarily rigid distinction. The result is an invigorating paradigm shift."

—*Publishers Weekly* (starred review)

"Urgent and uncompromising."

—*Kirkus Reviews* (starred review)

"A deft and compelling history of protest against white supremacy that gives the use of force due recognition." —*BookBrowse*

"Unsparing, erudite, and incisive, *We Refuse* is an insurgent history. Kellie Carter Jackson has produced a book that is every bit as urgent as the subject matter she so brilliantly writes about."

—Jelani Cobb, staff writer, *The New Yorker*

"Kellie Carter Jackson is fearless. She is not afraid to tell you want she thinks, share what she knows, or challenge prevailing wisdom. *We Refuse* is proof. She taps the wellsprings of memory, archives, oral histories, literature, imagination, and personal experience to tell a very Black story of armed resistance, strategic retreat, unbreakable resolve, and joyous rapture. Reading this book will cause discomfort in some folks, provoke cheers in others. But I doubt anyone will be able to put it down."

—Robin D. G. Kelley, author of *Freedom Dreams*

"What does it mean to use violence as a means of resistance? How has violent resistance shaped Black radical freedom movements, despite the popular notion that peaceful pleas for humanity or moderate negotiations with white supremacist oppression are the only path to racial justice? In *We Refuse*, Kellie Carter Jackson provides a cogent, provocative, and ultimately inspiring reevaluation of how violence—in all its forms—has been used by Black people to resist slavery and its afterlives. Both radical history and racial reckoning, this book is sure to become a canonical text. Through extensive research and brilliant analysis of Black communities and our politics, *We Refuse* is a timely rewriting of the African American past, one that forces us to reframe our discussion of our beloved civil rights icons, our assumptions about our politics, and our collective understanding of what it means to resist."

—Kerri K. Greenidge, author of *The Grimkes*

"From one of our generation's most exciting historians, *We Refuse* changes the way we understand the contours and legacy of the Black freedom struggle. Blending fierce analysis with touching personal vignettes, Kellie Carter Jackson's essential new book enhances the most pressing debates of our time and will stay with readers long after they finish."

—Elizabeth Hinton, author of *America on Fire*

"Kellie Carter Jackson tells a nuanced and textured story about how African Americans, over many centuries, have refused racism by any means necessary. Her book thoughtfully reveals that nonviolence is just one of the many strategies Black people have used to assert their humanity and achieve full equality in this country. It is a must-read for all of us committed to understanding and, hopefully, joining the long freedom struggle."

—Salamishah Tillet, Pulitzer Prize–winning critic

WE REFUSE

Also by Kellie Carter Jackson

Force and Freedom: Black Abolitionists and the Politics of Violence

Reconsidering Roots: Race, Politics, and Memory (coeditor)

WE REFUSE

A FORCEFUL HISTORY OF BLACK RESISTANCE

KELLIE CARTER JACKSON

SEAL PRESS

New York

Seal Press

Hachette Book Group
1290 Avenue of the Americas, New York, NY 10104
www.sealpress.com
@sealpress

Printed in the United States of America

First Edition: June 2024
First Trade Paperback Edition: November 2025

Published by Seal Press, an imprint of Hachette Book Group, Inc. The Seal Press name and logo is a registered trademark of the Hachette Book Group.

The Hachette Speakers Bureau provides a wide range of authors for speaking events. To find out more, go to hachettespeakersbureau.com or email HachetteSpeakers@hbgusa.com.

Seal books may be purchased in bulk for business, educational, or promotional use. For more information, please contact your local bookseller or the Hachette Book Group Special Markets Department at special.markets@hbgusa.com.

The publisher is not responsible for websites (or their content) that are not owned by the publisher.

The Library of Congress has cataloged the hardcover edition as follows:

Names: Carter Jackson, Kellie, author.
Title: We refuse : a forceful history of Black resistance / by Kellie Carter Jackson.
Other titles: Forceful history of Black resistance
Description: First edition. | New York : Seal Press, 2024. | Includes bibliographical references and index.
Identifiers: LCCN 2023046379 | ISBN 9781541602908 (hardcover) | ISBN 9781541602915 (ebook)
Subjects: LCSH: African Americans—Civil rights—History. | African Americans—Politics and government. | Government, Resistance to—United States—History. | White supremacy (Social structure)—United States—History. | Racism against Black people—United States—History. | United States—Race relations—History.
Classification: LCC E185.61 .J1515 2024 | DDC 323.1196/073—dc23/eng/20240118
LC record available at https://lccn.loc.gov/2023046379

ISBNs: 9781541602908 (hardcover), 9781541602915 (ebook), 9781541601598 (paperback)

LSC-C

Printing 1, 2025

To my three free, beautiful Black children,
William, Josephine, and Charlotte.
You bear the names of ancestors, abolitionists, and activists.

"We are the children of those who refused to die."

CONTENTS

PREFACE

In December 1934, W. E. B. Du Bois completed what I believe is the crowning jewel of his scholarship, *Black Reconstruction in America, 1860–1880*. With over seven hundred pages of forceful writing, the book is a sweeping narrative that centers the contributions of Black men and women who fought to liberate the enslaved during the Civil War and, afterward, to reconstruct the United States as a democracy that would uphold and protect workers and their labor.[1] On the first page, Du Bois writes a letter to his readers, a preface of sorts, in which he claims this is a book for those who believe Black people are human beings. "If [the reader] believes that the Negro in America and in general is an average and ordinary human being, who under [a] given environment develops like other human beings, then he will read this story and judge it by the facts adduced. If, however, he regards the Negro as a distinctly inferior creation, who can never successfully take part in modern civilization and whose emancipation and enfranchisement were gestures against nature, then he will need something more than the sort of facts that I have set down."[2] In America, Du Bois asserts, the interplay between these ideas has given shape to every historical moment and movement affecting Black people. When Americans argue over who should have access to schools, jobs, food, clean water, voting, health care, or justice, we are essentially wrestling with the idea of Black humanity as either a fact, an aspiration, or an aberration. Du Bois was not interested in persuading people of Black humanity. Neither am I.

This is a book about the ways Black people in America have responded to white supremacy—including through force. The intrinsic belief in Black humanity is essential to understanding Black resistance to racial terror. While many stories of resistance involve extraordinary courage, most are about ordinary Black folk demanding basic provisions or protections. This book pushes against and beyond the dominant civil rights narrative that conditions us to see Black people as worthy actors because of their commitment to nonviolence. Like Du Bois, I am going to tell this story with the implicit assumption that Black people are ordinary human beings. In a world where speaking about Black Lives Matter is polemical, I am fully aware that this will greatly reduce my audience. Moreover, my audience will likely be additionally curtailed by the fact that I am writing about how Black people respond to white violence and refuse white supremacy.

Black liberation is actually not revolutionary for Black people, but it is to white people. To white readers, my writing might sound extreme, but that's because most, if not all, white people are intensely invested in maintaining their position. In *What Then*

Must We Do?, Leo Tolstoy wrote, "I sit on a man's back choking him and making him carry me, and yet assure myself and others that I am sorry for him and wish to lighten his load by all means possible . . . except by getting off his back."[3] The formula for full humanity and equality is not complicated. It's not a differential equation or even multiplication; it's *subtraction*. White people must be willing to relinquish and divest themselves from power structures that benefit only them. But often those in power cannot imagine change that is not amenable to their position or granted without a permission slip. *We Refuse* is not a permission slip, but it does show a way of winning equality and equity. Black liberation is possible. It can be accomplished and, equally important, sustained.

But just because something is possible and sustainable does not mean it is easy. In this book, I resist the urge to solve problems with three-point plans, slogans, DIY instructions, or how-to solutions. It combats the flimsy arguments that racism can be solved with a good idea, a kind word, or a stiff upper lip. Slapping "antiracist" on a work as though it can be certified and guaranteed like an organic fruit is a ruse. The work of liberation will not be solved or spearheaded by one person. The work of liberation will be collective, and once the work is concluded, it will not have to be done again.

Dear reader, in the spirit of W. E. B. Du Bois, I am writing to you not only with a belief in Black humanity but also with a belief that in the pursuit of freedom, courtesy is not a virtue. The Irish poet and playwright Oscar Wilde was right when he argued, "The worst slave-owners were those who were kind to their slaves, and so prevented the horror of the system being realized by those who suffered from it, and understood by those who contemplated it, so, in the present state of things . . . the people who do the most harm are the people who try to do the most good."[4] Liberation is hard for white supremacists and even harder for people who prefer to be benevolent masters. Many white people believe that if they are "nice," they can create a better world. While it may seem rational to prefer being a benevolent master to being a malevolent master, it's even more rational to ask why the system of slavery is presumed to be a requirement—that is, why does there have to be a master at all? In this sense, being nice is not only ineffective but dangerous to Black lives. Courteous words such as "please," "thank you," "you're welcome," and "excuse me" are empty. We should not believe in nice masters any more than we believe that white superiority is the natural order of things.

Racism in America teaches a prevailing scarcity, that there are not enough resources for everyone. It does not teach that that scarcity is created by white people hoarding unearned advantages and resources. This is the truth: We will not run out of homes if everyone has a house. We will not run out of jobs if everyone is properly educated. Homelessness is not required. Failing schools are not necessary. In a democracy, voting is not a privilege but a primary feature. Mass incarceration is not merely unfortunate but unjust. *We Refuse* calls bovine scatology on artificial shortages, white fears, good intentions, and nice masters. On this journey, we will refuse lies and resist the status quo. Together, headed in a new direction, we will walk, run, limp, or even skip toward the light.

INTRODUCTION

My Ancestor's Refusal

My great-grandmother Arnesta was about nine years old when she stepped on a rusty nail. Not long after, infection began to set in—likely tetanus. Her mother, Mary Bullard, was frantic. Arnesta was her only child, and she was going to lose her if she did not act fast. Mary sent Arnesta to the only doctor she knew, a white man who lived in a big house on the other side of town. The white doctor offered to help, but in exchange Arnesta would have to live with him for the rest of her life, working for his family. Growing up Black and a girl in 1915 left her vulnerable. In rural Alabama, during one of the worst periods of race relations in America, these were the detestable but predictable terms of engagement. Mary, panic stricken, agreed. Thankfully, Mary's mother,

Martha, a former slave, intervened and refused the doctor's proposal. She picked up her ailing granddaughter and took her home. There, Martha administered every natural remedy at her disposal. Arnesta survived, but for the rest of her life, she walked with a limp. Whatever space she entered, whatever path she took, she was marked by an imprint of racial violence.

My mother told me this story when I was a child to explain my great-grandmother's limp. It was not until I was an adult that I realized that rusty nail was not the root of her trauma. This story has always gripped me, for several reasons. First, Arnesta was a child, her mother's only child. How could a doctor refuse a dying child medical care when it was in his ability to heal her? He abandoned his oath, *Primum non nocere*—"First, do no harm." Second, nearly fifty years out from slavery, white folks still felt entitled to Black labor and life in perpetuity. Clearly, everything was transactional to this white doctor. Built into the deal he offered was a lifetime of servitude and likely physical and sexual abuse.

White supremacy in America can be summed up by these two diabolical options: live a life in bondage, or refuse and limp.[1] To be Black in America is to limp. My great-grandmother's gait had nothing to do with biology and everything to do with power—the power of the white doctor to neglect, and attempt to exploit, a little Black girl who came to him for help. But this book is not about the white doctor or the millions of white people like him. In many ways, this book is about my great-great-great-grandmother's response: her refusal. It is about how she saved my great-grandmother. It is about resistance to white violence that seeks to steal, kill, and destroy Black lives. Martha did not just say no, she said *never*.

Refusal is a forceful no. It is a no that is packed full of energy and meaning. "We refuse" is similar to Black colloquialisms such as "Nah." "Nope." "Not today, Satan." "Oh hell no." Refusal is about rejection. It abhors oppression and insists on setting the terms for how humanity should be understood and treated with dignity, respect, and decency. Nonverbally, refusal is a halting hand, a pointed finger waving from side to side, or a powerful raised fist. It is a barrier that prevents oppressed people from being consumed. Refusal can be enacted by an individual, but at its heart, refusal is collective, which is why the sentiment behind the phrase "We refuse" persists among subjugated people and is a key refrain in Black feminist politics as well as Native politics.[2] Black women have refused to be invisible or small. Native people have refused deceptive treaties, assimilationist labels, and even geographical boundaries. This entire book consists of examples of Black people refusing lies, violence, theft, mockery, or second-class citizenship. It shows how our refusal denies whiteness and white supremacy their power and unearned authority.

While on a trip to Ghana, I traveled to the Gold Coast to visit Elmina, one of the largest slave dungeons built by the Portuguese. Just adjacent to a cell in which they kept rebellious Africans, who were left to die a slow death, is a plaque that reads, "We are the children of those who refused to die." Yes, Black Americans are the descendants of African warriors and soldiers, but we are also the descendants of ordinary African commoners who refused to be bound, broken, and dehumanized.

Since the sixteenth century, Black history has been a history of refusal. From the moment slave ships left the coast of Africa for a new world, Black people refused to die or chose death rather than living in vile conditions created by their white captors. In the seventeenth century Queen Ana Nzinga of the kingdom of Ndongo, present-day Angola, refused the terms and broken treaties of the Portuguese and fought for decades against the enslavement of her people. In the eighteenth century, Elizabeth

Freeman, an enslaved woman living in Massachusetts, upon hearing the Massachusetts Constitution read aloud, refused to be denied her right to liberty. She took to the courts, sued for her freedom, and won. In the nineteenth century, Nat Turner's rebellion in 1831 was a collective refusal. During the uprising, enslaved people killed nearly sixty white men, women, and children. They killed their enslavers because they refused to be kept in bondage. They killed white children because they refused to let them perpetuate the system by growing up to become slaveholders. Enslaved people refused to be enslaved, even when their efforts to gain their freedom failed.[3]

Refusal is Black culture. It is our anthem, a mantra, a way of being, present in the novelty and genius of our vernacular, in the newspapers and literature we create to tell our stories, in the drum, banjo, and bass that permeate our music, in the vocals that refuse to be timid, diluted, or replicated. It is present also in our willingness to welcome, forgive, be hospitable, and care. We refuse and build ourselves up.

We Refuse offers a fundamental shift in how we understand and talk about Black people's responses to white supremacy. When it comes to progressive change in America, what matters most is what is effective, not what will appease white people. Nonviolence is the only form of Black resistance to white violence that has appeased white people or been approved by them. But nonviolence is not the only possible response to white violence. I believe we must rethink nonviolence. For too long, nonviolence has been understood as a "turn the other cheek" praxis. Nonviolence is based on the principle that one can morally persuade their oppressor to have a pang of consciousness or conviction regarding their wrongness. Nonviolence uses compassion, empathy, and morality to compel another's humanity.

But I take issue with how the binary of nonviolence and violence has controlled the praxis and narrative by which the oppressed combat their oppression. Nonviolence on its own is not at all expansive enough to rectify the harm that has been caused by racism. While Martha's remedy might fall under the category of nonviolence, since no one physically harmed the doctor for making his proposal, my ancestor's refusal was complex, and it is too reductive to throw it into a pile labeled "nonviolence." Furthermore, promoting and celebrating nonviolence as the only acceptable form of resistance is rife with handicaps. I am suggesting a much broader range of tools. One cannot build or even dismantle an entire house with only a hammer.

My ancestor's refusal was fundamental to her granddaughter's survival. First, Martha refused the doctor's offer. Then she sought every natural remedy she possessed to stop the infection and heal Arnesta's body. She did not plead or bargain with the doctor. She did not try to convince him that Arnesta was a child or human. Her refusal, remedy, and protection transcended violence or nonviolence. She took the doctor out of the equation. The doctor had no compassion for the child. He could not be morally persuaded. Violence against him would have been a death sentence for them, but nonviolence would also have ensured my great-grandmother's death. White supremacy and anti-Blackness are always violent, and the constant refrain is for the harmed to forgive violence, forget injury, and forfeit their agency. We have more than two options. Black people need not choose between certain death or a life in bondage. We have, throughout history, approached such violence with an array of responses and refusals.

Since the civil rights movement, nonviolence has been the only tool to gain prominence within the activist community and dominate the historical narrative, to the exclusion of all others.

Dr. Martin Luther King Jr. theorized his six principles of nonviolence in his 1958 book *Stride Toward Freedom*. Drawing inspiration from the Indian anticolonial activist Mohandas Gandhi, he described nonviolence as a way of life, a mode of radical love that seeks to defeat injustice and cultivate friendship and reconciliation to create the "Beloved Community." For King, nonviolence meant embracing "suffering without retaliation."[4] This unearned and unavenged suffering would educate and transform the oppressor. He believed, "Nonviolence is a powerful and just weapon. Indeed, it is a weapon unique in history, which cuts without wounding and ennobles the man who wields it."[5] In sum, King argued that nonviolence is courageous, seeks friendship and understanding, seeks to defeat injustice not people, promotes love over hate, and ultimately believes in the triumph of justice.

Many of King's beliefs have been diluted at best or perverted at worst. American society presents a whitewashed nonviolence that often speaks nothing of white supremacy, capitalism, or militarism. I often find that King's beliefs were not wrong, merely incomplete. They do not always encompass the full range of human responses that people engage in, particularly in the face of death. King's six principles do not address action steps for oppressors, only the oppressed. They do not address reparations—which may not be purely monetary—or how to repair the harm of white supremacy. How do people heal, not after breaking a bone or stepping on a rusty nail, but after losing a loved one, land, wealth, and health, and after psychological trauma? And in a spiritual and secular sense, King's principles do not address repentance. What does it look like to turn from the ways of an oppressor? What does it look like to relinquish power? These missing principles are what activists today are still trying to navigate—not how we employ Black harm for transformation, but how we mitigate harm.

Today, nonviolence has dwindled down to marches. When a Black woman, man, or child is killed by racial violence, people march. But marches do not keep Black people alive. Marches honor the dead. Marches are public mourning, not public policy. And whenever racial altercations gain traction in the media, pundits and politicians alike are quick to point to King as the model for doing protests "the right way." After racial violence results in a death, the media's question is "Will protests be peaceful?" Or, an even more egregious question, "Does the victim's family forgive the perpetrator?" Marches, forgiveness, and peaceful protest are all shorthand for callbacks to King. But nonviolence today means something different than what King intended. Now it is a performance of passive power that almost ensures those in power never structurally change. White supremacy does not believe in nonviolence because it does not believe in Black humanity. To white supremacy, nonviolence is a scarecrow, and racists rest like crows on its outstretched arms. Nonviolence alone could never sufficiently frighten or endanger political, economic, or social institutions.

Those against the practices of nonviolence, such as anarchist Peter Gelderloos, critique nonviolence as "ineffective, racist, statist, patriarchal, tactically and strategically inferior to militant activism, and deluded."[6] Gelderloos sees nonviolence as unable to achieve its purpose of a "Beloved Community." He contends that nonviolence promotes white complacency and state power (think of police departments as mini armies) and puts too much faith in morality's ability to convict oppressors. For some, Gelderloos's critique has a great deal of truth in it. For too long, scholars and activists have promoted tactics that have lost their potency or cachet. But Gelderloos is wrong to dismiss nonviolence entirely. The truth is, it's complicated. Another way of thinking about it may be through connecting the works of Audre Lorde and Frantz Fanon.

For some, Lorde is most famous for her essay "The Master's Tools Will Never Dismantle the Master's House." The title is a declaration that rings true. Oppression and exploitation will never dismantle white supremacy but only perpetuate more harm under different power structures. But what if the master's tool is nonviolence? Fanon would argue that force and violence are required because the master promotes nonviolence, cloaked in morality, as the only acceptable form of protest in order to maintain their power and authority. The work of resistance must be clever. Throughout history Black people have proven that the strategies underlying many of their claims to progress fall somewhere between nonviolence and revolutionary violence.

Violence is more than the engine of white supremacy. I understand violence as an entire ecosystem. Violence is a tool employed to harm, deny, restrict, neglect, separate, and deceive. Notably, it can be the means to various ends—it can both enforce white supremacy and subvert it, as when it's used to overthrow a government, for self-defense, or in support of withdrawing one's labor (meaning it disrupts capitalist productivity). Violence is slavery and segregation. Violence is theft and hoarding. Violence is replacing the truth with conspiracy. Violence is rupture and separation. Violence occupies the space of a system, an ideology, a culture, and a language. Violence is subjugation, which can take many forms. Black people spend much of their lives, if not their entire lives, combatting, addressing, avoiding, and subverting white violence.

We Refuse examines some of the ways that Black people have successfully engaged white supremacy beyond nonviolence: revolution, protection, force, flight, and joy. I readily admit that even these broad categories are not exhaustive. But in *We Refuse*, I hope to uncover them as a set of possibilities among many. One of my favorite films is *Burn!*, directed by Gillo Pontecorvo. Released in

1969, it tells the fictional story of a slave rebellion and stars Marlon Brando as the lead antagonist. In the film, the formerly enslaved rebel José Dolores declares, "It is better to know where to go and not know how, than how to go and not know where." The line has always stuck with me. African Americans have always known where we are going: toward freedom. Our struggle is in how to get there. Conversely, white people remain on a well-trodden path to destruction, often without a clue or a care about where it might lead. *We Refuse* aims to point people away from destruction and dead ends. Throughout these five chapters, I offer historical markers and stories that show us where the country has been and hopefully direct us toward possible paths forward. And, critically, there are many such paths. My great-great-great-grandmother refused the metaphorical fork in the road. She stomped out a new trail for Arnesta. She rejected dehumanization. I will examine the remedies of revolution, protection, force, and flight, but also the potency of joy. I contend that the opposite of violence is not nonviolence. In America, the opposite of violence is the fullness of Black humanity bound together with joy.

Understanding a different path forward means asking different questions and being willing to accept hard solutions. Let's start with asking different questions. Rarely, if ever, are activists asked about the violence of whiteness. The public is more consumed with how Black folks will find liberation *only* as it relates to nonviolence. Shifting these conversations is imperative. Scholar and activist Angela Davis was asked a similar question by a reporter regarding the use of violence. In 1972, during her incarceration, Davis was filmed for an interview that has become iconic. She wore a rust-colored turtleneck and matching pants with her signature large afro.[7] The journalist asked, "How do you get there [to freedom]? You get there with confrontation? Violence?" Davis nearly laughed. "Oh, is that the question you are asking?" She shifted in her seat to address him—or, really, school him. She told him that the media was asking the wrong questions. "When you talk about revolution, most people think [of] violence without realizing that the real content of any kind of revolutionary thrust lies in the goals you are striving for, not in the way you reach them." *We Refuse* will not question choices so much as examine the intended outcomes of those choices. If the goal is safety, the public should not ask why oppressed people used force but whether force helped keep them safe. If the goal is citizenship, it is less important whether Black people drove or flew to another place and more important whether they got to a place where they could belong. Again, the question is not *how* but *what*.

"On the other hand," Davis continued in her interview, "because of the way this society is organized, because of the violence that exists on the surface of every level, everywhere, you have to expect there are going to be such explosions. You have to expect things like that as reactions." She reasoned that for a Black person experiencing constant police brutality and racial profiling, "ask[ing] me whether I approve of violence . . . doesn't make any sense at all. You ask me if I approve of guns. . . . I grew up in Birmingham, Alabama." Bull Connor was the Birmingham commissioner of police safety, and he *encouraged* violence against Black Americans. Davis's childhood friends were killed in the bombing of the 16th Street Baptist Church. One of the four little girls killed was a student of Davis's mother's. Accordingly, when someone asked Davis about violence, she found it appalling and incredible because it meant that the person asking the question had no idea "what Black people have experienced in this country from the time the first Black person was kidnapped from the shores of Africa."[8] It is impossible to write a book that offers a critical analysis on racial violence and does not interrogate white supremacy as the lead perpetrator.

Most extremist violence in America comes from the political right.[9] In a report by the Anti-Defamation League, researchers found that between 2012 and 2021, out of 450 murders committed by political extremists, 75 percent involved white right-wing extremists and over 55 percent were connected to white supremacist groups.[10] The fear of white right-wing extremists committing acts of violence is prevalent and on the rise. For too long the GOP not only has refused to confront such violent ideology and practice but has become comfortable with it. In some cases, violence has become a clarion call. The American public demands that people of color remain nonviolent but fails to ask the more important question, "Why are white Americans so violent?" The responsibility of nonviolence should be on the oppressors, not the oppressed. An even more poignant question is the one my professor Manning Marable posed to me in graduate school at Columbia University: "Is oppression required for the preservation of white institutions?" If our answer is yes, then our work is to dismantle such institutions and replace them, in the belief that justice should be the foundation of power.

In 1984, NPR journalist Terry Gross interviewed Bishop Desmond Tutu just before he won the Nobel Peace Prize.[11] Gross asked Tutu about violence as it related to dismantling South African apartheid. Tutu stated that while he was not a pacifist, he was "deeply committed to peace." Yet he reminded Gross that in South Africa, "the primary violence [was] the violence of the apartheid system." He went on to detail this violence:

The government has uprooted settled Black communities and dumped them as if they were rubbish in poverty-stricken areas. . . .

I'm a bishop in the Church of God, I am fifty-two years of age, and maybe one or two people might be willing to be persuaded to think that I am reasonably responsible. I can't vote in my country, and yet a child of eighteen, because he or she is white, can vote. Now, I mean, how do any people justify that kind of denial of access to the political decision-making processes? It is the violence of the migratory labor system which undermines Black family life so sharply. It is the violence of an inferior education system. It is the violence that makes children starve in a country which is a net exporter of food. You know, I mean, and what we are really talking about is not so much a nonviolent struggle at home, because it is nonsense to talk about violence and nonviolence when children were killed as they were. It is, can we keep that—the level of violence—to the barest minimum?

As we also saw in Angela Davis's interview, white people cannot understand how incredibly infuriating and offensive it is to ask Black people about nonviolence amid such conditions.

In the interview, Gross also asked Tutu about his thoughts on Dr. Martin Luther King Jr., civil disobedience, religious tenets, and morality's collective influence on South Africa. Tutu described civil disobedience from the inception of the African National Congress. He contended, "In 1912, when the African National Congress was founded, it used peaceful means such as protests, petitions, deputations. And we even had a passive resistance campaign and commitment to using peaceful means." Tutu went on, "But then what happened? In 1960, our people were protesting peacefully against the pass laws. And on the twenty-first of March, 1960, at Sharpeville, sixty-nine of them were shot dead by the police. And many of them were shot in the back running away, clearly showing that they were not intent on harming the police." Then he spoke of the killing of schoolchildren in Soweto by the police. On June 16, 1976, sixteen children were singing in the streets of Soweto and protesting their inferior education when the police attacked them.

Tutu claimed that Dr. Martin Luther King Jr. could point to morality as a tool for his movement in America. The violence of colonization and white supremacy tugged at people's heartstrings there. But in South Africa, they did not have the backing of the state or religious morality to support their protests.[12] For Tutu, what shifted the movement were economic sanctions and international pressure. The truth was that civil disobedience and protest alone were insufficient, perhaps grossly insufficient, to combat apartheid. While sanctions can be read as a nonviolent tactic, they are essentially an economic force used to squeeze bad actors and restrict and penalize those directly or even indirectly complicit with an oppressive system. If violence is a tool designed to harm, then even economic sanctions, which do not directly cause bloodshed, can be understood as a form of violence. Certainly we would understand it as such if sanctions were applied to the oppressed.

Peaceful resistance during apartheid is nonsense, even to a child. Tutu recalled a moment when he was speaking in a meeting about peaceful change.[13] After the meeting, a twelve-year-old boy approached him. "Bishop Tutu, I heard what you said. Do you believe it?" Tutu said he began to hem and haw and evade the question. The boy, sensing his inability to answer him straight on, issued a challenge: "Can you people, with your eloquent talk about peaceful change, show us what you have achieved with your talk? And we will show you what we have gained with a few stones." The boy was referring to the Soweto Uprising of 1976, in which over twenty thousand South African schoolchildren protested the introduction of Afrikaans as the language of instruction in Black and Bantu schools. Hundreds of children were shot at or wounded, and sixteen were killed, by the police. The violence went on for three days and drew international attention. Thousands of children were harmed, but even though they were outmatched by police forces, they physically fought back and won the world's support. Tutu admitted that he did not have any evidence to show him. Yet the boy could point to the fact that Afrikaans was no longer the compulsory language of instruction. He could point to new school buildings that the South African government had put up as a result of all their activism. He could point to the fact that the South African government was putting more money into Black education than they had before, largely in response to what the young people had done. Tutu conceded, "And so in some ways, he was right." Even a child understood the efficacy of force and the limitations of nonviolence.

These are the kinds of hard conversations *We Refuse* seeks to foster. We must be honest about what actions produce structural results and what actions produce symbolic results. Nonviolence does not adequately capture all of the responses to white supremacy that have been effective at forcing new systems and ways of thinking that empower all people. This book reframes the conversation away from the rightness or wrongness of nonviolence and violence and instead focuses on what works by placing Black resistance and liberation at the center. I ask, How have the oppressed responded to their oppressor, and how should they respond? How do the powerless procure power? White violence is the perennial stumbling block to racial progress in America, but this is not a book about how white supremacy has impacted the Black community. Rather, it illustrates the Black community's response to racial violence. *We Refuse* makes a case for how we might understand Black humanity and rage in the pursuit of freedom.

Our culture's fixation on nonviolence has caused us to miss entire histories of Black responses to white supremacy. In fact, many of the forms of resistance we see today are built on more radical strategies than those in power wish us to know. Not every solution to racism involves a march, a hashtag, or a speech. In fact, most solutions do not require public relations.

The idea of nonviolent, peaceful resistance has always had its critics. George Jackson, a Black Panther Party member, critiqued King's belief in nonviolence as a hopeful but false ideal. Jackson contended, "It presupposes the existence of compassion and a sense of justice on the part of one's adversary. When this adversary has everything to lose and nothing to gain by exercising justice and compassion, his reaction can only be negative."[14] Whiteness is not compelled by suffering but consumed with inflicting it. White supremacy, at its core, in its symptoms and indirect manifestations, is violence. Building on Toni Morrison's famous 1975 Portland State University speech, in which she said that "racism is a distraction . . . because it keeps you from doing your work,"[15] literary critic Sandy Alexandre described the anti-Black racism that arises from white supremacy as "not merely a thorn in a person's side. It's also a suffocating knee on a person's neck."[16] Alexandre moved beyond the nuisance of racism to its equally basic tenet: "Racism is, in fact, also a serial killer. This is not sensationalism. This is not hyperbole." We can very easily find out that white people's racism has killed Emmett Till, Addie Mae Collins, Cynthia Wesley, Carole Robertson, Carol Denise McNair, Fred Hampton, Eleanor Bumpurs, Henry Dumas, Skye Mockabee, Amadou Diallo, Aiyana Stanley-Jones, Oscar Grant, Tamir Rice, Korryn Gaines, Freddie Gray, Sandra Bland, Eric Garner, Philando Castile, Atatiana

Jefferson, George Floyd, Breonna Taylor, and many more. For Alexandre, anti-Black racism has been on a killing spree. And during the summer of 2020, she argued, racism was so distracting, "it deprioritized a whole global pandemic—the gall." From the photographs of public lynchings to the selfies taken at the US Capitol on January 6, 2021, racism has been so flagrantly murderous that it has absolutely no qualms about being caught on camera—in fact, it will pose for it. In the altered chorus of a Negro spiritual, Alexandre asked, "Were you there when racism serial-killed Black people? Sometimes it causes me to tremble, tremble, tremble."[17]

White supremacy wreaks havoc on the lives of Black people and strips the souls of white people. One might convincingly argue that white supremacy renders white humanity void, bereft. Enslaved to a myth of their inherent goodness and innocence, white supremacy is in bondage to the absurd idea that white people are, if not divine, elevated human beings. White people are not inherently violent, but, in America and beyond, they cannot be separated from violence. The work of separating white people from the violent supremacist self of whiteness must encompass severance economically, politically, and socially. Freedom work is not reforming a system that exists but demolishing it and its toxic materials and developing a completely different world. Liberation is forceful and often violent, but that does not make freedom illegitimate; it simply makes it hard.

Too often we have exclusively examined white supremacy's terrorism against Black lives, from slavery to massacres and mob attacks. We know well the harm that has been inflicted on Black people in their attempts to live free and full lives. Historically, we have touted nonviolence as the appropriate, acceptable, and most suitable form of resistance. And yet, freedom—that is to say, full citizenship and enfranchisement—has not yet arrived for Black

Americans. When civil rights lawyer Bryan Stevenson eloquently stated that the opposite of poverty is not wealth but justice, we failed to realize that justice is costly, even more so than wealth. Justice is not about profits and payments but about forfeiting an identity and position that are grounded in domination. White people cannot understand themselves or their relationships to others without white supremacy. This lack of understanding explains why there is so little scholarship in this area. White scholars have ignored or dismissed a rigorous discourse in violence because to engage would be to indict themselves.

My ancestor's refusal was found not just in her no but in her remedy. A remedy is a treatment for disease. It is a concoction of sorts, organic, homegrown. It is not a cure. There is no cure for racism, and anyone who tells you they can end racism is selling snake oil. There is always someone who "won't do right," who refuses to stop harm. Often and wrongly attributed to Alexis de Tocqueville, "Americans are so enamored of equality that they would rather be equal in slavery than unequal in freedom."[18] Yet remedies can still be potent. They can stave off death and draw out poison. The poor and oppressed will always limp—in America and worldwide. Our gait is forever changed. But healing is possible. Healing is justice.

In this book, I follow five remedies by which Black people have responded to white supremacy: revolution, protection, force, flight, and joy. Each is a response to the violence of white supremacy, and each is distinct. No path is static. Each works when it builds on the others and informs how we might think about confronting white violence and dismantling structural racism holistically. A deep, nuanced conversation on the history and implications of white violence is overdue. We have failed to examine the violence that Black people are responding to in their communities. We have dismissed the rock thrower, the looter, the graffiti artist, and the poet. Not all Black responses are violent, but not all Black responses are nonviolent either. Throughout history, Black people have employed a plethora of tools to combat anti-Blackness. These categories do the work of expanding nonviolence and in some cases give credence to violence when it works.

Revolution is the clarion call of nearly all Black freedom struggles. What is a revolution? What does it entail? What does it mean? What revolutions are truly revolutionary? At the core of revolution is structural change, not violence. So before radical readers rally with the calls of, "We ride at dawn!" I am reminded of Gil Scott-Heron's lyric, "The revolution will not be televised." A revolution can be as ceremonial as a democratic transfer of power. A revolution is clean water, access to quality health care, sufficient shelter, equitable schools, safety, an end to mass incarceration, restorative justice, and the like. Revolution looks like everyday life for lots of white Americans. A revolution is an end to the hoarding of resources and wealth and the exploitation of human beings. The violence of a revolution is radical or forceful only in its undoing of whiteness. But ultimately, a revolution is not bloodshed; it is forfeiture and equitable redistribution. In this chapter, I examine both the violent bloodshed of the Age of Revolutions in the West and also the ways revolutions can be bloodless. Every example represents a period when people were grappling with the terms of freedom, citizenship, or basic humanity.

Protection was one of the first things denied to Black people in America. Black women could not protect themselves from sexual assault. Black families could not protect themselves from the auction block. Civil rights leaders could not protect themselves from attacks from the mob or the state. Resistance had to include a fail-safe for one's protection. Defense has always been a key aspect, if not the foundation, of resisting white supremacy. Protection explains how Black people used collective action to shield the oppressed and the vulnerable, kin and the community. During slavery, protection was about stealing security and procuring safeguards that often circumvented the law. In the twentieth century, protection could be found in securing a safe integrated education for Black schoolchildren. Mob attacks from white terrorists were always met with resistance. Black veterans returning from war fought back against the racism that terrorized their lives. The Deacons for Defense and Justice served as bodyguards for prominent figures in the civil rights movement. Even today, the Nation of Islam's Fruit of Islam, a highly trained security force, has been known to provide protective details for Black activists at public engagements. Protection was not only about defense. Many of the services developed by the Black Panther Party, such as the free breakfast program, the health clinics, food distribution, and ambulances, served the community in ways that the local, state, and even federal government denied Black people. Protection was about fortification of the mind and body. In the twenty-first century, protection serves to combat local and state violence. The work of protection is constant. This chapter expands our thinking about how protection does the remedy work of shielding individuals from both racial degradation and societal neglect spurred on by anti-Blackness.

Force, in America, is a powerful and sometimes deadly solution for arresting white violence. Force, like protection, has a range of uses. Force can be a strike. Force can be a boycott. Force can be a vote. Force can be armed self-defense. As I define force, it has two central components. First, force is strength born from anger—and anger, as Audre Lorde explains, is an appropriate reaction to

racism and disenfranchisement.[19] Black anger should compel us
to grapple with the grievances of slavery, segregation, redlining,
mass incarceration, and many other violent, oppressive systems.
Second, force is an energy that can influence or change a person or
a system. Force can push, pull, accelerate, or compel acquiescence.
Force snatches freedom back.

This chapter specifically focuses on how guns have forced white
people to meet the weapon of their own design. White Americans
have long considered it to be in their self-interest to keep Black
people unarmed. In 1857, one US Supreme Court justice argued
in the infamous *Dred Scott v. Sandford* decision that recognizing
Black people as citizens would allow them to "keep and carry arms
wherever they went." The premise was that citizenship meant the
right to bear arms, and gun ownership should be a right afforded
only to white people—another reason whiteness and violence cannot be separated. Though sanctioned gun ownership was withheld
from Black people as a sign of their subordination, this did not
prevent Black people from obtaining firearms for their defense. In
every American war, Black people have possessed guns. Black soldiers left the fields of the Civil War with their guns. Black people
armed themselves during race riots and urban rebellions. The
African Blood Brotherhood demanded that Black communities
arm themselves during the 1920s. Black people carried weapons while traveling throughout the South during the 1940s and
'50s. During the 1960s, groups such as the Deacons for Defense
and Justice, the Lowndes County Freedom Organization, and
the Black Panther Party used gun ownership as a direct threat to
white people's monopoly on individual and collective protection.
White supremacy meant Black people could be harmed without re-
course. Force proved Black Americans were entitled to defend their
humanity and, ultimately, their citizenship.

Flight is one of the most common forms of Black resistance. Flight is about enforcing choice. In many ways, flight is a refusal. Flight can be quitting a job or place. Leaving can be short-term or permanent. During slavery, truancy, short stints of absence, played a major role in the lives of enslaved people. Maybe running away to the North was not possible, but running away to the swamps, forests, or a neighboring plantation was. Truancy was a way of withholding labor or leaving without permission to visit a loved one. It can be argued that the American Revolution and the Civil War depended largely not on whether Black folks fought but where they fled. Their fleeing the plantation crippled slaveholders. In the twentieth century, flight became the Great Migration. Black folks moved en masse from rural areas to urban areas and from the South to the North or West. They left with their families. They left with their labor. They left with their skills, genius, and artistry. And flight is not always about being pushed out; sometimes it's about being pulled away for adventure and pleasure. This chapter examines the powerful tool of departure from white supremacists' spaces. It is about carving out spaces that serve as maroon societies. Flight as a refusal means departing for a break or departing for good. Ultimately, flight also allows us to understand how much of mobility is tethered to race.

Finally, *joy* is possibly the most important and strongest remedy that makes a push for Black personhood. While anti-Black violence has profoundly impacted the African American historical experience, it is not the totality of Blackness. While whiteness cannot be separated from violence, Blackness can be separated from oppression. The most powerful tool the Black Panther Party (BPP) employed was not guns but joy. Black pride invoked hope and happiness, which could be shields from the demoralizing and degenerative effects of racism. In jest and in truth, James Brown once said, "The one thing that can solve most of our problems is dancing." There is no civil rights movement without singing. What was the long freedom struggle without music? Dance, music, laughter, art, memes, gifs, roller skating, fellowship over a good meal— these are potent weapons needed to combat the violence of racism. Writer and mother Ashley Simpo wrote, "Some of us fight racism by raising our Black children to know joy. This matters too."[20] Black Americans have always held both jubilation and sorrow in their hands. Only Black folk who love themselves can chant "I can't breathe" at a protest and in the *same space* break out into a collective electric slide. As Imani Perry wrote for *The Atlantic*, "Racism is terrible. Blackness is not."[21] Joy is typically understood within a spiritual context and works in tandem with suffering.[22] Joy supersedes material accumulation and the fleeting feeling of happiness. Joy destroys the physical, emotional, intellectual, and spiritual onslaught of whiteness as aspirational. To be clear, joy is not oblivious to Black suffering; on the contrary, suffering informs joy and even fortifies it. The deep well of humanity that Black people must draw on is not pure optimism. Joy is rooted in radical love, hope, and the complete confidence in the capacity of Black people.

I chose these five categories of Black response—revolution, protection, force, flight, and joy—because throughout my life, I have researched, witnessed, or experienced the utility of them all. Their impacts can blend into one another. Sometimes revolutions involve force. Sometimes flight is motivated by protection. Sometimes flight and force are joyful. Many will remember the viral video footage of a brawl that took place in Montgomery, Alabama, at Riverfront Park in August 2023. A Black dock worker was attacked by several white men who refused to abide by his instructions to move their boat. The white attackers shoved the Black man and began to overwhelm him. In minutes, dozens of nearby Black men and women joined the fight to help the dock worker by jumping on the white assailants and landing blows, including one teenager who jumped from a boat and swam to the dock to defend him and another Black man who swung a folding chair at white attackers to fend them off from harming more people. Within hours, the internet exploded with gifs, jokes, reenactments, memes, and even merch to celebrate the Black resistance of white violence. Collectively, both in person and virtually, Black people were refusing the violent treatment of white boaters. The single event was revolution, protection, force, flight, and joy. Black people rejected ill treatment. They protected each other. They used force to stop their attackers. They ran toward trouble. And they celebrated, laughed, and memorialized Black refusal with relentless joy and mockery.

The path to liberation and full Black humanity is not easy. Comfortable solutions will not work. Empathy and guilt will not work. Taking a field trip to a museum or reading about a civil rights activist are grossly insufficient attempts to repair the harm of anti-Blackness. Charity and philanthropy will not work. In many cases, philanthropy only reinforces power hierarchies. Policy is a start, but if policy does not repair, restore, and redistribute the losses of Black people and the massive gains of white people, it will not be enough.

This book is not about advocating violence. But I am encouraging readers to grapple with the causes and consequences of it, and to think outside the binary of violence and nonviolence. The refusals and remedies offered are equally not about revenge. The work of revenge is ridiculous. Consider this: Never have Americans ever heard of Black men bombing a white church and killing four little white girls before a service. Never have Americans ever heard of a Black man assassinating a white man in his driveway, in front of his family. Never have Americans ever heard of a Black man being invited into a white church for a prayer meeting where they treated him kindly and then gunning down the white churchgoers. Only in fiction or film could one conjure a story where Black people take white folks hostage, blow up police precincts, and kill white people. Vengeance is a white imaginary project. Black people are not consumed with revenge but with justice. And white people are not afraid of revenge; they are afraid of justice. Justice is more costly.

I started this story with my great-grandmother for a reason. Many of my examples, if not a majority, will involve Black women. I want to point out this distinction because there is a tendency to treat violence and leadership as masculine. Fighting back is considered an act of manliness. In works of military history, scholars write as if all soldiers are men. They are not. Violence is not always gendered. Most violence takes place outside of war, and contrary to popular belief, Black women bear the brunt of it. Violence for Black women is the theft of their lives, the theft of their children, the theft of their wombs, the theft of their contributions, the theft of their ingenuity, then the theft of their voices and their value. Historically, Black women have been the primary targets of white supremacist violence. Inside and outside the institution of slavery, Black women had every reason to contemplate or resort to violence as a meaningful tool to combat their powerlessness. Often, instead of seeking protection, Black women positioned themselves as protectors, defending Black humanity from slave catchers, the Klan, or the police.

Millions of Black people fall outside the politically imposed spectrum between W. E. B. Du Bois's political activism on one end and Booker T. Washington's accommodationist approach on the other, or the spectrum between Martin Luther King Jr.'s "Beloved Community" and Malcolm X's "by any means necessary." Furthermore, choosing between two men is likely how we have missed the brilliant ideas of others who offered their communities viable tools for undermining and dismantling white supremacist structures. As far back as Queen Nanny of the Maroons and as far back as Queen Ana Nzinga of Ndongo and as far back as the Dahomey Amazons, Black women warriors have always been with us. In the long view of Black liberation, Black women are the vanguard. The women in these pages are their descendants. Frantz Fanon discussed the role of Black women during the Algerian war: "The woman does not merely knit for or mourn the soldier. The Algerian woman is at the heart of the combat. Arrested, tortured, raped, shot down, she testifies to the violence of the occupier and to his inhumanity."[23] Black women are never bystanders.

During slavery, Black women toiled in fields and were preyed on in the house. Their wombs served as the engines of American slavery, reproducing lives and labor. They were the original housekeepers and homemakers, who lived through the irony of being slandered as unfit mothers while nursing and raising white children for success. Enslaved Black women resisted their oppression and fought to end the institution of slavery. In fact, abolitionist Frederick Douglass was adamant that "when the true history of the anti-slavery cause shall be written, women will occupy a large space in its pages; for the cause of the slave has been peculiarly woman's cause."[24]

Black women do not merely fight for themselves; they fight for everyone. They do not just open doors for other women and marginalized people who come behind them; they help to close doors on the dark past of slavery, segregation, and sexism. They remain at the forefront of combatting police brutality, voter suppression, and public health, and they have long led the way in movements pushing for equality for all. There is no American activism without Black women at its forefront. There is no abolitionist movement, no women's suffrage movement, no movement for integration, no civil rights movement, no #MeToo movement, no #SayHerName, and certainly no Black Lives Matter movement without brave Black women.

Within the historiography, however, Black women are centralized primarily as victims of violence, or they are ignored and pushed to the margins of violent resistance as "helpers." Black women have fallen into blind groups where their involvement is, at best, vague. Phrases such as "Black residents," "colored crowds," "armed farmers," or even a "Negro mob" prevent readers from seeing gender. The assumption is that the mob is male or the resisting group is completely made up of men. Historian Leslie A. Schwalm contended that post–Civil War freedwomen's "involvement in even the most violent confrontations with planters and agents of Reconstruction have sometimes been obscured by the tendency of observers to describe participants as undifferentiated crowds of freedmen or 'negroes.'"[25] However, historical records illustrate freedwomen were arrested and jailed for their resistance to exploitation. Accordingly, scholars must pay special attention to who might be present in the absence of verbal or written references.

The historian Stephanie Camp argued, "Women's history does not merely add to what we know; it changes what we know and how we know it."[26] We cannot know the history of white supremacy in this country and the violent efforts to demolish it without

Black women. Their contributions to revolution, protection, force, flight, and joy change what we know about this country and how we know it.

Black response to white terror is about enforcing an interruption.[27] Force stuns the oppressor into a pause. So yes, we can legitimately root for the historical heroes in this book. We can and should champion their courage to fight back, slap down, and tear up white supremacy. We need not fear these acts. Too often white people are more horrified by Black people's attempts to defend themselves than by what or whom they are defending themselves against. Because white Americans have been trained to view Black people through a lens of criminality (the myth that all Black people are criminals), all their actions and behaviors seem like crimes. Prison abolitionist Mariame Kaba brilliantly argues that "not all crimes are harms and not all harms are crimes." What matters is not the crime; what matters most is what is harmful.[28] Historically and daily, white people cause harm but are rarely held accountable for harms or crimes. The white doctor who proposed a lifetime of servitude for my great-grandmother may not have committed a crime. Naysayers might even point out Mary Bullard's willingness to relinquish her daughter. But the oath of a doctor is "First, do no harm." The doctor's solution posed more harm than the rusty nail.

The intervention of Martha reminds us that we cannot do this work alone. By ourselves, the options are daunting and capitulating is easy. Together, we can be courageous. There is strength in solidarity. Together, we can refuse. The stories offered here are of racial healers and medics called to the battlefield. These are the stories of Black women and men who used all of the options available to them to arrest and heal the harms of white supremacy.

These are the stories of patriots living in a country built by them but not for them.

A serial killer is on the loose and American society is cautioning us not to apprehend it, restrain it, or kill it. We should not harm the serial killer or call attention to its heinous murders. The blame is placed on the victims: "What did you do to be killed?" *We Refuse* is not the story of the killer or its coconspirators. This is the story of what Black people have done and continue to do to confront, combat, and crush white supremacy. I believe Toni Morrison gave all of us clear instructions: "There is no time for despair, no place for self-pity, no need for silence, no room for fear. We speak, we write, we do language. That is how civilizations heal."[29] I would add,

We revolt.

We protect.

We fight.

We leave.

We sing.

We laugh.

We refuse.

We liberate.

Throughout history, we, like my ancestor, have chosen life with a limp over the social death of white supremacy. Until we all get free, America will continue to be a violent place and Black people will continue to refuse.

Chapter One

REVOLUTION

My brother, William, was born with sickle cell anemia, a disease that predominantly affects people of African descent. Sickle cell causes the body's red blood cells, which are usually round, to change into a C shape, becoming stiff and distorted. Because these "sickled" cells have difficulty passing through blood vessels, they obstruct blood flow throughout the body, causing an array of ailments. William battled fatigue and pain throughout his childhood. My parents were in and out of hospitals with him and spent many sleepless nights worried about his survival. But when my brother was sixteen years old, he was cured. Yes, cured.

His medical team discovered that a bone marrow transplant from a healthy sibling could cure someone with sickle cell, if—and this is a big if—the sibling's bone marrow cells perfectly matched the recipient's. It turned out that my sister, Crystal, was this perfect match for William. The process was long, hard, and complicated, but ultimately successful. My brother's abnormal stem cells were replaced with my sister's healthy stem cells, and his body began making healthy red blood cells. He was the second person in the state of Illinois to be cured of sickle cell and the thirty-second in the country. From then on, my brother lived a normal life. He did things he could never do before, like play sports, attend college, and join the military. For the first time he could have basic long-term plans for his life. William's healing was a revolution for my family. It completely changed the trajectory of his life, and ours, for the better.

Revolutions do not necessarily require bloodshed, but they do require sacrifice. My sister could have refused to donate her cells. But the procedure did not require her life. She spent a day or two in the hospital and was sore in the places where they extracted cells, but mostly, she was happy. She did miss her prom, but that was minor compared to what her sacrifice made possible. My brother was going to live. Everyone in my family got a fresh start now that William was healed. The writer and activist Vicky Osterweil reminds us that revolutions can demonstrate the "possibility of better lives for all of us."[1] A revolution requires sacrificial, life-altering, permanent change for the benefit of everyone, particularly those in most need. A revolution is not a revolution unless it pursues a better society for all. Accordingly, we can turn toward revolution with "joy, attention, and solidarity and fight to spread [these moments of political, economic, and social rupture] to every corner of the globe."[2] As a family, we embarked on my brother's

health journey with fear—*What if the procedure does not work?*—
and faith—*What if it does work?* If my brother had died, we would
have been changed forever. That my brother lived also changed
us forever. If my family had focused only on the technical details
of the medical procedures such as the surgery, extraction, or risk,
we would have missed all of the hope and benefits that came with
healing. We should not get stuck on the revolution as forfeiture
alone. What is possible is what matters: a better society for all.

Revolutions are complicated. Americans venerate the American
Revolution and the French Revolution, but other revolutions, particularly ones that involve violence committed by people of color,
are rejected and feared. There is a tendency to think that revolution is scary, full of merciless violence, akin to Armageddon or
some other apocalypse. But when I think of revolutions, I think of
new beginnings. I think of Frantz Fanon's hope to "combine our
muscles and our brains in a new direction."[3] Revolutions do not
necessarily ask for consent; they demand cooperation.

American society has trained people to believe not only that
white supremacy is the natural way of things but that white supremacy is the savior that ends revolutions begun by people of
color and the poor. Racism and classism has blinded Americans
so they cannot see white supremacy as their own Armageddon
against Black people. How might our thinking change if we considered mass incarceration an apocalypse? Or economic inequality
a catastrophe instead of the status quo? For Black people, the state
of Black health, wealth, education, and housing is the end of the
world in slow motion.

Revolutions are birthed from oppression. Thus, revolution is
first and foremost a response that seeks change for the benefit of

humanity. Revolutions are not needed to improve a system. They are needed to create a new world. And, unlike an uncontrollable asteroid headed toward Earth, white state violence is neither natural nor unstoppable. Equality, equity, and reparations are not impossible—they seem that way only when we believe that white people are omnipotent.[4]

Revolutions are how the powerless procure power and transform it to work to the benefit of everyone instead of a select few. Whether a revolution succeeds or fails, the attempt to gain recognition, insurance, and protection for human rights is at the heart of the struggle. The force and violence used to bring down exploitative systems and oppressive leadership do not determine a people's way of life, only their attempts to break free from violence.[5] Revolutionary violence is a means to an end. No one wants to live an existence fraught with constant violence. Historically, revolutionary violence in the hands of Black people was used to stop harm that white people refused to acknowledge as a crime. In short, revolutions create structural change by employing forfeiture to radically redistribute resources and foster an equitable society. Revolution speaks directly to landowners, slaveholders, and colonizers who hoard power, land, profits, and even dominate the law to ensure they have control over everything and everyone. Forfeiture is intended to redistribute power, wealth, land, and access to Indigenous people, Black people, people of color, women, and anyone who has been robbed, marginalized, erased, and violated as a result of slavery, capitalism, and patriarchy. It is about keeping the promises of democracy.

Civil rights activist and Student Nonviolent Coordinating Committee (SNCC) leader Ella Baker believed in revolution, what she might have called radical change. She claimed, "In order for us as poor and oppressed people to become a part of a society that is meaningful, the system under which we now exist has to be radically changed. That means we are going to have to learn to think in radical terms. I use the term 'radical' in its original meaning—getting down to and understanding the root cause. It means facing a system that does not lend itself to your needs and devising means by which you can change that system." Baker admitted that this work is "easier said than done." But she also understood that at the heart of revolution is asking hard questions about our own identity. "How much have we got to do to find out who we are, where we have come from and where we are going[?] . . . In order to see where we are going, we not only must remember where we have been, but we must understand where we have been."[6] The past, even a very distant past, is useful for understanding both who we are and where we might go. The past shapes our creative potential to think a new, better world into being.

This chapter examines the American Revolution, the Haitian Revolution, and revolution in the French Antilles, which teach us valuable lessons about the transformative work of revolution. Indeed, the late eighteenth century was referred to as the Age of Revolutions because of the political upheavals in the United States and France. The United States was breaking away from its mother country, England, and France was overthrowing its monarchy. The ideals of liberty, equality, and democracy were being wielded as weapons against aristocratic power structures.

In a hemisphere dominated by chattel slavery, emancipation was a revolution. In Haiti and on the Caribbean island of Guadeloupe, the enslaved population understood that liberty and equality were not aspects of revolution; they *were* revolution. On these islands, undeterred Black leaders employed violence in an attempt to make life better for everyone. Their actions gave life and legitimacy to the rhetoric the American Founding Fathers and European colonizers merely performed. The people of Haiti and Guadeloupe showed courage in the face of insurmountable odds. But the hardest work of revolution is sustainability.

The victory of the American Revolution appears sustaining, but only if we examine white power structures. The American Revolution, per my definition, was not revolutionary. It did not protect Indigenous peoples. It did not free the enslaved. It did not replace an exploitative system with an equitable one. It did not forfeit or radically redistribute power and wealth to the most marginalized groups. Revolution is possible; Haiti and Guadeloupe proved as much. In the United States, the real revolution was the Civil War. Americans do not speak of the Civil War as revolution because the American Revolution is what created the United States, but the Civil War was its rebirth. The United States, Haiti, the French Antilles, and other places in the Atlantic World struggle with the ongoing battle to maintain the victories of emancipation and the transformational power of justice.

The Taíno people were the original inhabitants of Haiti, before it was known as Haiti. When Spanish explorer Christopher Columbus arrived at the island in 1492, he set a course of destruction and disease that brought the Taíno people to the brink of extinction. Columbus named the entire island Hispaniola. The Spanish enslaved many of the Taíno people until 1697, when the French took over the western side of the island and named it Saint-Domingue. Building on the work of the Spanish, who continued to control the eastern side of the island, named Santo Domingo, the French created a colony with violence and sustained it with violence. They imported stolen African lives to work on Saint-Domingue's vast sugarcane plantations.

In a relatively short time, Saint-Domingue became the crown jewel of the Caribbean and the French colonial empire. It produced more sugar, coffee, cotton, and indigo than any other colony in the Western Hemisphere. By 1789, Saint-Domingue, the size of Vermont and even more mountainous, exported nearly half of the world's coffee and sugar. These exports totaled more than those of Jamaica, Cuba, and Brazil combined. Because of the massive amounts of labor that sugar and coffee plantations required, enslaved people vastly outnumbered French planters and officials. By 1790, there were close to half a million enslaved, constituting 80 percent of the colony's population.

The island was also notorious for its brutality toward enslaved people. It was said that if an enslaved person rebelled on another island, they were sent to Saint-Domingue as punishment. Sugar mills were run twenty-four hours a day, 365 days of the year. The work was long, hard, and dangerous. Cultivating sugar took place not on flat plains of land but on mountainsides and along steep hills. In the sugar mills, it was easy to lose a limb—or one's life. In fact, the labor was so intense and the violence so harsh that the average life expectancy for enslaved people was just seven to eight years after arriving on the island, and one-third of enslaved laborers died within the first few years. Diseases such as smallpox and typhoid were rampant.

In 1789, when the French Revolution began, the ideals of liberty, equality, and fraternity motivated marginalized groups such as poor whites and the *gens de couleur libres*, a group of free mixed-race people who desired citizenship alongside the ruling elite. Social and economic instability and flagrant inequality provoked rebellion among the lower classes. The goals of the French Revolution particularly resonated with enslaved populations of Saint-Domingue. Revolution in France spread to revolution in the colonies. On August 22, 1791, two religious leaders, a vodou *houngan* (high male priest) named Dutty Boukman and a vodou priestess, or *manbo*, named Cécile Fatiman, organized a rebellion. It began with a religious ceremony at the Bois Caïman, a clearing just removed from the French planter Lenormand de Mézy's plantation in the north part of the colony. Boukman prophesied that three enslaved people—Jean-François Papillon, Georges Biassou, and Jeannot Bullet—would be leaders of a resistance movement and revolt that would free all enslaved people of Saint-Domingue. A pig was sacrificed, an oath was taken, and Boukman and Fatiman urged their listeners to take revenge on their French oppressors. Boukman declared, "Throw away the image of the god of the whites who thirsts for our tears and listen to the voice of liberty which speaks in the hearts of all of us."[7] A week later, nearly 1,800 plantations had been destroyed and over 1,000 slaveholders killed.[8] The revolution was only getting started. Boukman was captured and beheaded, but the enslaved in Saint-Domingue were not deterred. They continued to burn down plantations and slaughter French planters and their families. Within two years, slavery was abolished throughout Saint-Domingue.

Knowing the French were vulnerable because of their losses, the British and the Spanish, who wanted part of the French Empire for economic and political gains, set their eyes on Saint-Domingue. But even they could not compete against the Black forces led by the former slave and trained soldier Toussaint Louverture, who had joined Georges Biassou, Jean-François Papillon, and Jeannot Bullet to take up the revolution after Boukman's death. In 1798, Louverture defeated the British. Two years later he kicked out Spain, successfully safeguarding the entire island of Hispaniola and freeing Santo Domingo, which later became the Dominican Republic, from the institution of slavery. By 1801, Louverture had taken control of Hispaniola and declared himself to be governor for life. The island was still to be connected to the French Empire, but Toussaint created a new constitution.[9] France was now under the rule of Napoleon Bonaparte, who was incredulous that Louverture could appoint himself governor for life. Napoleon sought to put an end to Louverture and reinstate slavery.

Napoleon ordered General Charles Leclerc to lead a military campaign to reestablish slavery in Saint-Domingue and reinstitute it as a colony of France. In December 1801, Leclerc set sail from France with the greatest show of force in French history to this day: over forty thousand soldiers on warships. (Later reinforcements would bring the total number of French soldiers fighting in Haiti to over eighty thousand.) Under the pretense of negotiation, Louverture was duped into boarding a French ship in 1802 and died the next year in Fort de Joux, a French prison primarily reserved for France's political opponents. He famously declared, "In overthrowing me, you have done no more than cut down the trunk of the tree of the black liberty in St. Domingue—it will spring back from the roots, for they are numerous and deep."[10] He was right. While Leclerc managed to capture Louverture and regain French control of Saint-Domingue, he did not disarm Louverture's former officers, believing that the rebellion hinged on one man alone and not the collective resistance of Black people.

Now freed, Black people refused to be enslaved again. The capture of Louverture rallied together the rebels, *gens de couleur libres*, and their allies. The fight was for not just freedom from slavery but independence from France. With the rebels now led by Black generals Jean-Jacques Dessalines, Alexandre Pétion, and Henri Christophe, the violence intensified. Dessalines picked up the liberation mantle and did something radical: in an act of revolution, he took the French flag, a vertical tricolor of blue, white, and red, and ripped the white stripe out, signaling an end to colonial white rule and the beginning of an all-Black nation. Shortly after, Dessalines declared himself emperor of the first Black independent nation in the Caribbean, which he called Haiti. Named by the Indigenous people of the island, "Haiti" or "Hayti" in the Taíno language meant "land of high mountains." Haiti became the first nation to grant universal emancipation. This was a revolution. Black men and women created a new world for the benefit of all oppressed peoples.

Napoleon, Leclerc, and the other French generals were incensed. After Christophe massacred several hundred Polish soldiers at Port-de-Paix, Leclerc ordered the arrest of all remaining Black Haitian troops in Le Cap, a city on the north side, and executed one thousand of them by tying a sacks of flour to their necks and pushing them off the sides of ships.[11] In October 1802, Leclerc wrote to Napoleon essentially encouraging genocide: "We must destroy all the blacks of the mountains—men and women— and spare only children under 12 years of age. We must destroy half of those in the plains and must not leave a single colored person in the colony who has worn an epaulette." In that same letter Leclerc also lamented his role in war: "My soul is withered, and no joyful thought can ever make me forget these hideous scenes."[12] The violence deployed by the Black Haitian troops was effective; it may have made the French think the cost of war was too high. Perhaps Leclerc realized that white colonialist violence harmed both the oppressed and the souls of the oppressors. Napoleon did not care. He wanted to secure dominance at any cost.

One month later, in November 1802, Leclerc died of yellow fever. Napoleon was still undeterred. He sent Donatien-Marie-Joseph de Vimeur, vicomte de Rochambeau, as Leclerc's successor. Rochambeau was the son of Jean-Baptiste Donatien de Vimeur, comte de Rochambeau, who had famously fought in the American Revolution at the Battle of Yorktown. The vicomte had served alongside his father as an aide during the American Revolution and was known for his brutal and barbaric tactics. In fact, before Leclerc died, he endorsed Rochambeau to Napoleon for his animosity: "He is a person of integrity, a good military man, and he hates the blacks."[13] Rochambeau was charged to restore French control by any means necessary. Extreme violence was the only tool Rochambeau thought to employ. He put to death five hundred Black people at Le Cap and buried them in a large hole they dug while they waited for execution. In response, Dessalines hanged five hundred French soldiers for Rochambeau and the white citizens in Le Cap to see.

The French habitually employed and even enjoyed public displays of political executions. During the revolution, three Black men were condemned to be burned alive before a huge crowd. Spectators claimed two of them screamed horribly, but the third prisoner was a young man, just nineteen years old, who refused to give the depraved crowd a show. Blindfolded and bound, he called out to the other two men in Creole, "You do not know how to die. See how to die." He then twisted his body out from his bonds and sat down, placing his feet in the flames. He was burned alive without uttering a groan. "I was there," said French Captain Jean-Baptiste Lemonnier-Delafosse, "spectator of the heroic death of this wretch, greater than Mucius Scaevola. . . . These were the men we had to fight against."[14] Another prisoner who was thrown to the dogs showed no anger but stroked them and encouraged them while he presented his limbs to be destroyed.[15] The violence revealed the French as the ultimate criminals. The French were barbaric, but the Haitians were brave. The revolution was a refusal to be stripped of one's spirit. The oppressive system was based on using fear of violence to keep Black people under control, but when the enslaved showed no fear of violence, they could not be kept under control and the system fell apart.

With Black women it was no different. According to Marxist cultural theorist and Pan-Africanist C. L. R. James, when a Black chief named Chevalier was to be executed by the French, he wavered at the sight of the scaffold. Standing by his side, his wife shamed him. "You do not know how sweet it is to die for liberty!" Undaunted, she embraced her death and refused to allow the executioner or the French the satisfaction of killing her: she grabbed hold of the rope and hanged herself.[16] Even in defeat, Black women's belief in the struggle never waned.

Structural change brought about by revolution requires recognition; in other words, the French would have to acknowledge their defeat and the wrongness of slavery. But instead of reckoning with the innate powerful human desire to be free, the French attributed Black courage to dark magic. C. L. R. James wrote, "The muscles of a Negro, they said, contracted with so much force as to make him insensible to pain. [The French] enslaved the Negro, they said, because he was not a man, and when he behaved like a man they called him a monster."[17] The French preferred to concede defeat to a monster or a myth than admit their own loss and liberate Black people.

In the end, Haiti's independence was won by its generals and its people. Former slaves burned the island beyond recognition. They razed nearly every plantation in sight. When a French soldier questioned a Haitian prisoner about the logic of arson, the rebel retorted, "We have a right to burn what we cultivate because a man has a right to dispose of his own labour."[18] The rebelling enslaved men and women met French terrorism and violence with courage and, as they saw it, justice. It took thirteen years for the enslaved to achieve independence for Haiti, but then, it was the first colonial island largely inhabited by enslaved people to overthrow an imperial power. As a result of the revolution, Napoleon lost the centerpiece of his empire and was forced to sell the Louisiana Territory to the United States to cover the war's expenses. Enraged, Napoleon cursed the collection of his woes: "Damn sugar, damn coffee, damn colonies."[19]

Revolutions create new standards. In Haiti, there were no longer slaves or masters. The revolution could have been summed up in one common Creole phrase: "Tout moun. Se moun," which loosely translates as "Every person is a person." This might seem obvious, but in the context of white supremacy and anti-Blackness, it was a revolutionary statement. Starvation, prejudice, and violence were not necessary to preserve social, economic, and political order, as Saint-Domingue's French colonizers had believed. In fact, Haitians lived free and well. They farmed their own land and, though briefly, claimed the second-highest standard of living in the Americas.[20] In Haiti, Black people were not merely liberated; they were fully human. Every person was a person.

Louverture's constitution established the framework of liberty and equality and prohibited slavery and all forms of racial discrimination. Moreover, it did something unique. Louverture did not refer to rights being conferred on "men" and "citizens" but on "inhabitants," meaning anyone who lived in Haiti was automatically entitled to the same rights as anyone else. Freedom was not applied arbitrarily or in the abstract. Louverture's constitution was a revolutionary reworking of existing so-called universal language, which had, until now, really only enshrined the rights of a few.[21] His constitution spread throughout the United States and arguably became the most widely read piece of literature authored by a Black person, and it may have remained so until the publication of *Narrative of the Life of Frederick Douglass* in 1845.[22] When Des-salines took power he pushed freedom further. He endorsed abolition, but unlike Louverture, he declared Haiti's independence from France altogether. The Haitian Declaration of Independence anchors the ideas of revolutionary nation-making and Black humanity in the early nineteenth century. Liberation meant untethering the island from its colonial ruler.

What happened in Haiti echoed throughout the Atlantic World. Over three hundred miles away, in neighboring Jamaica, enslaved people were singing songs about the revolution within one month of the 1791 uprising. It affirmed what they already knew about themselves. Jamaica held the record for the highest number of slave rebellions. A successful revolution meant fighting was not in vain and victory was possible. Within a few years of the Haitian Revolution, slave owners in the Atlantic World complained of "insolence" on the part of their enslaved property that they frequently attributed to awareness of the successful Black revolution. Enslaved Africans in Trinidad parodied a Catholic mass and declared, "The bread we eat is the white man's flesh. The wine we drink is the white man's blood. Remember St. Domingo."[23] In 1804, just six months after Haiti achieved independence, a group of Black Americans began to protest their exclusion from Fourth of July festivals in Philadelphia. They stormed the streets and knocked white people out of their way, "damning the whites and saying that they would shew [sic] them St. Domingo."[24] Songs, symbols, and political sentiments left no question that Haiti was a model for Black power and authority.

The same events terrified slave owners. To them, Louverture was a villain and murderer, not a hero. White people fleeing Haiti were traumatized by their experiences. Stories spread that white people were slaughtered during the revolution and Dessalines's subsequent rule as well. One eyewitness reported seeing "young children transfixed upon the points of bayonets." Others described former slaves "dragging white planters from their homes and tearing off their limbs one by one or strapping them to wooden racks and sawing them in half."[25] Some stories were true. Some stories were exaggerated. The revolution was violent. As white families fled to other islands throughout the Caribbean and to the United States, they carried their stories of terror and Black criminality with them. Few, however, responded to the war by questioning the institution of slavery. All violence committed by Black people was deemed unwarranted and evil. Americans disregarded the history that American patriots had sought their independence with the help of Haitian soldiers and that French peasants had overthrown the monarchy with the aid of the guillotine. American hypocrisy reasoned that violence was only legitimate if it supported their own political, economic, and social order. The West could not accept the success of formerly enslaved leadership and refused to acknowledge Haitian sovereignty for decades. For white people, violence should only operate in one direction. Because the West's highest allegiance is to whiteness, Haiti's very existence was catastrophic.[26]

While news of the events in Haiti terrified white people, Black people throughout the Western Hemisphere, both free and enslaved, continued to be inspired. In 1805, Black soldiers in Rio de Janeiro wore medallion portraits of the Haitian emperor Dessalines.[27] It was this spirit that sustained the revolutionary victory of Haiti. Throughout Brazil, protest songs were passed down that praised the leaders of the Haitian Revolution and inspired the people to pursue similar means of liberation.

| I will imitate [Henri] Christophe | Hurrah! We will imitate his people |
| Qual eu imito a Cristovao | Eia! Imitai a seu povo |

| The immortal Haitian Leader | Oh, my sovereign people! |
| Esse imotal haitiano | Oh, meu povo soberano![28] |

In 1812, a free Black Cuban named José Antonio Aponte began plotting a slave revolution and encouraging the overthrow of slavery in Cuba. Aponte told the story of the Haitian Revolution to those who joined him and assured them that Haiti would support their efforts. "Word ran through Havana," according to one enslaved person in Cuba, that "generals and captains" from Haiti had come to seek "freedom for all the slaves on the island."[29] When Aponte was caught by colonial authorities, portraits of Henri Christophe, Toussaint Louverture, Jean-François Papillon, and Jean-Jacques Dessalines were found in his home. The help from Haiti was not forthcoming; it was only a rumor.

Simón Bolívar, the first president of Colombia, befriended Alexandre Pétion, then president of Haiti. Pétion convinced Bolívar to abolish slavery in all of the territories he controlled. To support his efforts, Pétion sent supplies and money to Bolívar to defeat the Spanish. Bolívar credited Haitian resources for his successful revolution. Haiti wanted an end to slavery everywhere. It shared resources with any country that shared its revolutionary goals.

No issue having to do with slavery and the role of Black people in society was discussed "so many different times, in so many different ways, for so many different reasons as the lessons of the Haitian Revolution."[30] The events in Haiti helped to advance legislation in some American states that would not otherwise have been passed. For example, New York and New Jersey passed moderate emancipation laws in 1799 and 1804, respectively.[31] New

York had one of the largest enslaved populations. One out of every five people was of African descent. It is likely New York did not want to be the site of a revolution. Similar proposals had failed in both states in the 1780s.[32] The federal government's closing of the slave trade in 1807 was also a direct result of the Haitian Revolution. Though the law ended only international (not domestic) slave trading to the United States (the illegal pirating of slave ships continued for some time), it represented a larger trend of scaling back the use of African labor. These changes were reforms, but they stemmed from revolutionary change. The United States did not move to abandon slavery, as the Haitians had done. For the moment, white people's terror of Black equality trumped their fear of Black violence. On the whole, white Americans continued to peddle the horrors of the Haitian Revolution and refused to give diplomatic recognition to Haiti.

Black people, particularly Black Americans, were never convinced by the attempts to dismiss or downplay the outcome of the Haitian Revolution.[33] Samuel E. Cornish and John B. Russwurm, the founders and editors of *Freedom's Journal*, America's first Black newspaper, routinely published supportive sentiments about Haiti.[34] "There are very few events on record which have produced more extraordinary men than the revolution in St. Domingo," they wrote in May 1827. In terms of Black leadership, Haiti had produced "the most incontestable proofs, that the negro is not, in general, wanting in the higher qualifications of the mind." Cornish and Russwurm understood that the same desire for the "advantages of liberty, independence and education, as their white brethren of Europe and America" could be found in Black people as well. Especially in the aftermath of the American and Haitian Revolutions, they wrote, the leaders of the United States should not be surprised by their desire to be free—all men deprived of liberty will make attempts to recover their inalienable rights. "We may delay the evils of insurrections and revolutions; but like the eruptions of Vesuvius, they will burst forth more awfully amid the horrors of midnight."[35] Through force and revolutionary violence, Black Haitians wielded the sword of war and swayed an empire. *Freedom's Journal* warned that calamity would come to anyone connected with the institution of slavery and wherever slavery was tolerated.[36] It cautioned that the day would come when the horrors of Haiti would be enacted before American eyes.[37] For Cornish and Russwurm, an independent Haiti represented the impossible made possible. Throughout the antebellum period, abolitionists used the success of the Haitian Revolution to threaten the institution of slavery.[38] For decades, the revolution was sustained not only by its victory but by the threat it represented to any slaveholding country.

Haiti's revolution endured, but Guadeloupe is the story of revolution delayed. If you travel to the small, butterfly-shaped island of Guadeloupe, you can visit the commune of Les Abymes, the largest urban area with nearly sixty thousand inhabitants. Located on the west side of Grande-Terre, the eastern part of Guadeloupe, the town buzzes with people preparing for work or going to school or shopping.[39] While there, you might drive past murals and sculptures representing the history of the island: images of the slave trade, scenes from colonial plantation life, and Guadeloupean figures of slave resistance. La Mulâtresse Solitude is unquestionably the most striking of these statues, a warrior who gave her life during a major rebellion against the French. She stands tall and fierce with her hands on her hips and her protruding pregnant belly centering her planted stance.[40] She is positioned looking west, facing the coast. She represents the precarity of freedom in the New World, a life that was stolen, then recovered, and, in the cause of freedom, lost again.

Solitude's mother was transported from West Africa to Guadeloupe in 1772. Before slave ships docked in the New World, slavery began at sea.[41] African men, women, and children were packed onto ships up to and often over capacity. From infants to the elderly, Black people were torn away from all they knew to face a world of labor and hell. Over 15 percent of enslaved Africans never survived to see the New World. Murder, neglect, and suicide stole the lives of millions. Enslaved women were constantly starved, beaten, and raped by sailors. Rape was so common during the Middle Passage that one in three women were impregnated by a European sailor.[42] An African woman could arrive in the New World just as she was entering her second trimester. Such was the case for Solitude's mother. She would have likely worked the lucrative sugar plantations that made the island a prized jewel for the French, alongside Saint-Domingue. In the eighteenth century, Guadeloupe was dominated by sugar, one of the most labor-intensive commodities of the slave trade. The Atlantic slave trade was a cruel irony. Sugar-sweetened tea, coffee, and other confections were produced by bitter and brutal exploitation of Black bodies.

Sometime during 1772, Solitude's mother gave birth. She named her daughter Solitude, perhaps to signify all of the things she felt: alone, isolated, and violently cut off from all she knew. It was said that Solitude had fair skin and gray eyes, revealing that she may have been conceived by rape. While she was referred to in history by the moniker La Mulâtresse Solitude, being mixed race afforded her no favors or rights. She spent all of her childhood and adolescence in bondage, trapped by a dangerous life of domestic work, where sexual and physical assault were common given the proximity to white slave owners and their families. Both Solitude and her mother were strangers in a world that sought to violate them at every turn. However, in 1794, at age twenty-two, Solitude had reason to hope. Saint-Domingue, the crown jewel of the French Empire, was three years into a full-fledged revolution. When it was rumored that the enslaved in Guadeloupe might also win their freedom, they did not hesitate to commence their own revolution. Historian Antoine Métral wrote, "These were no longer timid slaves. Women, children, and the elderly had all experienced the perils of slavery for a considerable period and regarded war as indispensable to liberty."[43] Oral history claims Solitude immediately escaped the plantation and went to live with the maroons, a group of former slaves who had found protection and haven in the mountains. They created communities that were often impenetrable to their white owners, who might come seeking to retrieve them.

But even in isolated regions, word spread fast that slavery was ending in the French Empire. The enslaved took their cue from Saint-Domingue, which in 1794 had abolished slavery and was in the midst of revolution, and freed themselves through violence and by abandoning plantations. However, amid chaos, Britain sought to gain control of the French islands, just as it had with Saint-Domingue. In April 1794, British troops arrived in Basse-Terre and gained temporary control. Just two months later, Victor Hugues, a representative of the French National Convention, arrived in Guadeloupe with a decree officially abolishing the institution of slavery. Hugues enlisted the help of the formerly enslaved to fight against the British to ensure their liberty. Empowered and mobilized, the formerly enslaved banded together against the British. By December 1794, the struggle with the British ended. Freedom won and hundreds of white slaveholders lost their lives. For a brief period, the Black men and women of Guadeloupe lived as free people. The revolution was settled in Guadeloupe earlier than in France, where people were still fighting to dismantle the monarchy.

While the citizens of Guadeloupe were able to maintain control of their island and their freedom, their neighboring island Martinique was still under British control and enslavement. In 1799, Napoleon—newly risen to power in the aftermath of the French Revolution—sought to retake control of all of France's former colonies and reinstitute slavery there. In 1802, he managed to regain sovereignty over Martinique from the British. On May 6, he sent General Antoine Richepanse and 3,400 troops to Pointe-à-Pitre, the capital of Guadeloupe, with specific orders to enslave the people, again.[44] Saint-Domingue may have become a lost cause for him, but Napoleon felt confident about Guadeloupe.

Having lived in freedom for eight years, no Black person on Guadeloupe was going to go back to the plantation without a fight. The Martinique-born, mixed-race colonel Louis Delgrès led an army of formerly enslaved men, women, and children, including Solitude. Pregnant but undeterred, she actively participated in the battle against the French, as did scores of other Black women. Black women were crucial to every battle, transporting food, supplies, and ammunition to those wielding arms. Historian Bernard Moitt wrote that rebel women "served as messengers, cared for the sick, acted as cover for men under fire, and chanted revolutionary slogans," which kept spirits high in the insurrectionary forces of Delgrès and other Black leaders.

Guadeloupean historian Auguste Lacour wrote that during the battle, while the city was barricaded, Black rebel women could be heard singing the French national anthem as they transported ammunition, mocking their oppressors. In describing the women warriors, Lacour claimed, "It was not their fault if their fathers, their sons, their mothers, and their lovers were not endowed with superhuman courage. When a bullet whistled above their heads or a bomb exploded near them, they sang loudly, holding hands while making their hellish rounds interrupted by the chant: 'Vive la mort!' (Long live death!)."[45] The Black people of Guadeloupe knew well what they were fighting for and what they were fighting against. Death was always preferred to a life in slavery.

Mothers who gave birth to enslaved children, who experienced the grief of bondage, were perhaps most motivated to combat the violence they so desperately sought to eradicate. This was what Solitude fought for: her life and the liberty of her unborn child. One of the few stories scholars have of Solitude is telling and comes from Lacour's *History of Guadeloupe*:

> La mulâtresse Solitude, who came from Pointe-à-Pitre to Basse-Terre, was then in the Palermo camp. She let her hatred and fury burst out on all occasions. She had rabbits. One of them having escaped, she armed herself with a pin, ran, pierced him, lifted him up, and presented him to the prison women: "Here," she said, by mixing with her words the most offensive epithets, "this is how I will treat you when it is time!" And this unfortunate woman was about to become a mother! Solitude did not abandon the rebels and remained close to them, like their evil genius, to excite them to the greatest crimes.[46]

Solitude hated slavery. She hated her oppressors. She hated the evil that Europeans perpetuated during the slave trade in the New World. Her genius was in her desire to create not just a better world but a new world, where freedom was a God-given right bestowed at birth and impossible to take away. She was bent on fighting until the end.

Despite the courage and heart of the Black rebel fighters, French forces overwhelmed them. On May 28, 1802, Delgrès and his men and women took their last stand in the battle of Matouba. They lined their outposts with gunpowder and placed explosives around the plantation where they were stationed, then waited for French soldiers to storm their posts. As the French approached, Delgrès and over five hundred men, women, and children shouted "Vivre libre ou mourir!" (Liberty or death!) In one of the greatest acts of solidarity that revolutionary violence has ever seen, they set the gunpowder on fire. The explosions killed some four hundred French soldiers and nearly all of Delgrès's rebelling force. Certain accounts claim Delgrès played the violin as shells and gunpowder exploded around him.[47] In the words of Dessalines, Black Guadeloupeans extended "their concern into the future and, dreading to leave an example of cowardice for posterity, preferred to be exterminated rather than lose their place as one of the world's free peoples."[48] In Guadeloupe they lived free, for a moment, and then chose death.

On July 16, 1802, the French successfully reestablished slavery on the island. Solitude was captured and sentenced to death, but given her pregnancy, officials agreed to execute her after the birth of her child. This was no act of mercy. It is likely Solitude's former owners claimed the child as their property. On November 28, Solitude delivered her baby. On November 29, she marched to her execution. Some stories say she died with breast milk stains on her clothes. Solitude had conceived her child in freedom and fought valiantly all throughout her pregnancy. And yet she could not promise her child a life of freedom. Solitude's actions were no less revolutionary despite her inability to win against her oppressors.

Solitude was not alone in her bravery. A woman named Marthe-Rose was known as Delgrès's mistress, and the French held her liable for inspiring Delgrès to incite the enslaved to rebel and for killing white prisoners held as their captives. Though she suffered from a broken leg, the French brought her before the tribunal on a stretcher. They condemned her to be hanged publicly. As the rope was placed around her neck, Marthe-Rose condemned her onlookers: "Having killed their king and left their country, these men have come to ours to bring trouble and confusion. May God judge them!"[49] She correctly described the Revolutionary Era. During the French Revolution, nine years before Marthe-Rose's execution, King Louis XVI was beheaded by guillotine. After achieving victory for his nation, Napoleon could not contemplate ruling without violence and slavery. No white people in the Western world could imagine their own revolutions without the suppression of Black people. Black equality was unthinkable. Rather than acknowledge Black agency, the West employed "trouble and confusion" by promoting categories of race. Marthe-Rose was right.

Two weeks before his last stand at Matouba, Delgrès wrote a final proclamation. His address "To the Entire Universe" was written to be a powerful republican plea for racial equality. He reasoned that "resistance to oppression is a natural right. Even the divinity cannot be offended that we defend our cause; it is that of justice and humanity: we will not defile it by the very shadow of crime. Yes, we are resolved to keep ourselves on a fair defense; but we will never become the aggressors."[50] Delgrès was not addressing Napoleon or the French or even Europe. He was addressing *the entire universe* in a message that slavery was warfare and racism was inhuman. He believed no one should be born into a world with adversaries. Moreover, he adamantly refuted the idea that revolution and revolutionary violence, as an act of collective defense against oppression, were not just. Today, there remains no original copy of his proclamation. We know of its existence only because of Lacour's history and copious interviews with survivors. But Delgrès's message and meaning echo to this very day.

During the late 1990s, officials in the French Antilles and the public grappled with how to commemorate iconic figures of resistance to slavery. The people wanted their historical heroes to be acknowledged. Several sculptures were installed in public spaces to honor the Black women and men who fought against slavery in the French Antilles. Sculptures of the heroic figures such as La Mulâtresse Solitude, Joseph Ignace, and Louis Delgrès were placed around the city center. Though the statue of Solitude was commissioned to represent a heroine, history, resistance, and marronage in Guadeloupe, its placement was political. The statue of Solitude, created by Black artist Jacky Poulier, and bust of Delgrès were not placed in central squares, parks, or gardens for people to contemplate. Solitude stands in the middle of a roundabout. Many other statues of revolutionaries were placed in the middle of multilane highways and hectic thoroughfares. Critics have argued that "this type of historical representation does not promote a sustained engagement with the past, but instead encourages one to simply 'drive by' the past with little reflection."[51] Guadeloupe's French road system prohibits the kind of large collective gathering that would allow these statues to serve as meeting places.

Sociologist Jean Casimir recognized that the challenge many scholars face is "to extract the vision of the vanquished from historical circumstances in which the vanquishers worked constantly to silence and destroy the elaboration of even the most basic means of expression on the part of the colonized."[52] In other words, the sustainability of revolution is dependent on not just victory but how that victory is remembered. Statues are not superficial. They offer a shortcut to the past, a way of valuing what was accomplished. Extracting history is difficult and preserving memory can be even more fraught. The violence of white supremacy is also bound up in forgetting. That Black revolutionary victories have been marginalized and forgotten is not accidental. The French did not just want to eliminate Black leadership; they sought to erase Black history because history often serves as a road map to a possible future. In marginalizing the past, white people were attempting to make Black people beholden to an identity stuck in subordination. These revolutionary leaders became footnotes because of their attempts to maintain freedom. But not all revolutions end in failure or suppression. Where Guadeloupe failed, Haiti succeeded, in the most powerful example of revolution ideals the Western world has ever seen. And even in failure, white supremacy is weakened, its fallibility exposed. The Black men and women of Guadeloupe were not afraid of failure; they feared the inability to live free. There is honor in failure; integrity, too. The story of Solitude is a powerful portrait of revolution.

In 1848, France abolished slavery in Guadeloupe, Martinique, and their other enslaved colonies. The efforts were led by Victor Schoelcher, a writer and staunch abolitionist. It could be argued that Schoelcher was a revolutionary. He understood that revolution requires sacrifice and forfeiture. He sold his father's business and his inheritance to dedicate himself to the abolition of slavery. After Haiti won its independence, Schoelcher was the first white abolitionist to visit the island. He was vehemently against the heinous debt France collected from Haiti to compensate former slaveholders. He also adamantly believed that any form of gradual emancipation was unwise. He feared slave rebellion was imminent in France's colonies without immediate emancipation. He was right. Before abolition, on May 20, 1848, enslaved people in Martinique began to rise up, motivated by the French Revolution of 1848. Claude Rostoland, Martinique's interim governor, knew he could not control the ensuing rebellion among the enslaved. He quickly moved to declare immediate emancipation throughout the island. Knowing word and violence would spread, Guadeloupe's governor followed suit.[53] Slavery in France was finished. On June 3, the French government abolished slavery legally, but the work had been accomplished on the ground by the enslaved, who forced their hands.

Revolutions do not require violence, but violence can ensure certain guarantees. For Black people in the French Antilles, violence and even the threat of violence guaranteed that liberation could not be ignored or delayed. A long-lived man or woman from Guadeloupe might have, over the course of their life, experienced slavery, then freedom followed by enslavement for another fifty years, and then finally liberation. All the while, Black people refused to give up. They were certain that, while revolution can be delayed, it cannot be denied.

In America, revolutions and violence belong to powerful white men alone. To be clear, there is a social contract between poor white men and wealthy white men in support of white supremacy. White women are also included in this social contract. Despite misogyny and distinct socioeconomic standings, white men and women are united in their racial identity. Together, these categories share varying forms of domination and an unrepentant sense of pride. Since the beginning of this country, riots and violent rhetoric have been markers of patriotism and whiteness. When the Founding Fathers fought for independence, violence was the clarion call. Phrases such as "Live free or die," "Give me liberty or give me death," and "Rebellion to tyrants is obedience to God" echoed throughout the American colonies and in many ways continue today. Force and violence have always been used as weapons to defend liberty because—as John Adams once said in reference to the colonists' treatment by the British—"we won't be their Negroes."[54]

In the Founding Fathers' minds, revolution was never intended to benefit the general public or to extend rights to all people. While not all Founding Fathers thought similarly about slavery, they all maintained a belief in Black inferiority. Among the prominent Founding Fathers, fourteen out of twenty-one owned Black people. Washington enslaved over three hundred people by the end of his life. Thomas Jefferson enslaved over six hundred men, women, and children. It should surprise no one that four out of the first five presidents (George Washington, Thomas Jefferson, James Madison, and James Monroe) owned Black people. Hypocrisy was not a hidden agenda. And yet, the Founding Fathers and the Enlightenment thinkers they quoted are credited with creating the most comprehensive and noteworthy ideas about liberty and equal humanity.

During the Revolutionary Era, Black Americans sought revolution as well, to create new terms for full humanity. Throughout the colonial period, Black essayists, some known as the Sons of Africa, were writing formal petitions demanding their freedom and the abolition of slavery, using the Revolutionary rhetoric favored by white political thinkers to point out the hypocrisy of these men calling themselves slaves to England while still enslaving Black people. Caesar Sarter was one of the earliest African American leaders to speak out on the evils of slavery before the American Revolution. Born in Africa, he was kidnapped, sent to the New World, and lived for over twenty years in bondage before becoming emancipated, after which he lived as a free man in Newburyport, Massachusetts. In a 1774 essay, Sarter asked, "If you are sensible, that slavery is in itself, and in its consequents a great evil, why will you not pity and relieve the poor distressed enslaved Africans?"[55] When Patrick Henry wrote that he could not do without his slaves' labor, Sarter disproved this idea by clarifying that patriots could not do without "the profits of their labor."[56] The ideals of the revolutionary moment were, in fact, not liberty and equality but greed and self-preservation, which prevented white Americans from believing the ideals of liberty and equality should extend to everyone. Western enlightenment was always rooted in the subjugation and enslavement of African and Native peoples. Sarter concluded that patriots' first step should be to liberate the enslaved. He warned that, should slaveholders continue in their oppression of Black people, the Bible was clear: "And he that stealeth a man, and selleth him . . . shall surely be put to death."[57] In this sense, revolution only belonged to the enslaved.

Another "Son of Africa," name unknown, wrote, "Are your hearts not also hard, when you hold them in slavery who are entitled to liberty, by the law of nature, equal as yourselves?"[58] The Sons of Africa called on scripture, specifically the book of Matthew, chapter seven, which discusses calling out the sins of another without addressing one's own. The Bible verse describes hypocrites who tell their brother to "remove the mote [sin] from his eye" without first removing the sin from their own eye. The Sons of Africa charged the colonists with this hypocrisy. The anonymous author wrote, "Pull the beam out thine own eyes." Not only is the author referring to the gross imbalance of scale (beams and motes), but he saw the weaponization of Christianity as a "cloak to fill their masters' coffers and to screen their villainy."[59] Both writers believed that slavery violated the laws of God, and they cautioned the colonists of God's retribution.[60] The patriots were not God's chosen people of Israel. No, they were Egyptians, and the Founding Fathers were pharaohs. For Black people in what would become the United States, revolution was not freedom from England; it was freedom from bondage.

However, in America, Black people who believed in freedom and used violence to achieve it were killed. The first Black Revolutionary hero credited in the American Revolution was also its first casualty: Crispus Attucks. Born into slavery, Attucks lived in Framingham, Massachusetts, before fleeing for his freedom on September 30, 1750. His enslaver, a white man named William Brown, quickly published an ad for his return. Brown described him as a "Molatto Fellow, about 27 Years of Age, named Crispas, 6 feet two inches high, short curled hair, his Knees closer together than common." Ten pounds was the reward for his return.[61] No one was ever able to claim this prize because Attucks was never caught. While he was legally a fugitive, he lived another twenty years as a free man. Attucks represented the contested nature of slavery in colonial New England. He was enslaved but also "acted as free."[62] So many in Boston at the time were people like him— African, Native, and living in some category of unfreedom.[63]

Attucks worked as a sailor and ropemaker in Boston. About 20 percent of the sailors employed on American ships during the colonial period were Black Americans. The whaling ships sailing in and out of Boston Harbor gave Attucks something he had never had as an enslaved person: mobility. Attucks did not just flee; he traveled the world. On the night of the Boston Massacre, he had recently returned from the Bahamas. Had he not been killed, his next trip would have taken him to North Carolina.[64] Attucks had obtained a living that was full of possibility.

The context for the Boston Massacre is worth noting. First, for over a year, the British Crown ordered that soldiers be housed in the homes of Boston citizens. Impressment or quartering of troops drew intense resentment from those citizens. Second, because British soldiers were paid poorly, many of them sought to supplement their income with additional jobs when they were off duty. They often took up the jobs of the propertyless, those who could not vote or participate in town meetings, such as sailors, ropemakers, and tavern workers, or any role that involved menial labor. Sailors and ropemakers, like Attucks, despised competing with British soldiers for economic opportunities. The labor grievances against the soldiers caused riots throughout the Eastern Seaboard, including New York and Newport, Rhode Island, where after weeks of impressment from British soldiers, over five hundred seamen, many of them Black, rioted because they were unable to earn a living.[65] All these years after fleeing slavery, Attucks was not going to relinquish his livelihood and ability to live freely.

On the evening of March 5, 1770, Attucks was with other seamen drinking at a pub in Boston. When a British soldier walked into the tavern to inquire about a part-time job, Attucks and his fellow seamen were incensed. They began to curse at the soldier and threatened him until he left the pub. Historians have argued that Attucks was not thinking about revolution in the ideological sense that night, but I disagree. If we rethink revolution as I have here, as a response to oppression and an attempt to establish an equitable and new social and political order, then his decision to confront the soldier was indeed a revolutionary act.

Attucks had zero interest in maintaining a system where British soldiers could upend his livelihood. He, along with the other seamen, had good reason to be defiant and even hostile. They allegedly chased the soldier into the street, where the skirmish began to turn violent. Witnesses claimed Attucks was the leader of the mob that confronted the British soldier. Historian Douglas Egerton reasoned, "The prudent thing to do for a man like Attucks was to back away from that confrontation, but he did not."[66] According to trial testimony, Attucks brandished two wooden sticks. At once, several other British soldiers arrived, formed a semicircle, and pointed their cutlasses and bayonets at the growing crowd. One enslaved man named Andrew was a witness to events. He recalled that Attucks was a "stout man" who tried to punch one of the officers. Andrew claimed Attucks snatched the soldier's bayonet from his hand and then yelled for the crowd to "kill the dogs, knock them over."[67] In that moment, the soldier regained control of his firearm and shot Attucks in the chest.

Interestingly, the deaths of Attucks and four other men who also were killed by the British that night were met with a wave of solidarity. Samuel Adams, member of the Sons of Liberty and an eventual Founding Father, took it upon himself to organize the procession to move the five bodies to Faneuil Hall, where they lay in state for three days before their funerals. An estimated ten thousand to twelve thousand people attended the procession. At the time, that was more than half of Boston's population. His Black and Indigenous ancestry would have kept Attucks from being buried in the same plot as the white colonists, but for Attucks the city made an exception. He was buried along with the four other victims at the Granary Burying Ground.[68]

The public may have embraced Attucks, but the elite did not. The trial for the British soldiers involved in the massacre is telling. The lawyer tasked with defending the soldiers was none other than John Adams. When presenting his case, Adams described the men the soldiers killed as "a motley rabble of saucy boys, negroes and molattoes [sic], Irish teagues and outlandish jack tarrs."[69] Race and class are the essential factors for each group: Adams pointed to racial and class categories to emphasize that they were men of no consequence. Black men, teagues (a slur referring to Irishmen), and "jack tarrs"—seamen—were all expendable, probably criminal. These men were "saucy," or irreverent, and could not be assumed to be up to any good.[70] That Attucks was forty-seven years old, not some adolescent rabble-rouser, did not matter. His ancestry, skin color, and perhaps his height were enough to make him the lead culprit.

Adams built his defense of the British soldiers on the charge that Attucks struck the first blow and led the "dreadful carnage." Adams concluded that Attucks's "mad behavior" provoked the soldiers' response, saying that Attucks's group was "under the command of a stout molatto [sic] fellow, whose very looks, was enough to terrify any person."[71] Adams used Attucks's race, and specifically his Blackness, to arouse sympathy for the terrified British soldiers. He argued that these soldiers were rightfully (and racially) afraid. Essentially, Adams argued that Black people cannot employ violence, revolutionary or not. However, it was acceptable for white people to use lethal force to "defend themselves,"[72] particularly when threatened by Black people.

When the trial concluded, six of the eight soldiers involved were acquitted after two and a half hours of jury deliberation. The remaining two soldiers were found guilty of manslaughter for firing into the crowd. But both sentences were eventually reduced from death to the branding of their thumb in court, a proverbial slap on the wrist. Adams's anti-Blackness was counterrevolutionary; it served to support the institution of slavery and the violent subjection of all Black people in the United States.[73] The work of revolution could never be complete if it did not extend to include African Americans. Seminal moments in US history that historians have defined as patriotic were also moments that denied patriotism to Black people. Crowds in Boston considered Attucks a symbol of the revolution, but the irony was that the "revolution" was only to benefit white men. Interestingly, not only is Attucks known for being the first casualty of the American Revolution, but in the telling of the Boston Massacre, he is the only casualty known by name. Who readily recalls the names of Samuel Gray, James Caldwell, Samuel Maverick, and Patrick Carr? Most people cannot even remember how many people were killed. While Attucks might show up in history as a mere reference point for the Boston Massacre, he has become a hero for Black Americans. According to author Eric Hinderaker, Attucks became a symbol in the 1840s for Black abolitionists.[74] African American leaders and activists promoted him as an example of a Black patriot. In the spring of 1858, nearly one hundred years after the Boston Massacre, Black abolitionists gathered in Boston to honor Attucks with the first-ever Crispus Attucks Day. Black efforts and activism are why we remember Attucks to this day. Black leaders such as Lewis Hayden and William C. Nell were in attendance for a festival at the famed Faneuil Hall. White abolitionist Wendell Phillips was in attendance as well and gave a speech acknowledging Black people as pioneers against British tyranny. Phillips declared, "Who set the example of guns? Who taught the British Soldiers that he might be defeated? Who first dared look into his eyes? Those five men!" He claimed, "The 5th of March was the baptism of blood. . . . I place, therefore this Crispus Attucks in the foremost rank of the men dared. When we talk of courage, he rises, with his dark face, in the clothes of a laborer, his head uncovered, his arm raised above him defying bayonets. . . . When the proper symbols are placed around the base of the statue of Washington, one corner will be filled by the colored man defying the British muskets."[75]

Black and white abolitionists attempted to reorient the genesis of the American Revolution from Lexington and Concord to the streets of Boston. They were attempting to make a Black man the true face of the rebellion that culminated into a revolution, reminding all that it was Attucks's defiance and death that rallied colonists. In the twentieth century Attucks remained a model of Black resistance. In 1964, civil rights leader Martin Luther King Jr. wrote to Black schoolchildren, "Know that the first American to shed blood in the revolution that freed his country from British oppression was a Black seaman named Crispus Attucks."[76] But radical leaders like Black Power spokesman Stokely Carmichael took Attucks's example even further. In 1966, Carmichael praised participants in racial social unrest and argued that the "[Black] man who goes out and throws a brick at a white cop is taking part in an uprising as Crispus Attucks, another Black man, was when he threw rocks in the American Revolution at Boston."[77] Enslaved, free, and fugitive Black people were the true revolutionaries of the Revolutionary Era because they believed in abolishing slavery and establishing a society that worked for everyone.

Attucks was courageous. In the face of armed authority, he risked everything by physically engaging with British soldiers. Though he had lived as a free man for more than twenty years, capture was always a possibility. He was not content to simply flee. He traveled, he labored, and he fought to preserve his freedom. He had no control of how history would use his memory or interpret his intentions, but that is not the point. He was unwilling to live a life in subordination to anyone. Author Mitch Kachun contends, "It does not matter whether or not he was a leader, or a friend of Revere and Hancock, or well-read in political philosophy, or a good Christian, or active in the Sons of Liberty, or merely a drunken dockworker." His presence and actions on March 5, 1770, "embodied the diversity of colonial America and the active participation of workers and people of color in the public life of the Revolutionary era."[78] When the Revolution came, Attucks may have been the first casualty, but he was far from alone in his stance for life and liberty unmarred by slavery and tyranny. And as a former slave, he had more claim to these ideals than the Founding Fathers.

When America's war for independence commenced, some Black men and women contributed to patriotic efforts. In many cases, the role of Black soldiers was transformative in shifting the victory of war both on the ground and strategically. Black soldiers enlisted because they hoped for or were promised freedom. Achieving the goals of the Revolution had to include them. While some white leaders might have been reluctant to arm Black men, enslaved labor was a mainstay in the military: enslaved people served as cooks, porters, skilled tradesmen, sailors, spies, and valets. But George Washington was appalled to find the large numbers of enslaved Black men besieging British troops in the battles of 1775. He condemned their service and outlawed additional recruitment of Black troops. He feared that permitting the enslaved to bear arms might threaten the institution of slavery itself. Indeed, a democracy is antithetical to slavery. But Washington was not fighting for revolution; he was fighting for independence from Britain.

Black soldiers never acted in the way the Founding Fathers predicted or desired. Despite planter paranoia, there were no rampant slave rebellions and insurrections. Only after a brutal winter at Valley Forge did Washington change course on the enlistment of enslaved men. He was desperate. He and the Continental Congress allowed Rhode Island to recruit enslaved men. The First Rhode Island Regiment was made up entirely of Black soldiers, and Washington chose this all-Black company to lead the Continental army in the final battle at Yorktown. However, fighting in exchange for freedom was a precarious deal, and being placed on the front lines of a battle only signaled that one was disposable. In 1778, Rhode Island recruited the enslaved with the promise of freedom only to later rescind the promise.[79] For Black Americans, this was not a revolution; it was a charade. The government made it clear that Black men were merely slaves in service of the military, not free men fighting for a cause. Liberty was touted to entice their participation but never materialized as a reward.

At the conclusion of the American Revolution, nothing had changed for the marginalized or those without power. For the oppressed, the Revolution was not revolutionary. Some might argue that the Revolution inspired gradual emancipation in the North. For example, the enslaved woman Elizabeth Freeman of Massachusetts (also known as Mumbet) was able to sue for her freedom after hearing the Massachusetts Constitution read aloud. Her successful case served as a legal precedent and eventually led to the abolition of slavery in Massachusetts, the first state to abolish slavery. But the liberation of most enslaved people in all of the southern states was not complete. And in places like New York and New Jersey, slavery continued until the threat of revolution in Haiti pushed them toward gradual emancipation.

Revolution involves the total transformation of society and the liberation of all people, not a few. Thus, the American Revolution did not radically transform colonial society in a way that lived up to the principle fought for: that all men are created equal and have unalienable rights to life, liberty, and the pursuit of happiness. In the aftermath of the Revolution, the overwhelming majority of Black Americans were still enslaved, Native Americans had no protection for their western lands, white farmers who had been given cheap incentives to fight were still largely cut out of the economy by the planter class, and women, who made major contributions to war efforts, saw no changes in their social or political status despite their overwhelming support of white supremacy in the new nation. Americans had merely supplied the rhetoric of Black freedom efforts, but they never intended to extend freedom to the masses. For Black Americans, the Revolution replaced a distant white supremacist tyrant supportive of Black enslavement with local and electable white supremacist tyrants empowered to preserve the existing social, political, and economic order, which was grounded in slavery and anti-Blackness. The Revolution was not merely imperfect; it was not true.

Former slave turned abolitionist Frederick Douglass offered the most famous speech regarding America's incomplete revolution. "What to the Slave Is the Fourth of July?" is a scathing critique of American hypocrisy as the land of liberty. Douglass asks,

> What, to the American slave, is your 4th of July? I answer: a day that reveals to him, more than all other days in the year, the gross injustice and cruelty to which he is the constant victim. To him, your celebration is a sham; your boasted liberty, an unholy license; your national greatness, swelling vanity; your sounds of rejoicing are empty and heartless; your denunciations of tyrants, brass fronted impudence; your shouts of liberty and equality, hollow mockery; your prayers and hymns, your sermons and thanksgivings, with all your religious parade and solemnity, are, to him, mere bombast, fraud, deception, impiety, and hypocrisy.[80]

He referred to the war as a "thin veil to cover up crimes which would disgrace a nation of savages." America's revolution was guilty of violence and bloodshed; it was not a legitimate response to oppression. As Douglass argued, "There is not a nation on the earth guilty of practices more shocking and bloody, than are the people of these United States, at this very hour." For Douglass, a delayed revolution such as Guadeloupe's was better than a farce. Throughout the Black Diaspora and in the Western world, successful revolutions were the Haitian Revolution and Simón Bolívar's war for South American independence because they abolished slavery and were fought for better lives for all people. Douglass added, "The brave stand taken by the black sons [and daughters] of Haiti" was transformative. "Striking for their freedom, they struck for the freedom of every black man [and woman] in the world."[81] Because of Haiti's influence, South America was not just free from Spain; it was free from slavery. America accomplished nothing of the sort.

Like Solitude, Delgrès, Louverture, Attucks, and others, Black people have continued to die for the cause of freedom. And like Solitude, Delgrès, Louverture, and Attucks, few have died without first putting up a fight. When it comes to slavery and white supremacy, Douglass was right about this too: "It is not light that is needed, but fire; it is not the gentle shower, but thunder. We need the storm, the whirlwind, and the earthquake. The feeling of the nation must be quickened; the conscience of the nation must be roused; the propriety of the nation must be startled; the hypocrisy of the nation must be exposed; and its crimes against God and man must be proclaimed and denounced."[82] Black people mobilized to fight against their oppression. Black people strove to be the fire and the thunder, the storm and the earthquake. In revolutions, whether we consider the success of Haiti, the delayed liberation of Guadeloupe, or the incompleteness of the United States, one thing remains: revolutions require transformational change to improve the lives of all people.

It can be argued that America's revolution began not in 1776 but in 1863. The true American revolution did not start with the Civil War. It began when the demise of slavery was chosen as the determinant for winning the war. The Emancipation Proclamation sanctioned what enslaved and free Black Americans were already doing, freeing themselves. Hundreds of thousands of enslaved people abandoned plantations, and over 250,000 Black soldiers fought valiantly against a slaveholding South. When the war ended, slavery was over. The real work of revolution in America was Reconstruction. Three new amendments known as the Reconstruction Amendments were added to the US Constitution between 1865 and 1870. The Thirteenth Amendment (abolishing slavery), the Fourteenth Amendment (establishing citizenship for all), and the Fifteenth Amendment (prohibiting discrimination in voting rights) were revolutionary. For the first time in the nation's history Black men were free, were citizens, and had guaranteed suffrage. The revolutionary work of Reconstruction went further than any other country in the Western Hemisphere. And yet this revolution still did not extend to women.

In less than a generation, just several years, Black men went from being enslaved to being elected officials. Robert Smalls was born into slavery in Beaufort, South Carolina. During the Civil War, he managed to steal a Confederate ship with his family on board and sail it undetected to Union strongholds. His contributions helped convince Lincoln that Black men should be enlisted as soldiers to help win the war. When the war was over, Smalls returned home and invested in his communities. He entered politics and won an election as a Republican to the South Carolina legislature. He then ran for the United States House of Representatives and won. In 1861, Smalls was still enslaved. By 1868, he was serving in his first elected office. He was not alone. Over 1,500 men served in elected offices during Reconstruction, from local municipal roles to United States senators.

Political revolution was taking place. Black people did not have tremendous power, but they had influence, and they used it to benefit all Americans. The first universal public schools were established during Reconstruction. Education had been a privilege primarily for the elite. Now, for the first time, poor white children and Black children could obtain literacy and a formal education. The first public health departments were created to combat tropical diseases such as smallpox and typhoid, which had taken so many lives during the war. Schools, sanitation departments, roads, and infrastructure were implemented to reconstruct the entire country, not just the South. And in 1875, Congress passed the Civil Rights Act. The bill, which was sometimes, and interestingly, referred to as the Enforcement Act or the Force Act, was in response to white violence and terrorism occurring against Native Americans and thus was designed to "protect all citizens in their civil and legal rights."[83] The act aimed to provide for equal treatment in public accommodations and public transportation, and to prohibit exclusion from jury service. It was passed in honor of radical Republican senator Charles Sumner, who had drafted the bill in 1870 but died before its passage. Nearing the end of Reconstruction, Black South Carolina congressman Thomas Miller summed up the contributions of Black leadership: "We were eight years in power. We had built schoolhouses, established charitable institutions, built and maintained the penitentiary system, provided for the education of the deaf and dumb, rebuilt the ferries. In short, we had reconstructed the State and placed it upon the road to prosperity."[84] Finally, the work of revolution was beginning to take shape. But Reconstruction was not permanent, and it was not protected. If Haiti, Guadeloupe, and the United States have taught us anything about revolutions, it is that the hardest part of revolution is not winning; it's protecting and sustaining what was won.

I learned this lesson with my brother, William, who was cured of sickle cell anemia. From age sixteen to twenty-seven, he lived a full life. He graduated from high school and went on to college. He joined the Reserve Officers' Training Corps and graduated from his university as a commissioned officer in the United States Army. He fell in love and got married. He traveled the world. He was deployed to the Middle East and served his country with honor. He returned home with big plans for his life and with his wife. But when he was twenty-seven years old, he suddenly became ill. He told his wife he was having trouble breathing. He was admitted to the hospital, and doctors quickly determined that he had an infection of pneumococcus bacteria, which bone marrow transplant recipients like him are more susceptible to. They gave him a 50 percent chance of survival. After four days of battling and medical intervention, William died. He had lived over ten years sickle cell–free.

My brother's loss was devastating. In some ways, I felt like Guadeloupe, having experienced a short-lived freedom that was taken away. But the work of revolution is never dependent on one person. When Toussaint was captured and left to die in a French dungeon, he proclaimed that the fight would continue. I hate that I lost my brother, but I am grateful that research on sickle cell anemia did not stop with his death. In fact, researchers and doctors have come up with new ways to treat and cure sickle cell disease. It is possible that with time, resources, and work, sickle cell anemia can be eradicated. Cures are not about individuals; cures are about the community. Similarly, revolution is never intended to help one life but to help all lives. Many people have been cured of sickle cell anemia and gone on to live long, full lives. All oppressed people are in a constant struggle to reclaim what has been lost, protect what has been gained, and work to perfect equitable change.

Revolutions are the beginning of something new and just. Socially, politically, economically, we need revolutions. With revolution we are set up to walk down a better path, but the journey is long and hard and ongoing. If revolution were all that was needed, Black people would have won years ago, but as we'll see in the following chapters, revolutions must be protected and enforced.

Chapter Two

PROTECTION

I come from a large family. My great-grandparents, James and Rosa Price, and their sixteen children moved from West Feliciana, Louisiana, to Darlove, Mississippi, in a move James later called one of the worst decisions of his life. The opportunities throughout the South were bleak. James and Rosa raised their children on a farm where resources were in constant scarcity. Mouths had to be fed. Children had to be clothed. Bills had to be paid. Despite the hardships, James and his family had a good reputation. James was beloved and highly respected in the community. He was a godly man and a deacon in his church. Even white folks respected him.

One summer day in the 1930s, tragedy struck. James was out driving his car around town when a little white boy ran into the street in front of him. He was hit by the car and killed instantly. James was horrified. He ran to the child's aid, and people all around, Black and white, began to gather. They had witnessed the accident and seen the boy run in front of James's car too quickly for him to have possibly stopped the car in time. But a Black man had killed a little white boy with his car. In the 1930s, this was surely grounds for a public lynching. James would have been dragged out of his car, beaten, and lynched for all to see without apology. Rosa would have been left to raise all the children on her own, and exile might have been necessary for their own safety. Yet remarkably, nothing happened. The crowd saw what had occurred, recognized James, and immediately understood it was a tragic accident. Word spread around town that James was innocent, that there was nothing he could have done to prevent the collision. Even the parents of the little boy did not fault him. No one blamed him or harmed him. In fact, word spread fast around town specifically to prevent violence against James. He was publicly protected . . . sort of.

I have sat with this story for years. Why did white people let my great-grandfather walk away unharmed? My family will tell you it was "the Lord" and "a miracle." Others speculate that it was James's impeccable reputation as a good, earnest man who meant no one ill. But I suspect that the reason was something else. I return to James's confession that moving to Mississippi was "one of the worst decisions of [his] life." During the 1930s, the Great Migration was nearing its peak. Millions of African Americans were leaving the South to pursue better opportunities or to flee racial oppression. The South was struggling for laborers. Places like Detroit and Chicago were like vacuums pulling all Mississippi's skilled and unskilled workers away. Protection in a white supremacist world is an anomaly. Mercy is an exception. In a capitalist society, the greatest allegiance is to capital. If James and his family had been harmed, or even if they had left town for fear of retaliation, valuable and exploited labor would have been lost. The defense of James was not about protecting him as a human being but about protecting an asset. The need to preserve his labor meant inducing the Price family to stay where they were. James, Rosa, and their sixteen children had no land or significant resources the town could confiscate. What the town could exploit was their labor. Black labor was Mississippi's lifeblood, and the state could not afford to lose good, cheap workers. Protection is collective action to shield the oppressed and vulnerable. What James experienced was not protection; it was intended to perpetuate his exploited labor. Perhaps James felt both indebted and trapped by the town's grip on his family. He likely understood that in this instance, capitalism made the white boy's life expendable. In the small town of Darlove, the boy should have looked both ways.

While revolutions seek offensive solutions, protection is about a defensive stance. In other words, revolution breaks down the door of the oppressor and demands a new world order. Protection is about barricading the oppressor from the safe spaces that offer Black people reprieve. For Black people, the "war" against slavery, anti-Blackness, and white supremacy required a defensive strategy as much as an offensive one. The institutions of slavery and systemic racism were assaults on Black humanity; protection encapsulated the greatest expression of resistance to oppression because it is typically the first response to violence. Protection is like a reflex. It does not always require strategy or planning. Much like revolutions, protection can be violent, but it cannot be oppressive.[1]

Self-defense cannot create powerful structures and systems that deprive people. It is not retaliation or revenge. Protection stems from urgency, the immediate need to strike down, hit back, or arrest an onslaught of terrorism. Accordingly, protection has been a constant method of survival from the days of the slave trade to today.

To be clear, protection is more expansive than self-defense because in the Black community protection is collective. Protection seeks to protect all vulnerable people and even entire communities. Protection has included sheltering fugitive slaves, writing, giving speeches, providing or withdrawing financial support, and offering legal services, and in extreme but necessary cases, it could involve the murder of a slave catcher or rapist. During slavery, Black vigilance groups did the work of protection; they patrolled Black neighborhoods in packs looking for slave catchers or suspicious people. They attempted to recover kidnapped people from the state. Among the enslaved, protection was about minimizing the violence of slavery: slowdowns, deceit, threats, poison, arson, destruction of property, and physical altercations were used against slaveholders to stunt the institution and secure protection for oppressed Black people. Even after slavery, similar tactics have been employed to shield Black people from the eroding and harmful effects of racism. For example, bystanders record police interactions with Black people. With protection, sometimes large groups protect individuals and sometimes individuals protect large groups. Protection is the antithesis of policing because it is about securing freedom, not denying it.

Authors Zoé Samudzi and William C. Anderson contend that "white supremacist logic has been so convincing that we oppressed people have largely come to believe that self-defense is violence."[2] Protection explains the collective defensive tactics taken up by

Black abolitionists, activists, civil rights leaders, and ordinary folks in the Black community. It is a collective act to defend the oppressed and the vulnerable, kin and the community. Protection is about stealing security and procuring safeguards that often circumvent the law and can build up to or on the work of revolution. Slave catchers, police officers, and white terrorists are always met with resistance. With protection, the corollary to white supremacy is not turning the other cheek but pivoting from a blow and even landing one in return.

This chapter is about how Black Americans sought protection during slavery and after emancipation. These examples of protection are especially useful for us to consider because slavery offered zero protection. A slaveholder could legally murder, rape, beat, or sell away their human property. Enslaved people, free Black people, and their allies had to circumvent the law often in order to secure their safety. The nineteenth century poignantly illustrates how protection worked around the law and how Black leadership forced politicians to create equal protection under the law. The activism and courage of the nineteenth century established a blueprint for the activism of the civil rights movement of the twentieth century and even today's social and political movements.

When I think about protection in the antebellum period, I think of someone like Lucy Stanton, who was likely the first African American woman to graduate from a four-year institution, Oberlin Collegiate Institute, now known as Oberlin College. Located in Ohio, which was becoming a safe haven for free Black people, Oberlin was unusual in that it was one of the few institutions that admitted both men and women as well as African American students. Though it remained 97 percent white, it was known as a beacon for abolitionist and progressive politics. Stanton stood out. As the president of the Oberlin Ladies Literary Society, she was invited to give an address at commencement. She was just eighteen years old.[3] In many public spaces, women were shunned, booed, or even had objects hurled at them for speaking out in public, but not at Oberlin. And Stanton, well respected as a writer and a leader, was equipped for the task. On August 27, 1850, a warm summer day, Stanton stood at the podium facing a crowd and gave a speech she wrote entitled "A Plea for the Oppressed."

Her speech was essentially about employing protection for Black people. She knew well the political environment around her. Her stepfather, John Brown, was a wealthy Black barber and business-man in Cleveland who was active in the Underground Railroad. From a young age, he and her mother, Margaret, raised her with the scriptures to "do justice, love mercy and walk humbly with [her] God." Throughout her childhood she witnessed her parents harboring fugitive slaves and caring for those who could not help themselves. At one point, they housed as many as thirteen run-away slaves in their home. Stanton likely aided her parents, spoke with the enslaved, gave them supplies, and prayed for their safe journeys. Working on the Underground Railroad carried great danger for everyone involved. Though Stanton was born free and to some extent privileged, slavery and anti-Blackness and even pa-triarchy put her endeavors at considerable risk. As she prepared for her speech, she knew that the federal government was about to pass the Fugitive Slave Act, which would make all Black peo-ple potentially susceptible to capture and enslavement. No Black American would be really free or protected.

The Fugitive Slave Act held that slave owners maintained their property rights not just in the slaveholding South but throughout the country.[4] Those owners had the backing of the US government to retrieve their "stolen property." The law put Black folks who escaped slavery and sought haven in northern states at risk of being sent back to their slaveholders. Furthermore, any child born of a fugitive mother was also considered property of the slave owner. To reclaim an enslaved person, the owner needed only to make his plea to a court commissioner and the process could begin. Once captured, the accused had no right to trial by jury. The edict made clear that no hearing under this act could allow the testimony of the alleged fugitive to be admitted as evidence; except in cases involving mistaken identity, the master's testimony was all that was allowed.[5]

There were also significant financial incentives for returning fugitive slaves. US Marshals could gain hefty rewards for retrieving a person, and they could deputize white northerners on the spot to assist them in doing so. If a white person refused to assist, they could be fined up to $1,000 or face six months in jail. Court officials were compensated according to the judge's decision: ten dollars if the judge returned the slave to the proclaimed owner and five dollars if the judge decided there was insufficient proof to do so. The law exploited people's greed. In addition to threatening fugitive slaves, the law also put free Black people at risk. Because they had little to no say in a court of law, they could easily be kidnapped and enslaved. Thus, Black people encountered two options, and neither was satisfying: flee to Canada's border, America's new Mason-Dixon Line (Canada refused to return runaway slaves), or stay in America and be prepared to protect themselves. And protection required collective action to sustain individuals' safety.

Much of the abolitionist movement was operating on a nonviolent ideology promoted by white abolitionist William Lloyd Garrison during the 1830s and '40s. Garrison believed in moral suasion, the idea that slaveholders could be morally persuaded to relinquish their enslaved property. But morality among thieves was moot. Who could be persuaded to relinquish their property even if they believed slavery was a sin? Famous abolitionist Frederick Douglass contended, "Moral considerations have long since been exhausted upon slaveholders. It is in vain to reason with them. One might as well hunt bears with ethics. . . . Slavery is a system of brute force. It shields itself behind might, rather than right. It must be met with its own weapons."[6] For former and fugitive slaves, pacifism, or nonresistance, was an ideology or even a luxury they could not afford. Empathy had failed to drive progressive change. Racism and exclusion were profitable to those in power. Combatting them meant making anti-Blackness and white supremacy costly and dangerous instead.

When Stanton gave her speech, she knew the only topic worth speaking about before a largely white audience was how to persuade them, or, really, mobilize them, to act in defiance of laws like the Fugitive Slave Act. Urgency was the theme of Stanton's speech. "The freedom of the slave and the gaining of our rights, social and political, are inseparably connected, [so] let all the friends of humanity plead for those who may not plead their own cause."[7] Abolition would take more than just Black Americans calling out the wrongness of slavery. White Americans also needed to understand the violence slavery caused. "Will you not raise your voice in behalf of these stricken ones?" Stanton admonished. "Will you not plead the cause of the Slave? Slavery is the combination of all crime. It is War."[8]

Stanton was making an intellectual or philosophical case for protection. Her speech was a call for securing protection for the enslaved. For Stanton to refer to slavery as war was no small thing. She was not being colorful; she was being emphatic. And not only was slavery war, but it was violent and catastrophic theft. Stanton argued that slavery robbed Black people of their homes, liberty, education, and life. Slavery was not mere labor. Because slavery was evil, Stanton argued, one could not hold on to virtue and refuse abolitionism as a cause. Actions and values needed to be coupled together for meaningful impact. In other words, she was calling out white northerners who were comfortable saying slavery was wrong but then did nothing to end it. This was unacceptable to Stanton. "Ye that advocate the great principles of Temperance, Peace, and Moral Reform . . . will you not plead the cause of the Slave?"[9] She called out the hypocrisy she saw in the social and political agenda. At such a time, the reformer's only cause should be the end of slavery because it impacted everything in society. Slavery, for Stanton, was "pollution."[10]

During slavery, Black women recognized early on that their lives under and outside the law were not encased by the culture's "true womanhood" or deemed worthy of protection. Black women were never included in the nineteenth-century ideas regarding societal standards for women. This made them an easy target for violence. In history books and popular culture, we see enslaved women and fugitives risking everything to give themselves and their families better lives. Much less discussed are the free Black women who employed force and violence and risked their freedom, if not their lives, to ensure the freedom of others. Moreover, their resistance was specific: slave owners, slave catchers, snitches, and anyone who interfered in the pursuit of freedom was at risk of facing Black women's armed position. Violent resistance did not belong to men alone. Black women have never been afraid to use violent force to protect themselves and their loved ones. Inside and outside the institution of slavery, Black women had every reason to contemplate or resort to violence as a meaningful tool to combat their powerlessness. More often than not, instead of seeking protection, Black women positioned themselves *as* protectors.

In July 1836, an event known as the Abolition Riot took place in Boston. Two enslaved women, Eliza Small and Polly Ann Bates, had run away from their master, John B. Morris of Baltimore. When the two women were caught and brought to trial, the abolitionists in the community sought to rescue them. A commotion in the courtroom began when someone shouted, "Go, go!" Multiple people rushed to the bench, seized the two fugitive women, and shoved them into a carriage that was waiting for them at the steps of the courthouse. When an officer attempted to grab one of the women, another Black woman intervened. She was described as a woman "of great size" who scrubbed floors for a living. The unnamed woman threw her arms around the officer and immobilized him. She held on to him long enough for Small and Bates to escape. The two women found their freedom and were never recaptured. No one was charged for aiding in their escape.[11] A Black woman's protection saved them.

In the Midwest, Black women were likewise vigilant against slave catchers. Anyone they did not recognize or who spoke with a southern accent sent them into high alert. In one instance, an elderly Black woman recognized two slave catchers policing the area where she lived. It is not clear whether enslaved people were hiding nearby, but in any case, the woman clearly did not want anyone to be captured. She cornered the two men and threatened them with her knife. She then forced them into a corncrib as a makeshift holding pen. What fortitude would allow an elderly woman to take on two men? Her courage and protective actions allowed any fugitives being pursued by the men to continue on their journey to freedom.

Stories like these were countless. In 1848, Black women in Cincinnati protected themselves with shovels and washboards to fend off slave catchers, and in Boston, Black women flung stones at men they suspected of kidnapping fugitives or free men and women.[12] While the names of these women and the full accounting of their courageous acts may never be revealed, it is recorded that Harriet Tubman was not above packing a pistol for her journeys in and out of slave territory. It changes our perspective on Black women, self-defense, and protection if we no longer see someone like Harriet Tubman as the exception but the rule when it came to security in Black communities. Even freeborn Black leaders proclaimed they were prepared to resort to arms in defiance of the Fugitive Slave Law. In 1855, a Black Oberlin student named Mary Ann Darnes gave a short speech in Cincinnati. She warned, "The time is not far distant when the slave must be free; if not by moral and intellectual means, it must be done by the sword. Remember, gentlemen, should duty call, it will be yours to obey, and strike to the last for freedom."[13] Gentlemen were not the only ones to answer the call of duty and strike for the freedom of African Americans: Black women were also ready and armed.

In 1817, Eliza Ann Elizabeth Howard was born into slavery in Maryland. She managed to escape to Pennsylvania and married William Parker, a local activist and former fugitive himself, having run away with his brother, Charles, from Anne Arundel County, Maryland. As a fugitive, Eliza knew what was at stake in procuring protection for herself and her family and community. Eliza had been instrumental in her own escape to freedom; she had to brave great dangers and uncertainties. Together, Eliza and

William formed an organization for fugitive slaves offering mutual protection against slaveholders and kidnappers in their new hometown of Christiana, Pennsylvania.[14]

Geography played a major role in protection. Because Pennsylvania bordered the slave state of Maryland, many runaways sought safety and freedom over the Pennsylvania state line. Scholars believe Pennsylvania had the highest percentage of runaways in the North.[15] Slave catchers, aware of such safe havens, monitored them closely, making quite a business of returning runaways. In Christiana, a border town, a group of men notoriously known as the Gap Gang terrorized both fugitives and free Black residents. In response, Eliza and William Parker banded together with other fugitive men and women to form their own group, the Lancaster Black Self-Protection Society.[16] It's one of the few times the word "Black" was used to define a group in the nineteenth century. The society resolved to "prevent any of our brethren being taken back to slavery, [even] at the risk of our own lives."[17] Allies such as white Quakers agreed to be of assistance if needed.

On September 11, 1851, the Parkers' reputation brought four fugitive slaves—Noah Buley, Nelson Ford, George Ford, and Joshua Hammond—to their door. The men sought safe haven in the Parkers' home in Christiana on their path north. The Parkers agreed to house and protect them. But it was not long after their arrival that Maryland slaveholder Edward Gorsuch arrived with his son, his nephew, a deputy marshal, and his assistants to claim his fugitive property. When Gorsuch and his men confronted the Parkers at their home, words were exchanged, and a standoff ensued. Parker instructed the fugitive slaves not to be afraid or give in to any slaveholder: he would fight for them to the death if necessary.[18] Eliza's brother-in-law Alexander Pinckney, also a fugitive who lived with the Parkers, was on the brink of turning himself in. "Where is the use of fighting?" he moaned. "They will take us anyway." Eliza immediately armed herself with a corn cutter, a tool she undoubtedly knew how to use. She threatened to "chop off the head" of the first member of their band who tried to give up.[19] Protection violence was not reserved for white people; it also was faced by anyone who stood in the way of liberation. Eliza would have just as easily used her corn cutter on cowards as she would have on slave catchers. It was one thing to be afraid; it was another to be a coward. Surrendering was not an option.

Eliza and William had prepared for such altercations. In the event that slave catchers were near or trouble arose, Eliza was responsible for sounding the alarm to alert the Lancaster Black Self-Protection Society. When it became clear that Gorsuch was unwilling to forfeit his property, Eliza suggested to William that assistance was needed. She thought now was a good time to signal their friends to come to their aid. William agreed. Without hesitation, Eliza moved into action. She headed to their small attic and proceeded to blow a loud horn. One of Gorsuch's men began to question what was happening. They asked Parker, "What do you mean by blowing that horn?" He did not answer. It was nearly 7 a.m., and the blowing of the horn continued. Standing with Gorsuch was Henry H. Kline, a US Marshal and professional slave catcher who was notorious for kidnapping Black people, free or fugitive. Kline ordered his men to shoot at anyone blowing a horn. Two of his men then began to climb a peach tree that stood by the end of the house. As the two men climbed, they spotted Eliza and started shooting at her. Shot after shot, they aimed at her and missed. Eliza continued to blow her horn, tucking herself into a ball just below the window seal and resting the horn on top of it. William later recalled that the men "blew blast after blast, while the shots poured thick and fast around [Eliza]." He believed they must have fired their pistols ten or twelve times. But the Parker home was made of stone and impenetrable to the slave catchers' bullets. The stone house and the deep windows preserved Eliza's life.[20]

What followed was one of the most significant violent altercations before the Civil War. As the demands between William and Gorsuch escalated, William heaved pitchforks and axes at the slave catchers to keep them from breaking in the house. At that moment, members of the Lancaster Black Self-Protection Society, eighty Black women and men along with two white Quakers, arrived on the scene. Armed with guns and farm equipment, they surrounded Gorsuch's men and the US Marshal. Outnumbered and outgunned, Kline fled in terror as shots were fired. Gorsuch was unwavering, and William later claimed that "his slave struck him the first and second blows; then three or four sprang upon him, and, when he became helpless, [they] left him to pursue others."[21] Gorsuch's son, Dickinson, was lying on the ground not far away, severely wounded. Gorsuch lay on the ground near the house in a pool of blood. William wrote that as Gorsuch lay on the ground, "the women put an end to him."[22] The women were not afraid to use violence to finish him off. It could have been Eliza or her sister, Hannah Pinckney, or any of the other women who arrived on the scene to help. Perhaps they used a corn cutter; regardless, they ended his life quickly. What Gorsuch's slaves started, these women finished, and now Gorsuch was dead. At the time, Eliza was just twenty-one years old and the mother of three children. With the exception of Eliza and Hannah, the other women are nameless in this story, but they reveal the remarkable role Black women played in defense. Women had no trouble putting an end to Gorsuch. The fact that William later declared that women were involved validates the solidarity among

Black residents regarding violent protection. Both Black women and men were susceptible to kidnapping and assault. Both women and men and their children were terrorized by the Gap Gang and the tyranny of people like Kline. The confrontation in Christiana, Pennsylvania, is significant because it represents a collective act of resistance in which both women and men acted heroically. Furthermore, had it not been for Eliza's quick thinking to alert the Lancaster Black Self-Protection Society, the Christiana Resistance could have ended quite differently.

After the fight, William wrote, Eliza had to go into hiding as he went on the run. She took their three children to her mother's home to be cared for by her mother and the charity of their neighbors until she could ensure her own safety. Friends told William that officers were looking for him to arrest him and would not relent until he was caught, so he made plans to leave right away. As he headed back to his home, likely to gather up supplies for his departure, a group of Black women stopped him. "Forty or fifty armed men," they relayed, were at his house searching for him. He could not go home, not even for a moment. William and the four fugitive slaves who had escaped from Gorsuch fled farther north on foot and by boat, briefly stopping at safe houses, until they made it to Canada.[23]

For their final stop, the men stayed at Frederick Douglass's house. Even Douglass, who earlier in his abolitionist career had allied with Garrison in his support of moral suasion, recognized the legitimacy of protection violence. The Fugitive Slave Law was a game changer for Douglass. He wrote about their short visit to his home in Rochester, New York: "I could not look upon them as murderers. To me, they were heroic defenders of the just rights of man against mansteelers and murderers. So I fed them, and sheltered them in my house." Furthermore, Douglass admitted that had the authorities come to his house that night, his "home would have been stained with blood."[24] Given the inhumanity of the Fugitive Slave Act, violence could not be off the table. When asked about the act, William Parker claimed, "The Laws for personal protection are not made for us, and we are not bound to obey them. . . . We have no country."[25] William believed that Black people should not be forced to obey laws until they had the right to shape laws. Several years later, in 1857, the Supreme Court would validate William's stance, holding in the *Dred Scott* case that Black people had no rights or protections as enslaved or free people. Black abolitionists grew more isolated from their white allies who saw moral suasion as the only retort to slavery. Violence would be the inevitable response.

Douglass accompanied William Parker and the four other fugitive slaves as they boarded a steamer headed to Toronto. Once on the ship, William presented Douglass with the revolver that had fallen from Gorsuch's hand when he died. William described the weapon as "a token of gratitude and a memento of the battle for Liberty at Christiana." Douglass concluded, "I returned to my home with a sense of relief which I cannot stop here to describe."[26]

The Christiana Resistance became national news and a symbol of the political transformation of a Black community bound together by protection. The border along Pennsylvania and Maryland was significant not only as a place where Black Americans suffered violence but also as a place where they managed to use violence to redeem their sense of self, community, and value.

Though he had safely made it to Canada, William could not rest until he knew his family was safe. He thought of the thirty-five Black women and men and five white people who had been arrested for treason for their role in the Christiana Resistance and were being held in the Moyamensing Prison in Philadelphia to await trial.

He began to relax when he received a letter that Eliza and their children were safe. William was still illiterate, and as the letter was being read to him, he asked the reader to stop. He wanted his wife at his side desperately. William and Eliza were partners and were equally committed to protecting the lives of the enslaved, but just as important was protecting each other. Two months from the day William landed in Toronto, Eliza arrived. But she was alone. Her path to Canada had been a treacherous one, but Eliza was both brave and undaunted. Twice, authorities had placed her under custody as she attempted to escape to Canada.[27] Escape was much more difficult for women than for men, and one can only imagine the violence she must have suffered during her detainment, but the details of her experiences are not known. When Eliza learned that her former master was seeking to retrieve her, she managed to slip free a third and final time. But her hasty escape did not allow her to bring their three children with her; she had to leave them with her mother.[28]

As months passed, the events in Christiana remained in the public discourse. The North blamed the slaveholders for their own demise. The *New York Independent* attributed Gorsuch's death to all advocates of the Fugitive Slave Law: "The framers of this law counted upon the utter degradation of the negro race—their manliness and heroism—to render feasible execution" and, according to the paper, they foolhardily "anticipated no resistance from a race cowed down by centuries of oppression, and trained to servility."[29] Many slaveholders believed the Fugitive Slave Law would solve their problems. Instead, it exacerbated national tensions over slavery.

The political ramifications of the Christiana Resistance were significant. Internationally, the influx of Black Americans into Canada caused tension in the diplomatic relationship with the United States because Canada was not interested in aiding the United States in the return of fugitive slaves. The Christiana Resistance also came at a great monetary cost. The US government spent $50,000 ($1.47 million in 2012 dollars) trying to find justice for Gorsuch, to no avail. Nearly every political faction had an opinion about who was to blame. Nonradical white abolitionists attempted to distance themselves from the event, claiming that the Black residents of Christiana were "acting independently of the guidance by whites."[30] No doubt the Parkers found this sentiment to be complimentary. Black self-determination was necessary to move beyond the failed practices of moral suasion and white paternalism.

Democrats saw the Christiana Resistance as a tool for berating their enemies and presented false or exaggerated details that were reprinted in southern newspapers. In particular, the Democratic Party blamed Pennsylvania governor William F. Johnston for the increase in violence committed by Black people. Democrats were determined to defeat Johnston, a Whig, in the October election. Exploiting racial tensions over slavery, his opponents argued that Johnston was partisan to Black residents and abolitionists because he would not support the Fugitive Slave Law and refused to repeal the state's 1847 antikidnapping act.[31] Democrats also accused Johnston and the state's "notorious abolitionists" of having responsibility for Gorsuch's death.[32]

Southerners were beginning to discover that Black men and, especially, Black women "who have tasted liberty, soon learn to prize it, and are ready to defend it."[33] Eventually, the Christiana Resistance was a major victory in the fight against the Slave Power.

The charges against the accused were dropped, and Eliza and her husband were reunited with their three children. They lived out the rest of their days on a fifty-acre settlement in Buxton, Ontario, where the Parkers' descendants still live to this day. Arguably, more than any other event apart from John Brown's raid, tensions from Christiana helped to precipitate the Civil War. According to the scholar Thomas Slaughter, the soil of the Civil War was fertilized with Gorsuch's blood.[34] And it was Black women who sounded the alarm, rose to the occasion, and shed that blood.

The Fugitive Slave Law increased violence both along and far away from the borders of free and slaveholding states. Corporately, Black people were willing to risk their lives to ensure the protection of their communities, but the roles women played in protection societies were central. For example, in Cleveland, Black women made up four of the nine members of the all-Black vigilance committees. "Their track record was impressive. Over the course of just eight months, the committee assisted 275 enslaved people to freedom in Canada."[35] Boston and Detroit also had all-Black vigilance societies. In Boston, the New England Freedom Association existed only from 1842 to 1847, but during its short tenure, two of its seven directors were Black women, Judith Smith and Mary L. Armstead. The Black vigilance group in Detroit had tremendous success: during a two-week period in 1854, they aided fifty-three of their Black brothers and sisters in bondage. Over the course of seven months, from May 1855 to January 1, 1856, they assisted an additional 1,043 enslaved people.[36] One by one, free Black communities were undermining the planter's ability to retrieve his lost property.

During the 1850s, there were countless stories of Black women and their allies employing axes, pistols, rifles, and other weapons to combat slave catchers throughout the North. These groups were also run as a labor of love. Lack of sufficient finances was a constant impediment, and all their efforts placed them at significant risk, particularly after the passage of the Fugitive Slave Law. But as domestic workers, many Black women in the North had the mobility to serve as the eyes and ears of the vigilance committees. During their daily chores, Black women could overhear conversations and keep tabs on suspicious southern visitors. Black women bore the burden of some of the most daring tasks: caring for and hiding fugitive slaves. Mary Myer, a Black woman living in Philadelphia, owned a bakery and used her business to conceal fugitives seeking temporary shelter until they could move farther north. Another Black woman, Henrietta Duterte, took over her husband's undertaking business when he died and aided fugitives by hiding them in caskets.[37]

Records of the heroic stories of fugitive slaves who successfully resisted a return to slavery were circulated widely. William Still, known as the father of the Underground Railroad, who was responsible for the successful escape of over eight hundred slaves, made a point of recording the stories of his encounters with runaways.[38] One of these was the story of Margaret Garner. In January 1856, twenty-two-year-old Margaret escaped slavery with seven members of her family. They fled the Maplewood plantation in Boone County, Kentucky, during one of the coldest winters on record. They walked across a frozen Ohio River and into the free state of Ohio, where they found refuge in the home of Margaret's uncle, Joe Kite. After enjoying freedom for mere hours, slave catchers and US Marshals found the fugitives and attempted to break down the door to the home where they were hiding. In a moment of chaos and panic, Margaret begged her mother to help her kill her children. Margaret managed to slit her two-year-old daughter's throat and attempted to kill her other three children to prevent them from being taken back into slavery. Before she could, she was stopped and arrested. During her trial she declared, "I did the best that a mother could do. And I would have done better and more for the rest. I've done the best I could."[39] If given the chance, she would have killed all her children to prevent them from returning to the hell of slavery. For Margaret, if freedom could not be had, then death was the only form of deliverance. She loved her children so much, she refused to forfeit them to slavery. Nevertheless, she and her remaining family were eventually returned. But Margaret was not sent back to her master's plantation. Her family was split up and she and her husband were sent to the Deep South.

Margaret made national headlines when she killed her child to prevent her return to slavery. She illustrated what desperate lengths Black women were willing to go to in order to obtain either liberty or deliverance through death. She attempted to save her children from a fate worse than death. Black women gave Margaret's story a platform to dispel the myth of "happy and contented" slaves. American expatriate Mary Ann Shadd Cary was the leading Black woman in the abolitionist movement in Canada. She founded and ran a newspaper called the *Provincial Freeman*. When Shadd Cary learned about Margaret and her slain child, she published articles that spoke of her bold and desperate act in an admiring tone. She even suggested that Margaret's spirit should be cultivated. Not only did the *Provincial Freeman* support Margaret's sentiments and actions, but an article suggested that "all endeavors should have been made to cut the throats of the lawless pursuers, which would have been in compliance with the . . . scriptures." The paper also published James Madison Bell's poem "Liberty or Death," in which he declared, "Long live the name of Margaret in every freeman's breast." The poem illustrates how terrible enslavement was, particularly for mothers:

> *Go and ask of Margaret Garner,*
> *Who's now in prison bound,*
> *(No braver women e'er hath trod,*
> *Columbia's slave-cursed ground)*
>
> *Why did she with a mother's hand*
> *Deprive her child of breath?*
> *She'll tell you, with a Roman's smile,*
> *That slavery's worse than death.*

Margaret's case reached the governor of Ohio, Salmon P. Chase, and the president of the United States, Franklin Pierce, both of whom the abolitionists were quick to blame. The American Anti-Slavery Society accused Governor Chase of cowardice for not taking steps to protect and free Margaret's family. The society declared, "It is unfortunate for the fair fame of Ohio that she had not a Governor, who, in such a crisis was ready to override, if necessary, all forms of law, and assert the dignity and rights of the State."[40] For northerners, and abolitionists in particular, Margaret's plight was a tragedy and an indictment of American slavery. Margaret's return to slavery served only to heighten antislavery sentiments. For Black women, slavery was physically, sexually, emotionally, and psychologically violent. Slavery exploited Black women's wombs for capital and then robbed them of their children. In the face of slave catchers, Black women had the greatest reasons to resort to violence. Black people were willing to use violence against

their oppressors, or to turn the knife on themselves or their families if necessary to prevent their return to slavery.

In 1856, Frederick Douglass's newspaper published Black abolitionist, physician, and lawyer John S. Rock's lament for the often
helpless and hopeless position in which African American women
found themselves. Rock was deeply affected by the comments of
white abolitionist Theodore Parker, who remarked that if Margaret
had been a white woman, all the four hundred thousand white
men living in Ohio would have come to her defense. Interestingly,
Margaret's slain child had fair skin, or was phenotypically white.
Officials described the child as looking like a cherub with locks
of golden hair and fair skin. It cannot be proven, but it is likely
that her child was the result of sexual assault by her master. Rock
wanted Margaret's motherhood, grief, and actions to matter. Rock
challenged Black Americans to take on a "daring or desperate"
enterprise to demonstrate their courage. He wanted Americans to
see Margaret's family as more than property: as vulnerable people
fighting for freedom and worthy of defense.

After her murder trial, Margaret and her family were taken back
to slavery on a steamboat called the *Henry Louis*. Their Kentucky
master broke up her family. Her two older boys were sold away. Her
parents were sold away, too. Only Margaret, her husband, Robert,
and their infant child, Cilla, continued to the Deep South, which
would take them farther away from all that they knew. While en
route, something unexpected happened. Their ship collided with
another steamboat, propelling Margaret, who was carrying her
child, into the water. Margaret's hands were chained together; she
could not have saved her infant child from drowning even if she
had wanted to. However, it was believed that Margaret rejoiced in
the death of her only surviving daughter. Now childless, Margaret
was rescued and eventually sent with her husband to slavery in

New Orleans. In 1858, she died of typhoid fever. On her death-bed, she made her husband promise that should he marry again, he would marry a free woman, to ensure that their children would never be enslaved. Even on her deathbed, she wanted to protect Black children from slavery.

Lucy Stanton's 1850 commencement speech at Oberlin high-lighted the suffering of enslaved mothers. She called on white women to have compassion and to think of their own lives and families and imagine it all being taken away from them. She painted a vivid picture of a woman who toiled long, hot hours in the field and returned home to her child, "for to her it is the only ray of joy in a dreary world. She returns weary and sick at heart from the labors of the field; the child's beaming smile of wel-come half banishes the misery of her lot. Would she not die for it? Ye who know the depths of a mother's love, answer!"[41] Stan-ton wanted answers. But she seemed to get them only from other Black mothers, who understood the violence of slavery and sever-ance of families.

The violence of the Fugitive Slave Law energized Black leaders across the country, but perhaps no one more than Harriet Tub-man. The stories are true: she never lost a passenger on the Under-ground Railroad. Despite a traumatic brain injury as a child—she was hit in the head with an iron weight—Harriet had a brilliant mind. She knew how to read the stars for direction and identify plants that would quiet babies during long journeys. Tubman personified all of the attributes of protection. Moving along the eastern shore, she successfully rescued dozens of men, women, and children from bondage. She always kept a pistol on her and would not have hesitated to use it. Harriet threatened to shoot not only any slave catcher or dog but also any enslaved runaway who contemplated returning to the plantation and potentially spoiling her rescue efforts. In story after story, witnesses testified to Harriet's belief in the utility of forceful protection. During one rescue, when their odds of escape looked bleak, a man in the fleeing group said that he was going to return to his plantation. Harriet pointed her gun at the man's head and said, "You go on or die." Given these options, the man endured, and days later the group arrived in Canada.[42] Protection included preventing sabotage. As Eliza Parker had done during the Christiana Resistance by preventing her brother-in-law from surrendering, Harriet put the group above the individual.

The late 1850s were precarious times. Black and white leaders sensed a breaking point regarding the institution of slavery in America. Black men in the North were beginning to form their own quasi-military groups to protect their communities. A radical white abolitionist named John Brown believed he could use protection, flight, force, and, essentially, revolution to abolish slavery. His famous raid on Harpers Ferry, Virginia, was intended to start a wholesale exodus of enslaved people out of the South. He collected men and arms, and they planned to meet in Harpers Ferry to overtake the arsenal there. Only when his men met resistance would they shoot back. It was not the best-thought-out plan. How was Brown going to get hundreds or even thousands of enslaved people in the surrounding area to freedom? He could think of no better person for the job than Harriet.

Given her politics and her heroic and successful escapes, Harriet was just the kind of woman Brown wanted when he began to plan his monumental raid. He eagerly sought Harriet to enlist her talents to aid his grandiose plans of freeing the enslaved en masse and escaping to the Blue Ridge Mountains. While it is unclear how Harriet and Brown initially met, Brown wanted to have her as a possible recruiter and as a guide to help runaway slaves get to freedom in Canada. In April 1858, the two met at least twice in St. Catharines, Ontario, where Harriet lived in a boardinghouse on North Street. They discussed recruiting former slaves for the Harpers Ferry plot. Brown contended that her crucial knowledge of terrain in Maryland and Pennsylvania would be necessary for conducting a successful attack.[43] Brown admired Harriet's bravery so much that he gave her the highest compliment he could at the time: he called her General Tubman and sometimes used the pronoun "he" when referring to her.[44] As backhanded as it sounds, equating Harriet to a man was Brown's way of acknowledging her unwavering fearlessness. Harriet agreed to support Brown and his efforts. She began to recruit others as well.

However, Brown did not wait for Tubman or her recruits. No one knows why, but on October 16, 1859, Brown started the raid with his twenty-one-man army of liberators. The skirmish was over before it could really take off. Brown's men managed to take the armory but were trapped inside it. The local militia overtook them within a day and a half. Brown and many of his men were captured; others were killed. On December 2, Brown was executed for his crimes.

Because he had moved ahead without significant help, Harriet was not in attendance at the raid. Some historians speculate that she likely fell ill just prior to the raid.[45] Scholar Kate Clifford Larson contends that Harriet might have been unavailable because she was out recruiting for the raid; Larson also suggests that she may have begun to see the plan as unwinnable. Regardless, Harriet was willing. Douglass thought Brown's raid was suicide, but Harriet was likely an optimist when it came to freeing enslaved people. She expected resistance, certainly, but she never expected to lose. In many ways, Brown's raid had a delayed victory. It catapulted the South into secession and forced the North to confront the institution of slavery. Some historians argue that Brown's failed raid was the start of the Civil War.

When the Civil War began, protection reached a new pinnacle for Black people. Throughout the war slave catchers were still plaguing Black communities. In fact, during Lincoln's first inaugural address, he upheld the Fugitive Slave Law. On March 4, 1861, the day Lincoln was sworn in as president of the United States, he declared, "I have no purpose, directly or indirectly, to interfere with the institution of slavery in the States where it exists. I believe I have no lawful right to do so, and I have no inclination to do so."[46] Lincoln was behind the curve: enslaved and free Black people had already decided that this was not a Civil War but an abolition war, a war that would once and for all end the institution of slavery. Enslaved people were presented with two options: flee or fight. Many enslaved people left. Hundreds of thousands abandoned their plantations, particularly during the absence of their masters. They fled to Union lines and sought safe haven where they could find it.

Those who chose to fight expanded definitions of protection. Warfare in this case was not solely meant to protect the oppressed from oppression; it was also used to protect the entire country from slavery. War was used to protect the nation and present it with the truest form of freedom, one that fervidly defended the idea that all men are created equal. The American Revolution had been incomplete, unfinished, because it did not include transformative, progressive change for all people. The Civil War was a chance to complete the promise of democracy. In this sense, protection also completes the work of revolution. Once liberation is obtained and power is forfeited and redistributed to the benefit of all, protection is needed to sustain progress. Protection is the guardrail of revolutionary change.

Douglass used all of his advocacy to persuade Lincoln to issue the Emancipation Proclamation, immediately liberating three million of the four million people enslaved in rebellious Southern states (Missouri, Kentucky, Delaware, and Maryland were slave states still loyal to the Union). He also urged Lincoln to allow Black men to enlist in the war and pay them the same as white soldiers. Lincoln's executive orders to free the enslaved in the Confederacy and allow for Black soldiers were revolutionary: not only did they free many of the enslaved, but they empowered Black soldiers to fight and kill slaveholders with the full support of the nation. Over 250,000 Black soldiers fought in the war and helped turn the tide for a Union victory. Their bravery and skill were transformative. Mary Ann Shadd Cary, who had pledged she would never return to the States after emigrating to Canada, came back with the sole purpose of recruiting Black men for the war. Douglass's sons, Charles and Lewis, fought in the war. And Black men were not alone. Black women served as nurses, domestics, and cooks. They also served as spies, gaining valuable intelligence for the Union. And the most famous supporter of the war efforts was Harriet Tubman. She served as a spy and led troops into battle—the first time a Black woman led American troops.

In early June 1863, Harriet led 150 African American soldiers of the Second South Carolina Infantry on an expedition. Moving along the Combahee River in Beaufort, South Carolina, Harriet managed to bypass Confederate mines and thwart their forces. She planned the entire effort, guided the men fighting against Southern soldiers, and destroyed any resources that would have aided the enemy. Perhaps her greatest feat was helping to lead nearly seven hundred enslaved people to freedom once Union soldiers liberated Confederate camps. With her leadership they left the plantation in droves, never looking back. In fact, there was such a feverish attempt to get aboard the three Union ships used in the raid that they almost capsized. Absconding slaves did not want to bank on any promise of returning ships—they wanted out now. Panic was rising. An officer turned to Harriet and pleaded with her to calm the people. Harriet stood in the bow of the boat. She stared out at all of the enslaved people. She was them. Though they were strangers, she knew them well. She started to sing:

> *Of all the whole creation in the East*
> *or in the West*
> *The glorious Yankee nation is the*
> *greatest and the best*
> *Come along! Come along!*
> *Don't be alarmed.*

A wave of silence went through the crowd. The people listened intently. No one would be left behind, and no one would be harmed. In response to her singing, the enslaved began to shout out praises. "Glory!" they called out. Salvation had come. The boats managed to make several trips, dropping off enslaved people with Union soldiers and heading back to pick up more. "I kept on singing until all were brought on board," Harriet later recalled.[47] Hundreds of men, women, and children found freedom that day, and about one hundred of them decided to fight for the Union army.[48] What is so powerful about protection is that protected people protect people.

A reporter for the *Wisconsin State Journal* witnessed the raid. He saw the Union gunboats returning to their home base with Harriet at the helm. Perhaps he was unaware that he was watching Harriet Tubman. He merely wrote, "A Black woman led the raid."[49] The story went out across the nation and Franklin B. Sanborn, a Bostonian and friend of Harriet, realized it was her. As an editor for the *Commonwealth* newspaper, Sanborn rewrote the story to let the world know that the Black woman who led the raid was Harriet. He wrote,

> [Three hundred] Black soldiers under the guidance of a Black woman, dashed into the enemy's country, struck a bold and effective blow, destroying millions of dollars worth of commissary stores, cotton and lordly dwellings, and striking terror into the heart of rebeldom, brought off nearly 800 slaves and thousands of dollars worth of property, without losing a man or receiving a scratch. It was a glorious consummation. . . . The colonel was followed by a speech from the Black woman who led the raid and under whose inspiration it was originated and conducted. For sound sense and real native eloquence her address would do honor to any man, and it created a great sensation.[50]

Harriet was setting the world on fire. But when she returned from the raid, she was less concerned about credit and more concerned about continuing the mission to win the war in clothes that would allow her to run. Tubman requested that Sanborn let it be "known to the ladies" that she needed a "bloomer dress" so that she could run without tripping. During the raid she had fallen after stepping on her dress while trying to corral an enslaved person's pigs.[51] Through it all, Harriet was practical: for her, even fashion served a protective purpose.

Harriet was not the only Black woman to lead a raid. On March 26, 1865, a slave insurgency took place in Pineville, South Carolina. It was suspected that the leading rebel of the insurgency was an enslaved woman named Rose. A thorn in her mistress's side, Rose wreaked havoc in Pineville. When the raid was met by Confederate scouts, Rose, along with twenty-seven other armed Black people, was shot. Historian Thavolia Glymph argues that Rose "spoke to the long history of slave resistance and encapsulated the ways the gendered work of Black women in the plantation economy informed individual, family, and community resistance and the ways Union and Confederate policies made gender a critical touchstone of emancipation."[52] Rose was a ringleader. Moreover, it appeared that mistresses in the neighborhood were not surprised by the leading role Rose played in political and social violence. Accordingly, she was executed by local officials. They shot Rose and discarded her, just as any other Black soldier would have been shot and discarded in the slaveholding South. During war, labor was not valued the same. Rose would not have been spared the way my great-grandfather was. Rose's danger to white supremacy outweighed the value of her labor.

Thavolia Glymph argues that in America, enslaved women "waged war" against individual slaveholders and, eventually, the Confederate state in several ways. She explains that Black women "fought as combatants and noncombatants, civilians and partisans. But they were not men, and they were not White. They were not soldiers, and they were not citizens."[53] While victories they won or contributed to have been largely overlooked, they were essential to slavery's destruction.

Donating funds and supporting abolitionists' activities were primary practices of Black Northern women. Black readers largely financed newspapers such as William Lloyd Garrison's the *Liberator*. It was also common practice for Black women to organize bazaars, sewing circles, and fundraisers to finance antislavery newspapers, vigilance societies, and the Underground Railroad. Frederick Douglass was adamant that "when the true history of the anti-slavery cause shall be written, women will occupy a large space in its pages; for the cause of the slave has been peculiarly woman's cause."[54] But when the opportunity arose, Black women stood up to slaveholders, slave catchers, politicians, and anyone who opposed them. The Lancaster Black Self-Protection Society protected fugitive slaves at the risk of their own lives. When a slaveholder attempted to claim their "property," the women put an end to him. When Margaret Garner could not gain her liberty, she chose death at each opportunity. Harriet Tubman aimed a gun at a Black man's head for wanting to give up but then delivered him to freedom. No one was more committed to the politics of protection than Black Americans, men and women.

After the Civil War, Black people continued to use every tool at their disposal to resist oppression, racial terrorism, and white supremacy. When Northern troops pulled out of the South, ending Reconstruction, Black people were left vulnerable. Riots spurred by racial tensions erupted across the country. Black towns faced massacres, mob attacks, loss of life, and loss of land. Lynchings were common and horrific displays of white impunity. Two Black people were lynched per week over the course of decades. And while the trauma of this violence was felt in every corner of America, Black people still resisted. They continued to choose from the best options in front of them.

In one of a handful of extraordinary instances, a white man was lynched by the Black community. In 1887, a white man named Manse Waldrop assaulted and raped an eleven-year-old Black girl named Lula Sherman. Shortly after the assault, Lula died as a result of her injuries. Her community was devastated and outraged and planned to do something about it.[55] Waldrop was arrested and held in a local jail. When rumors began to spread that a Black mob might form to lynch him, the authorities thought it best to move Waldrop out of town. On their way, they were stopped by a collection of Black men, among them Lula's father and Black ministers. They demanded that Waldrop be released to them. Given the size of the crowd, the police released him into the hands of the angry Black community. They dragged Waldrop into the woods, beat him, and lynched him. Eleven-year-old Lula had had no protection, and neither did Waldrop. The Shermans would never get their daughter back, and they certainly could not expect to receive justice through the courts. Their act ensured that at least one man who harmed an innocent Black child was held accountable. Surprisingly, the Black men charged in Waldrop's death were all acquitted. The South Carolina governor saw their actions as equivalent to the stance white men took on lynchings and released them.

The rape of Black women by white men, which had been frequent and unpunished during slavery, continued after emancipation, usually without any consequences for the rapists. According to the best statistics available, there were only four lynchings of white men led by Black people.[56] The small number may reflect the fact that only in the most egregious and exceptional of circumstances could retaliatory violence take place. What most Black people wanted was justice. A lynching was not justice. Black towns wanted the violence against their communities to stop, and they wanted a judicial system that would guarantee them protection. Lula needed protection. In the wake of her death, her family did not get justice, merely the guarantee that one man would not commit crimes again.

As Reconstruction came to a close and more Black men were disenfranchised, the Black community shifted its hope of assistance from the political realm to the social and spiritual. Godly men and leaders in the Black community could not protect Lula, but they could fight to ensure that what happened to her never happened to anyone again. Much of the hard work in protection is about proving that a double standard exists in terms of who is awarded rights, citizenship, and humanity, and preventing the double standard from causing harm. Until Black and oppressed peoples are able to be and belong, protective collective action will be required.

More than one hundred years after the Civil War, it is easy to rationalize how an enslaved person would have been justified in using violence to fight off an oppressor. During the civil rights movement of the 1950s and '60s, also referred to as the "long freedom struggle," there was even some sympathy toward Black folk, who were facing down Bull Connors or the Klan. In 1964, the director of the Mississippi Student Nonviolent Coordinating Committee (SNCC), Robert Moses, proclaimed, "It's not contradictory for a farmer to say he's nonviolent and also pledge to shoot a marauder's head off."[57] Self-defense was always an option, if not a feature, of the civil rights movement, particularly when it came to voting. SNCC leader Stokely Carmichael enjoyed telling an anecdote about an elderly Black woman that he brought to vote in Lowndes County, Alabama. "She had to be 80 years old and going to vote for the first time in her life. . . . That ol' lady came up to us, went into her bag, and produced this enormous, rusty Civil War–looking old pistol. 'Best you hol' this for me, son. I'm a go cast my vote now.'"[58]

She had a reason to bring a gun to a polling place. In 1965, in Louisiana, the Deacons for Defense and Justice protected civil rights groups that were registering Black people to vote and facing violence and intimidation from the Klan. In Bogalusa, Louisiana, Black activists marching to city hall were met by angry white protesters. One protester threw a rock and hit Hattie Mae Hill, a Black teenager. Hill fell and was attacked by the mob. The Deacons intervened to defend Hill when the mob refused to relent. Deacon Henry Austin pulled out his gun. He shot and hit a white man. Immediately, the crowd dispersed. No one died that day, including the white man who was shot, but Austin had proved a valuable point: armed protection worked in the face of a mob. When the Klan realized their own lives could be at risk when they were terrorizing Black communities, racial violence came to a halt.[59] Ordinary people without political, economic, or social power have always found empowerment in defending their lives and the lives of others. Collective protection is powerful. It not only saved lives but compelled people to reckon with the reasons for needing it. Why might a Black woman threaten to kill a coward alongside a slave catcher? Why might a mother be pushed to kill her own children? Why would a woman with no military training lead men into battle? Why might an eighty-year-old woman bring a pistol with her to vote? The answers should haunt us. Protection was a constant response to white supremacy. White power had become synonymous with violence.

One of the most potent collective responses to white violence during the twentieth century was the Black Panther Party's (BPP) definition and implementation of protection. In October 1966, the BPP developed their landmark Ten-Point Program and platform. Their first goal was freedom, their second was full employment for Black people, and their third was an end to capitalism and a start for reparations. It was not until point seven that guns were referenced and then mainly in relation to self-protection. Point seven reads,

> We want an immediate end to POLICE BRUTALITY and the MURDER of Black people.
>
> We believe we can end police brutality in our black community by organizing black self-defense groups that are dedicated to defending our black community from racist police oppression and brutality. The Second Amendment to the Constitution of the United States gives a right to bear arms. We therefore believe that all black people should arm themselves for self-defense.[60]

Guns were only needed for self-defense from the brutality of the state. In a capitalist world, scarcity is weaponized and guns are necessary to maintain power. The optics of Black Panthers with guns was powerful and even seductive to impressionable people wanting to immolate the perceived power of whiteness. But bravado was not necessary and in some ways was counterproductive. Young people were attracted to the power a gun held. Many Black Panthers kept their arms with great care. They knew how to clean, shoot, and secure their guns. Protection, and in particular armed defense, was not to be taken lightly. The stakes were high and lives were on the line because guns contributed to the FBI's attack on the BPP.[61]

In the public memory, the BPP is perhaps one of the most misunderstood political groups. Though historians and scholars have worked tirelessly to rehabilitate the history and memory of the BPP, too many are stuck on iconic images of black leather jackets, black berets, sunglasses, and shotguns. The BPP was founded in Oakland, California, in 1966 by Merritt College students Huey P. Newton and Bobby Seale, who originally called it the Black Panther Party for Self-Defense. The organization's initial purpose was to form armed patrols to "copwatch." They kept an eye out for police brutality and got involved if they believed the police stop might escalate. They observed police traffic stops while armed. Police brutality was devastating, and for decades the police persecuted Black communities through harassment, surveillance, and violence.

However, the Panthers found out rather quickly that the greatest threat to white supremacy was not Black armed protection. As historian Robyn Spencer notes, "In their first year of activism the Panthers had boldly and legally picked up the gun—and had been forced to lay it back down."[62] Guns created more controversies than solutions. The local and federal governments targeted the BPP in ways that threatened their image, goals, and existence. Instead of guns, leadership realized, the best defense to white supremacy was a fed, healthy, and educated Black populace, so over time the Black Panthers increased their community programming. Their most successful form of protection was their free breakfast program for children. Every morning young schoolchildren were provided with a hot and balanced breakfast to begin their day.[63] Not only did the Panthers serve breakfast, but they simultaneously worked to subvert gender roles that perpetuated patriarchy. Men flipped pancakes, stirred grits, and donned aprons and smiles while they served young people and encouraged them to have a great day. The program spread, and its success led to other necessary services that provided groceries for those who could not afford to pay. Food was medicine. Good health was political; food programs were a remedy to food scarcity. In addition to food, the Panthers offered health and education clinics, and treatment for sickle cell anemia and tuberculosis.[64] They even operated their own ambulance system.[65] When paramedics refused to respond to emergencies in Black communities, the Black Panthers showed up. Gun rights mattered, but protection attended to the whole body, the whole person. True liberation makes guns obsolete because when everyone is cared for there is no need to conquer, and certainly there is no need to hoard.

When it comes to protection, nothing is more powerful than the willingness to put one's body between someone else and the oppressor. On the afternoon of May 16, 2020, about a week before George Floyd was killed by the police, twenty-one-year-old Tye Anders was accused by the Midland, Texas, police of running a stop sign. He pulled over in front of his ninety-year-old grandmother's house. Standing outside on the front lawn, Anders was terrified.[66] Several police cars pulled up and the officers pointed their guns at him, all for an alleged traffic violation. Anders clearly was unarmed, with open empty hands and outstretched arms. Family members and friends soon formed a phalanx of witnesses with their phones in hand, recording the entire confrontation. A woman who claimed to be Anders's friend called out to him from the sidelines, trying to reassure him and calm him down. The friend shouted and then screamed at the cops: "He's scared. Y'all have guns on him. He's Black. Do you not see how many Black people are getting shot?! Do y'all not see that? And y'all have guns on him. He's only twenty-one. Of course he's fucking scared. Of course he's fucking scared!" The friend could barely maintain her composure while filming. "Y'all gonna find any fucking reason to shoot cause he's Black. Because the color of our fucking skin we get punished. We get fucking punished."[67] During 2020, nearly every week a hashtag named for a Black man or woman slain by the police circulated on Twitter—Breonna Taylor, Andre Hill, Manuel Ellis, Tamir Rice. Often they were killed after a routine traffic stop or other nonviolent encounter. Black folks knew that little, if anything, of substance needed to happen for a Black person to be shot and killed by authorities. Black people were on the edge of a glass filled with injustice. Less than two weeks later, the murder of George Floyd in Minneapolis would cause that glass to overflow.

Anders was pleading and screaming through tears at the police: "Put the guns down. I'm scared. I'm scared." The scene was chaotic and gripping to watch. Every bystander was trying not to panic, but they could barely contain their fears and disbelief at the police's irrational response to a young, unarmed Black man lying flat on his grandmother's front lawn. Anders was not just crying; he was wailing and pleading for his life. Not a single cop lowered their weapon. Suddenly, Anders's ninety-year-old grandmother stepped outside the house. She was praying. Her prayers were inaudible, but her hands were outstretched toward her grandson's prone, wailing body. She was standing with a cane just a few feet from her Anders, wearing a pale-pink housedress, her head topped by white and gray hair. She walked toward her grandson while guns were pointed in her direction.

The family, friends, and neighbors surrounding the lawn were still screaming at the police to put their guns away. Over and over again, like a chant, the friends and family yelled, "Put your guns up!" Finally the cops began to lower their guns, and four officers approached Anders. One leading officer was still pointing his gun as he walked toward Anders with a team of other police officers. Anders was still panic-stricken, his grandmother now standing over him. The officers circled Anders and began to try to arrest him, but his grandmother was not convinced they would not shoot him. The police tried to push her back. She refused to move. In that moment, every onlooker was apoplectic at the imminent violence. The grandmother, in an attempt to rescue her grandson, fell on top of him. Perhaps she reasoned that the police would not shoot Anders if she threw her body on top of his. Or perhaps, at ninety years old, she intended to sacrifice her elderly life for Anders's young one. Not long after she collapsed on top of Anders, with police piling and pushing all around her, she lost consciousness.

In the end, Anders was arrested and charged with fleeing from a police officer. His grandmother was taken away in an ambulance. One of Anders's friends posted her roughly three-minute footage on Instagram and it went viral. People were outraged to see an elder treated in this way. The dismissive and even aggressive behavior of the police toward a ninety-year-old woman with a cane remains unconscionable. However, I tell this story not to dwell on the abhorrent behavior of the police but to point to the grandmother's protection, both spiritual and physical.

Anders's grandmother reminds me that one might even make a solid argument about the connection of care work and rest as a form of protection. When we tend to the mental, emotional, and physical needs of Black people, we are equipping them to defend themselves against a hostile, grinding world. All parents want their children and their children's children to experience an absolute sense of safety. Her collapse was not a coincidence. Protection is powerful, beautiful, and sacrificial because protection is love. But she should not have needed to put her body between the police and her grandson to protect him.

Anders's grandmother would have been born in or around 1930. If she was born and raised in Midland, a small city in western Texas largely known for its connection to former president George Bush and his family, she would have seen some things. She would have known about at least a handful of the over seven hundred documented lynchings that took place in the state of Texas from 1882 to 1945.[68] She would have known that the local Midland high school, perhaps the one her grandson attended, was named after Confederate general Robert E. Lee.[69] In the midst of a violent police altercation, she would have known that there were few forms of protection she could have employed to stave off the police and defend her grandson. So she used the most powerful things she had: prayer and her own body.

Tye Anders did not die that day, but he came dreadfully close. If the best protection Black people can provide each other in this day are our cell phones, our screams, or the sacrifice of our very bodies, then that should remind everyone that we are still living in a country that is grossly unjust. Protection alone has its limitations. Perhaps the best complement to protection is force.

Chapter Three

FORCE

I n November 2003, my grandmother Reader Carter died after a short battle with colon cancer. My family flew to Detroit, where she and so many other family members lived, for her funeral, and afterward we gathered to clean her apartment and distribute her possessions. Her apartment was small, just one bedroom, located inside a retirement community. As we emptied out kitchen cabinets and closets, other relatives came by to pick up items they wanted, or just to pay their respects. We decided to tackle her bedroom last. I remember it was nearing the evening. Some of us sat on her bed or leaned against the wall. My dad slowly opened her nightstand drawer. What he found shocked him. Lying in the nightstand drawer was a box full of bullets and a tiny, pretty .22 pistol. It had a brown handle with a gold medallion, and it was fully loaded. We all sat there open-mouthed, watching him hold it, and then . . . we erupted in laughter. Almost in unison, we bellowed, "Grandma has a gun!"

I did not grow up with guns in my home. Neither did my dad, as far as he knew. I had a very narrow understanding of gun ownership. I thought guns were for criminals or southerners. I also did not realize how intimidated I would be by a gun until I saw one up close. But my grandmother's gun ownership should not have surprised me or any of us that day. She may have spent most of her life in the North, but Reader was a transplant. Like millions of Black southerners, she migrated north to Detroit for better opportunities and to flee racial violence. She had grown up in rural Louisiana, one of eighteen children. I recall her telling me that her brothers would spend their weekends in jail there.

"Why did they go to jail? What did they do?" I asked.

"Nothing," she responded. "It was just safer there."

I was incredulous. "What do you mean, 'safer'?"

"Well," she sighed, "the white men in town used to get drunk on the weekends and hang Black folks, so if you was already in jail, you were safe."

She told stories of my uncle Clement, who as a teenager once was running behind the caravan of cars and was frantic. He did not want to be left behind as the menfolk headed off to jail on a Friday night. This was the world in which Reader and millions of other Black people lived. The violence of white supremacy was daily and heightened on the weekends—so heightened that even jail was a refuge. However, jail should not be understood as protection. Confinement is not freedom. Protection is liberatory. Jail, in this case, was more of an alibi. If you were in jail, you could not be accused of anything that happened outside of the cell walls that might attract the attention of a white man or mob eager to dole out extrajudicial punishment.

My grandmother could have kept the gun for a number of reasons. She was an elderly widow living alone in Detroit. But I have no doubt that the genesis of her gun ownership began in Louisiana. In the South, guns were tools, used to hunt to provide supplemental food for a large family maintained on meager wages. Guns were also force, a bulwark against a hostile, white supremacist world. Guns were not foreign to my grandmother but familiar and highly respected.

This chapter illustrates the powerful relationship between Black women and force in the face of anti-Black violence. Force is the energy needed to influence or change a person or a system. Force allowed Black people to have their demands met. In this chapter I examine the effectiveness of force, particularly through the use of guns to defend Black humanity. Few know better the utility of guns for Black liberation than Black women. For them, force secured liberation and reinforced their citizenship. When Black women made use of force as a tool for liberation, they never antagonized white people or attacked them unprovoked. In response to white terrorism, Black women used guns to stop trouble, not start it. Rarely were guns fatal; instead, they nearly always served as warnings—bullets fired in the air to quickly quell the violent desires of the mob. This is the most important difference between white supremacy and Black liberation: for the latter, the sole purpose of force was to halt violence or suppress it.

Guns were not just about exerting force; they were also an expression of freedom, independence, and courage by Black women. Their use against the brutal vagaries of white supremacy was both rational and necessary. I feature the stories and courage of three Black women in particular who employed guns to protect, protest, and proclaim Black humanity: Carrie Johnson, Daisy Bates, and Mabel Williams. They exemplify the power of force through armed defense. Each woman confronted white violence and threats to end their lives.

Throughout history, force was a remedy to the violence of white terrorism.[1] Just as it was for my grandmother, for many Black Americans, force was not boastful; it was serious. Black women were not ashamed of owning a gun, but they had to exercise discretion for their own safety. Guns were kept secret, undiscussed, stashed in closets or hidden compartments of pocketbooks and regarded as "grown folk's business." My grandmother Reader and her pretty .22 pistol with its chocolate-brown handle and gold medallion mean something different to me now. Her gun ownership should not have been surprising. I only wish she could have told her story.

As Carol Anderson's excellent scholarship on the denial of Second Amendment rights to Black Americans has shown, the refusal to acknowledge and protect Black gun ownership and self-defense is entangled with white supremacists' ideas and power.[2] From the origins of American colonization and slavery, white Americans' relationship to guns was birthed from a seductive romance between power and whiteness. In their lasting relationship, guns are loving partners white people can openly hold hands with in public spaces. Their possessive monopoly on gun ownership is also a way of conveying to Black people, "She's mine! You can't have her!" Denying them this romantic partner is akin to denying them companionship with power. Furthermore, in America, white supremacy's most tangible representation of power is not nuclear weapons but guns. There is a reason the Second Amendment is the second in a long list of constitutional amendments. In the founding of the United States, violence was prioritized. Guns became a part of American identity. And, as Anderson argues, guns were intended to keep Black people from power.

Accordingly, many white Americans have considered keeping Black people unarmed to be in their self-interest. In 1857, Supreme Court justice Roger B. Taney argued in his majority opinion for the infamous *Dred Scott v. Sandford* decision that recognizing Black people as citizens would allow them "to keep and carry arms wherever they went."[3] He feared rebellion or revolution. The decision that Black people were not citizens established legally the premise that gun ownership was a right only afforded to white people—another reason whiteness and violence cannot be separated. Citizenship meant the ability to bear arms. Black people were not citizens in 1857. The government denied gun ownership to Black people as a sign of their subordination. However, this did not prevent Black people from obtaining firearms for their defense.

And nothing was more forceful than the inclusion of Black men in the Union army. Over 250,000 Black men fought courageously against slavery and white supremacy, armed with bayonets, rifles, and revolvers. Guns served to complete the process of emancipation. On March 21, 1863, Frederick Douglass published an editorial in his own paper, the *Douglass' Monthly*, urging Black men to join the war for abolition. He wrote, "A war undertaken and brazenly carried on for the perpetual enslavement of colored men, calls logically and loudly for colored men to help suppress it. Only a moderate share of sagacity was needed to see that the arm of the slave was the best defense against the arm of the slaveholder."[4] For the first time in American history, Black soldiers could legally take up arms against slaveholders.

Before Douglass convinced Lincoln to allow Black troops, Douglass knew well the stakes of taking up arms. Throughout most of his abolitionist career he, along with William Lloyd Garrison, preached moral suasion and nonviolence, but after the passage of the Fugitive Slave Act and certainly with the war raging, he declared in a passionate editorial, "I now for the first time during this war feel at liberty to call and counsel you to arms."[5] What is most interesting about the conclusion of this piece is that Douglass referred to Black revolution as the precedent for liberation. He listed the leaders of slave rebellions and participants in John Brown's raid: "Remember Denmark Vesey of Charleston; remember Nathaniel Turner of Southampton; remember Shields Green and Copeland, who followed noble John Brown, and fell as glorious martyrs for the cause of the slave. Remember that in a contest with oppression, the Almighty has no attribute which can take sides with oppressors."[6]

On April 4, 1865, Lincoln offered up ideas for what Black people should do in regard to their newfound freedom, brought about by force: "In reference to you colored people, let me say God has made you free. Although you have been deprived of your God-given rights by your so-called masters, you are now as free as I am, and if those that claim to be your superiors do not know that you are free, take the sword and the bayonet and show them that you are; for God created all men free, giving to each the same rights of life, liberty, and the pursuit of happiness."[7] Lincoln was doing several things here. First, he acknowledged that he was, in fact, not the great emancipator: "God made you free." Second, he recognized that Black people were wrongly denied their humanity and rights by "so-called masters." He called out the illegitimacy of the ability to own someone. Third, he acknowledged that Black people were free, as free as Lincoln himself. There are no levels to freedom; to be as free as Lincoln was to be as free as possible. Fourth and finally, Lincoln was sanctioning force to protect one's humanity: "Take the sword and the bayonet." Black people knew this and cultivated these beliefs from the beginning of the slave trade to the Civil War. Force saved lives, arrested violence, and then permanently ended American slavery.

Carrie, Daisy, and Mabel all used force and guns to defend not only themselves and their families but their communities. These women came from long lines of Black women and men, from the nameless women and men who took up arms in slavery to kill their enslavers to the most famous Black woman of the nineteenth century, Harriet Tubman. Even conservative, accommodationist Black leader Booker T. Washington was a gun owner. In fact, in 1915 the faculty at the Tuskegee Institute presented Washington with a shotgun as a gift. While Washington never publicly touted armed self-defense, his faculty's gift of a gun likely served two purposes, recreation and protection.

Gun ownership was not limited to Black southerners. W. E. B. Du Bois was born and raised in Great Barrington, Massachusetts. He once confessed, "I have never killed a bird nor shot a rabbit. I never liked fishing and always let others kill even the chickens which I ate. Nearly all my schoolmates in the South carried pistols. I never owned one. I could never conceive myself killing a human being. But in 1906 I rushed back from Alabama to Atlanta where my wife and six-year-old child were living. A mob had raged for days killing Negroes." Du Bois admitted that he bought a Winchester double-barreled shotgun and two dozen rounds of shells filled with buckshot. He claimed, "If a White mob had stepped on the campus where I lived I would without hesitation have sprayed their guts over the grass." Du Bois's stance was a direct response to the Atlanta race riot of 1906. During the massacre, white mobs lynched Black people, hanged them from light posts, beat them, and stabbed them to death. Black homes and businesses were destroyed. It was reported that over ten thousand white men and boys attacked and killed dozens of Black people over the course of three days. The race riot quickly became international news. One scholar later wrote that Du Bois's possession of arms was unusual only in that he was "late to the game."[8] In 1886, his Fisk University classmates carried arms with them regularly, especially when traveling to Nashville, Tennessee. The following stories are of women who also employed force to remind white people of their freedom and to stop the madness of white terrorism.

Benjamin Johnson and his daughter, Clara, known as Carrie, lived at 220 G Street NW in Washington, DC. Little is known about their family. There are no records of Benjamin's wife or Carrie's mother. There is no record of other children. Benjamin was likely raising Carrie as a single father, unusual for the social climate of the day. She was eleven years old when thousands of women descended on Washington from all over the country to march for their right to vote the day before Woodrow Wilson's presidential inauguration. Perhaps she thought about attending Howard University because of her familiarity with the city; she would have known the spaces in DC where she would be welcomed and the spaces she should avoid. As a young Black person, being in the wrong place could have deadly consequences.

Alongside Harlem, Washington, DC, was an exceptional place for African Americans to live during the twentieth century. Washington boasted large Black populations and enclaves of Black affluence. Black people flocked to the city for education and employment. Working for federal agencies meant more than just having a "good government job"; it was a path to prosperity. Before 1913, when President Woodrow Wilson instituted segregated labor practices in government agencies, Black people worked alongside white people in federal offices. Though public schools were racially segregated, public school teachers were considered federal workers, so Black and white educators were paid equally. Black middle-class families could send their children to excellent schools. The famous M Street High School, later known as Dunbar High School, was a preeminent place for Black youth to learn. Howard University was also attracting the best and the brightest. During the summer of 1919, educator Carter G. Woodson, the father of Black History Month, had just moved to Washington to serve as the new dean of liberal arts, professor of history, and head of the graduate faculty at Howard. Carrie might have had dreams or hopes about attending these schools. She may have known other students who did. At seventeen, she was in her last year of high school and may have had ideas about where her life would take her next.

Washington was full of promise, but the possibility of white supremacist danger curtailed the full realization of Black people's freedom. When Black soldiers returned from World War I, their presence sparked animosity among some white people, who resented having to compete with them for jobs. In fact, the possibility of advancement prompted much of the precarity for Black people. According to one scholar, "The trigger for white rage, inevitably, is Black advancement. It is not the mere presence of Black people that is the problem; rather, it is Blackness with ambition, with drive, with purpose, with aspirations, and with demands for full and equal citizenship."[9] The reason is simple. Equality threatens the myth of white supremacy, and excellence destroys it completely. Washington was full of promise, but the possibility of white supremacist danger curtailed the full realization of Black people's freedom.

All throughout 1919, the exercise of Black freedom—Black veterans wearing their military uniforms in public, Black children swimming in the "white section" of Lake Michigan, Black sharecroppers in Arkansas organizing for better wages and working conditions—was met with white mob terror broadcasting the message "Stay in your place!"

By 1919, President Wilson's segregationist policies had restricted new employment opportunities for Black workers and ushered in a Jim Crow climate in Washington that emboldened white residents. Parks, streetcars, and sidewalks all became contested public spaces. In a May 1919 issue of the NAACP newspaper *The Crisis*, W. E. B. Du Bois described Black soldiers returning home to a resurgence of anti-Black violence. Lynchings and mob attacks on Black communities were picking up momentum as spring turned into a long, hot, and violent summer. "We return. We return from fighting. We return fighting," Du Bois wrote, aptly describing the deplorable conditions in which Black soldiers transitioned from defending their country to defending their communities from white riots and mobs.[10] That summer—which was dubbed "Red Summer" for all the blood that was shed—Black people took on new, assertive, and forceful stances to protect themselves. Black soldiers had returned home with their guns in tow.[11] Their force was an expression of justice. Black people demanded that America live up to its democratic principles. And in July, the race riots came to Carrie's doorstep.

For four days, from July 19 to July 22, white Washingtonians raided Black communities because of a rumor that a Black man, Charles Ralls, had sexually assaulted Elsie Stephnick, a white woman who was married to a civilian who worked for the navy. For months, white newspapers had been printing salacious stories about crime and fostering an atmosphere of fear among their white readers. Though Ralls was arrested, white Washingtonians believed he was not going to be held accountable. They took to the streets, destroying Black businesses and homes. They pulled Black people off streetcars and beat them. White mobs, many of them composed of veterans, armed themselves with sticks, pipes, and guns with the intent of terrorizing Black people. The police did nothing to stop the mobs and, in some cases, assisted the mobs in attacking Black residents. Compelled to defend themselves, Black people fortified their homes and shot at white attackers.

The mob attacks on Black communities in Washington, DC, were relentless. The *New York Age* reported that scores of Black people had been seriously hurt, with injuries ranging from broken bones to deep lacerations and internal bleeding. The week brought a series of violent attacks on Black people. By Monday, Black Washingtonians were no longer willing to see the violence continue without police intervention. An estimated five hundred firearms were sold that day. By that evening, the city's Black community had—by the estimate of the head of Washington's Black teachers' union—spent a collective $14,000 on guns and ammunition. The surge prompted police to ask weapons dealers to suspend sales. But when the gun dealers complied, Black bootleggers turned their attention from liquor to guns, driving to Baltimore to buy weapons and ammunition and then handing them out to Black Washingtonians.[12] Carrie's father could have been among the Black men who picked up a gun. Everyone needed to be protected. The streets were not safe.

During the riot, Carter G. Woodson was walking home from Howard University's campus when he witnessed a Black man being chased by a mob. They caught him and executed him in the middle of the street. Woodson was terrified. The unspoken rule was that Black people could expect to be overpoliced and white people could largely commit crimes with impunity. Black Washingtonians had had enough. According to Woodson, "The lack of police response outraged Black members of the community who made extensive preparation for the retaliatory onslaught of the Whites." Woodson added, "This mob has misjudged the Washington Negroes. . . . Weapons were bought, houses were barricaded, and high-powered automobiles were armored for touring the city late in the night."[13]

Drawing from local newspapers and historical scholarship, on July 22, the fourth straight night of rioting, Carrie and her father were alone in their home when the mob came to their neighborhood. Their home was a modest two-story brick house with shutters on the windows and four porch steps before the front door landing. It was located east of Judiciary Square, on a crowded block with several alley dwellings.[14] The immediate neighborhood was Black, but it was surrounded by white neighborhoods, and white residents greatly outnumbered Black ones. Around one thousand white people stormed the streets headed toward Black homes such as the Johnsons'. Armed with pistols and rifles, the Black community was doing all it could to keep the mob at bay. Black women and men shot at marauders from their windows, rooftops, and front doors. Sitting in her window overlooking New York Avenue, Carrie took potshots at the white mobs prowling the streets below. She clearly knew how to load a gun and understood the advantage of being higher up: her position on the second floor allowed her to see everyone below her as well as from a distance. She also had good aim, shooting and hitting one of the white men storming her block. It would not be long before Carrie was outnumbered and outgunned, but she gave all she had.

Carrie's father must have been outside initially. It was nearly 10:00 p.m. As the riots continued, two white police officers noticed a Black man, allegedly Carrie's father, run from his porch into his home as the mob approached. Bent on arresting as many Black people as possible, twenty-nine-year-old detective Sergeant Harry Wilson and his fellow detective Patrick O'Brien headed toward the Johnson home. No police officer was interested in stopping the white mobs from destroying Black property and harming Black people. The Johnsons' home was their only refuge. They knew they could not overpower the hundreds of white people on the streets. Benjamin met Carrie in her room and they quickly hid under her bed.

When the two officers arrived, they did not knock or announce themselves. Instead, they broke down the front door. Within minutes five other detectives and policemen had joined in the search. The home was dark and quiet. They decided to start looking upstairs for Johnson. "I'm younger than you. Let me go first," whispered Wilson to his partner. They quietly crept up the staircase with their guns ready. They made it up to the second floor and pushed their way into a dark bedroom. As the officers opened the door, shots rang out. Carrie was shooting from under the bed. Bewildered, Wilson and his partner shot at the dark walls. Carrie, meanwhile, was relentless. She took several shots and hit Wilson twice. He lay on her bedroom floor dying. A bullet struck Carrie in her thigh, and another struck Benjamin in the shoulder. But they were alive. When the gunfire finally ceased, officers dragged Carrie and her father from under the bed and marched them to the street in handcuffs. Their survival was nothing short of a miracle. Had the officers known they were hiding under the bed, it would have served as no more than a holding pen for them to aim at. During an investigation, officers extracted nineteen bullets from the bedroom walls, none from the floor.[15] The Johnsons' wounds—likely a result of bullets that had ricocheted off a wall—were treatable.

Outside, the riot began to dissipate. The rampant gunfire let white people know that as they terrorized Black residents, they put their own lives at risk. Perhaps white people also saw that if a police officer could be shot and killed, they could be next. It was one thing to throw a rock, quite another to catch a bullet. Witnesses and Black neighbors, and likely white people who had intended to mob the community, gathered outside the Johnson home. Carrie was waiting for an ambulance to arrive and transport her and her father to the hospital. Somehow people in the community must have heard that Carrie had shot and killed the officer. A bystander offered up his unsolicited thoughts regarding the entire debacle: "Only the fear of more trouble was keeping a rope off her neck."[16] That the bystander referred to "her" neck implied that he knew Benjamin was not the shooter. His comment also implied that any lynching mob would be met with Black resistance. The authorities, for their part, were likely baffled that a teenage girl had committed such an act of forceful armed defense. As people stood around wondering what might happen next, it began to rain and then pour. The shooting of the police officer had caused the gathering white mob to pause, but the rain broke their will to continue.

The riot lasted a full four days in the heat of the summer, from July 19 through July 22. On the final day of the riot, President Wilson belatedly mobilized two thousand soldiers to disperse any remaining crowds from street corners, close theaters and bars, restrict auto traffic, and bring in tanks equipped with machine guns from Fort Meade, twenty-five miles away in Maryland. Limited violence arose that night, but what had really brought calm to the capital was the hot summer night's rainstorm.[17] In the end, fifteen people died in the riot, ten white people and five Black people. Fifty people were seriously wounded and one hundred less severely wounded. It was one of the few twentieth-century riots in which white fatalities outnumbered those of Black people. Six Metropolitan Police officers and several marine guards were shot during the riot. Two of those shootings were fatal. Carrie was responsible for one.

It did not take long for the local newspapers to pick up what happened. The white newspapers quickly created a narrative of victimhood for Wilson. The *Washington Post* published large side-by-side photographs of his widow, Alice, and their daughter, Margaret. The headline read, "Wife and Baby of Young Detective Who Gave His Life in Line of Duty." Their images were centered at the top of the page with a caption that read, "MRS. ALICE WILSON AND LITTLE MARGARET WILSON left virtually without means of support, when a negro's bullet killed Detective Sergeant Harry Wilson, during the recent rioting." The *Washington Post* established a fund for the family. The caption is telling. Nowhere is Carrie's name mentioned. The phrase "a negro's bullet" hid the fact that a teenage girl shot Wilson. In earlier articles, Carrie had been referred to as a "negress," but if the Wilson family was to gain sympathy and dollars for their fund, Wilson's death would need to be honorable, even heroic.[18] For Wilson to be a hero, the public could not know it was a Black teenage girl who killed him; perhaps his family and the press did not want him to look weak.

However, in the Black press, every attempt was made to center the gender of Wilson's murderer. Various headlines in the *Washington Bee* read, "Girl to Be Tried in Murder," "Girl Faces Murder Charge," "Girl Is Convicted in Wilson's Death," and "Girl Gets New Trial."[19] In an article in the *Bee* titled "They Started It," the writer claimed he regretted the death of Detective Wilson but then added, "He can only blame himself. At the corner of Seventh and

Florida Avenue, the evening of the riot, he was vindictive toward the colored people. Did he have the right to invade the home of the person who shot him? Did he see a felony committed? Did he witness a murderous assault? If he did, he was justified in entering and his assailant should be punished; if not, he had no right to enter this home."[20] At the forefront of the media's attention was Carrie's right to use force against a home invasion. Had the police been working to protect and serve Black communities, Wilson might have survived. Carrie would not have killed him.

Unfortunately, scholars know very little about Carrie. Her voice is absent from newspapers and scholarship. By all accounts, she shot first and it was her bullet that killed Officer Wilson. Immediately, her legal team claimed self-defense. Carrie was, after all, a minor, and she was hiding in her home when officers burst unannounced through her door. How would she have been able to tell the difference between police officers and the white mob that was terrorizing her community? Carrie employed the tenets of force and protection. Force was taking shots at the oncoming mob and any intruder. She was conveying to the mob, "Retreat or else." Protection was hoping that the space under the bed would serve as a refuge.[21] And given the odds stacked against Carrie as a teenage Black girl, her actions were nothing short of brave.

The violence in DC marked a flashpoint in American racial dynamics. African Americans were empowered by opportunities that their own grit and endurance created. Black veterans would not relinquish their claim to citizenship, and neither would young Black girls. Following the Washington riot, a "southern Black woman," as she identified herself, wrote a letter to the NAACP magazine *The Crisis*. She praised Black people for fighting back. As she read about the Washington riot, the woman said, she wept tears of "gladness and madness."[22] She felt a sense of solidarity and pride. Since this woman was from the South, she knew about the race riot in Atlanta in 1906. Amid the massacre, white mobs attacked and killed Black people. The displays of violence ranged from property damage to hanging bodies from light posts. Over the course of three days, scores of Black people were assaulted or murdered by more than ten thousand white men and boys. Now, a little over a decade later, racial violence was erupting across the country in places such as Charleston, South Carolina; Longview, Texas; Bisbee, Arizona; Knoxville, Tennessee; Omaha, Nebraska; and Elaine, Arkansas. In the summer of 1919, it felt like each day brought a new story of a Black town that had been destroyed. Accordingly, the deadly resistance that white people faced in Washington felt like justice to this southern Black woman: "The Washington riot gave me a thrill that comes once in a lifetime. . . . At last our men had stood up like men. . . . I stood up alone in my room . . . and exclaimed aloud, 'Oh I thank God, thank God.' The pent-up horror, grief and humiliation of a life time—half a century—was being stripped from me."[23] Although the writer didn't mention Carrie specifically, she played an active role among Black men in imparting pride and dignity to this southern Black woman.

Those who knew about Carrie turned her into a folk hero in the Black press. Several people wrote poems in her honor, but perhaps the most poignant was a poem written by an eleven-year-old Black girl named Martina Simms. In August 1919, Martina's poem was published in the *Afro-American*, the Black newspaper in Baltimore. She wrote about the riot and Black veterans returning from war only to fight again, but she singled out Carrie's bravery.

Washington Riot

You have heard about the riot
In Washington, D.C.

You can't come fooling around
Aunt Dinah's boys you see.

They went to France and fought
For Democracy
They might as well shed their blood
For their rights in Washington, D.C.

You read about Carrie Johnson
Who was only seventeen
She killed a detective, wasn't she
Brave and keen.

They will fight,—of course they will
fight
If the white folks don't give Aunt
Dinah's boys their rights.[24]

Martina saw Carrie as strong and courageous. Her act of force was inspirational. Even at her young age, Martina was aware that the detective's murder was not unwarranted. She understood the hypocrisy in white supremacy: Black soldiers could fight for American democracy and still be denied the privileges and protections of citizenship at home. While the poem's tone is thrilling, the young poet notes that the violence was not about revenge. Black veterans and Carrie were forcefully claiming their rights. Force was rational to Martina: "Of course they will fight." But it is also clear that the threat "If the white folks don't give Aunt Dinah's boys their rights" was a warning to stop the discrimination and violence that white people inflicted. Black children were not shielded from the harm white people caused in Black communities either. Their parents, caregivers, and loved ones instructed youths about the dangers of white terrorism and the absence of legal accountability. Oppression forced Black people to take defense into their own hands.

Washington's African American community, and indeed Black people around the country, embraced Carrie and celebrated her actions as heroic, sending money for her legal defense and writing to Black periodicals in her support. Ella Rice, treasurer of the New Jersey Federation of Colored Women's Clubs, wrote a letter to Moorfield Storey, the president of the NAACP, in hope of securing aid for Carrie. Written on the letterhead of the Rice Industrial School, the letter stated that the federation wished to send a contribution "to the young girl implicated in the recent race riot at Washington."[25] The note signaled that Black women held Carrie in high regard and considered the harsh punishment she might face. In Rice's mind, Carrie was a "young girl" caught up in a horrible situation. She had compassion for her. During an era of respectability politics among the Black community, it would have been easy to cast Carrie aside. But at nearly every turn, the Black community showed empathy for her circumstances and admiration for her actions. Fighting back was not easy or cheap.

Both Carrie and her father, Ben, were charged with first-degree murder. They were held separately in the DC jail. Ben, who was a member of the Freemasons, reached out to a fellow Mason and lawyer named William Hart and asked him to represent his daughter. Hart began to shape a narrative for reporters. He described Carrie as "the little heroine" and "our Joan of Arc, our Charlotte Corday," a nod to the French revolutionary who murdered Jacobin leader Jean-Paul Marat. He dramatized her actions, claiming, "Carrie Johnson faced death like a little rabbit in a corner, fired upon point blank by Officer Wilson and others."[26] Everything Hart said contradicted accounts given by the police and newspapers. But it turns out Hart was of little help to Carrie. It is not clear why, but as her trial began, he was no longer her lawyer.

Facing a possible death sentence if convicted of first-degree murder, Carrie's father placed all of the blame on his daughter. He allegedly agreed to testify against Carrie in exchange for having the charges dropped against him. In November 1920, Ben appeared on a list of witnesses for the government, and after he paid a $200 fine, he was free to go.[27] Carrie remained alone in jail. She desperately needed support.

The Legal Committee of the Washington branch of the NAACP offered its services to Carrie and others who, as a result of the riot, were facing first-degree murder charges in the Supreme Court of the District of Columbia, but she found new representation by two attorneys named B. L. Gaskins and T. M. Watson. Her legal team claimed Carrie had acted in self-defense, but the judge on the case barred her lawyers from using this defense. Therefore, her lawyers pushed for reasonable doubt: "In a pitch-dark bedroom, several detectives wielding revolvers, who could know beyond a reasonable doubt whose shots had killed Wilson, let alone that Carrie had planned to kill Wilson?"[28] They had a point; first-degree murder was a stretch. Sensing the jury might be sympathetic, the prosecuting attorney, John E. Laskey, reluctantly relented and dropped her charges down to manslaughter. The all-white, all-male jury found Carrie guilty of the reduced charge. Immediately her two lawyers requested a new trial in order to push for self-defense. When a new judge took on the case, he allowed Gaskin and Watson to claim self-defense, at which point Laskey decided against prosecution and dropped the charges.[29] It had taken a year and a half, but in June 1921 Carrie was a free woman.

Throughout American history, it is difficult to find a case in which a young Black woman killed a police officer and walked away a free woman. Yet her release was met with little fanfare. The white press was confounded. How could people make sense of a young Black woman who used gun violence against a cop to protect her family and survived? Perhaps Carrie could not make sense of the situation herself.

It was summer again, and on June 21, 1921, the *Post* buried a tiny story on an inside page: "RELEASED IN RIOT KILLING: Carrie Johnson, Colored, Freed in Death of Detective Wilson." The records of Carrie Johnson's life, however, are scant. One city directory revealed that she obtained a job as a janitor. But by 1930, her name did not appear in the census. She might have gotten married, moved away, or died. Ben Johnson was no longer listed either. In time, the public and the press forgot about Carrie, and yet, she represents something instructive. The public was not interested in remembering a young Black girl who killed a cop in self-defense and was cleared of all charges. In history, forgetting is political. The Washington riot should stick in our minds not only because trained Black military veterans fought back but because young Black girls equipped themselves to fight off white terrorism. In history, scholars can easily gloss over events or people that do not fit neatly within narratives of resistance or where voices are irrecoverable. But force in defense of Black lives had a deep impact. In fact, it changed laws.

The spectacle of armed Black men after World War I compelled Congress to pass DC's strongest gun control law ever, which required the registration of all guns and imposed stiff penalties for carrying firearms in public.[30] To white lawmakers, Black veterans and even Black civilians with guns represented a threat. The circumstances of the law's passage warned cities with growing Black populations that gun control was an extension of white supremacy. But Carrie stands out as an outlier. Legally, socially, and even politically, no one knew what to do or what to make of an armed young Black woman.

Daisy Bates knew violence from birth. When she was an infant, her mother, Millie Riley, was raped and murdered by three white men. The men threw her mother's body into Millpond, a small lake not far from where Daisy grew up in Huttig, Arkansas. The murder upended her father's life. Unable to parent, he left Daisy under the care of Millie's best friends: Susie Smith and her husband, Orlee Smith, a World War I veteran.

Returning from the war was tumultuous for Black veterans in 1919. Elaine, Arkansas, experienced white terrorism that rivaled anything seen in Washington, DC, that Red Summer. Located just two hours east of Little Rock, Elaine was a small, rural Black community that was historically made up of cotton plantations cultivated by enslaved labor. When slavery ended it was replaced by sharecropping, an economically exploitative practice that stunted Black wealth accumulation. When Black sharecroppers attempted to organize for better wages and improved working conditions, they were met with violence. Empowered by police and deputized by the governor, white men rained terror down on the Black community. They killed Black people on the street and inside their homes. They murdered a Black veteran who was celebrating his return home from World War I, dragging him from a streetcar and killing him in broad daylight. It is estimated that white vigilantes murdered anywhere from one hundred to over two hundred Black people in Elaine.

The town was hell-bent on suppressing what they concocted as a Black insurrection. White farmers even compelled Governor Charles Hillman Brough to delay sending in federal troops to stop the massacre. White southerners circulated false narratives, which were supported by the press, skewing public memory of the event. Black witnesses testified that they had been tortured into giving false statements regarding their participation and intent to bargain collectively. Every Black person in Arkansas knew that law would not be on their side. The twelve Black defendants charged with murdering a white deputy, known as the Arkansas Twelve, were convicted by an all-white jury in less than ten minutes and sentenced to death by electric chair.[31] The loss inflicted on the Black community by the fall of 1919 was incalculable. It is still largely unknown how many people were killed or where their bodies are buried. Not a single white person was held accountable. Every Black veteran returning to Arkansas would have been aware of what happened.

Daisy was just five years old at the time of the riot. Much of the violence during Daisy's youth was shielded from her. Her adoptive parents kept many of the details of her past a secret from her, even the fact that she was adopted. When another child teased Daisy about her "real parents," Susie and Orlee sat her down to tell her the truth. Daisy was eight years old when she learned that her parents were not her biological parents. They told her the truth about the violent death her mother had suffered by three local white men. Even then, she vowed to get revenge. She recalled later that as a child, she had a secret goal: "To find the men who had done this horrible thing to my mother."[32]

Daisy eventually claimed to have identified one of her mother's killers. It was a small town; perhaps someone told her who the men were. She believed she found one of them at a commissary and stared him down. Her eyes told him that she knew what he did. Whenever possible Daisy would go to the store and belittle him, just with her eyes. She never spoke to him and to others referred to him only as a "drunken pig." After a while, likely burning with guilt, the man began to plead with Daisy to leave him alone. He was an alcoholic, and not long after their initial encounter he drank himself to death; he was found dead in an alleyway.[33] Daisy was somewhat satisfied. She wanted her mother's assailants to pay and knew the law was never going to hold them accountable. So each time Daisy met one of her mother's murderers, she convicted him with her eyes. She was gripped by her hatred for the white men who had killed her mother and disdained and distrusted white people in general.

Daisy's adopted father, Orlee, was disturbed by her bitterness. He did not want his teenage daughter to be consumed by her pain. He advised her from his deathbed, "You're filled with hatred. Hate can destroy you, Daisy. Don't hate white people just because they're white. If you hate, make it count for something. Hate the humiliations we are living under in the South. Hate the discrimination that eats away at the South. Hate the discrimination that eats away at the soul of every black man and woman. Hate the insults hurled at us by white scum—and then try to do something about it, or your hate won't spell a thing."[34]

She never forgot her father's words. By age twenty, Daisy realized she did not want revenge. She wanted justice. And Daisy knew that if she wanted justice, she had to take it by force.

In 1957, nine African American students sought to integrate Little Rock Central High School in Little Rock, Arkansas. The presence of Black students brought the town and the nation to a crisis. School segregation was the foundation of Jim Crow laws. Nine Black children and those who supported them faced insults, physical assault, and constant threats of violence. Arkansas governor Orval Faubus claimed, "Blood will run in the streets . . . if Negro pupils should attempt to enter Central High School."

Daisy Bates, now a civil rights activist, and her husband L.C. were at the forefront of the struggle to integrate Central High School. They were the founders and editors of the town's Black newspaper, the *Arkansas State Press*, an eight-page paper that covered local news such as Black social events, religious gatherings, and sporting events. The *Arkansas State Press* was the most successful Black newspaper in Little Rock. Daisy also served as the president of the NAACP's Arkansas Conference. She knew now that she could not merely stare her opponents to death, so as the battle for school integration heated up, she armed herself. Daisy's home became a fortress.

Educating Black children has always been a political act. From the moment literacy was banned for enslaved people, the work of getting Black children educated could be met with danger and even deadly force by white supremacists who wanted a subjugated Black class. When Daisy and her husband L.C. agreed to take on the battle of integrating Central High School, they wanted their home to be a safe space for the students. Because the Bates were leaders in their community, their home served as headquarters or gathering location for both the press and the students. It also made their home a target for white supremacists. Accordingly the Bates worked hard to make sure their home was warm, welcoming, and secure. Each day they greeted students before and after school at their ranch-style house at 1207 West Twenty-Eighth Street. The Bateses took their time making sure they could protect themselves and everyone who sought safe haven in their home. At first, Daisy was uncomfortable with guns in her home: "It took many weeks for me to become accustomed to seeing revolvers lying on tables in my own home. And shotguns, loaded with buckshot, standing ready near the doors."[35] But she believed she had few options. Ted Poston, a journalist for the *New York Post*, covered the Little

Rock story and remarked that the house "by necessity has become a fortress."[36] On August 27, 1957, a rock was thrown through the Bateses' front window. A note attached to the rock read, "STONE THIS TIME. DYNAMITE NEXT TIME."[37]

These were not empty threats. And not even children were exempt from terror. The iconic image of the Little Rock Nine is of the lone student Elizabeth Eckford, who attempted to attend school on September 4, 1957, not knowing that Daisy had instructed Elizabeth's eight Black fellow classmates to stay home for fear of violence. Elizabeth's family did not have a telephone, so she missed the vital message. Photographs and film footage from that day show white people harassing, taunting, and cursing Elizabeth while she clutched her notebook closely to her chest. She marched through a mob looking for her Black classmates. The scene that day terrified Elizabeth's parents. After witnessing the violent threats of the mob, Birdie Eckford, Elizabeth's mother, recounted to Daisy that she sent her husband to town to "buy me a gun with plenty of bullets."[38] She could have sent him to buy a telephone, but a gun was its own form of communication. Black women were willing to do whatever it took to protect their children. Eckford's instructions were clear: "Buy *me* a gun." It is likely that Daisy told Eckford about her own guns, too. Daisy remarked that Eckford had "the courage of Harriet Tubman." When Daisy stopped by her home, she saw Eckford's new purchase. There on her table, side by side, were the Bible and the gun. "I looked at the Bible and I looked at the gun and smiled," recalled Daisy. Responding to her inquisitive eyes, Eckford said, "Yes, the Bible is old, but the gun is new. God said wait as well as pray."[39]

Despite violent resistance, the experiment with integration continued. It took great bravery, sacrifice, perseverance, and activism, but school integration in Little Rock was finally enforced by the

National Guard. The children were in school, though they faced constant harassment, bullying, and isolation. In the years following integration in Little Rock, Daisy traveled around the country, speaking to audiences about the necessity of armed resistance to protect Black life and Black property. If she knew she had a receptive audience, she would disclose that she had her own gun and proudly state that she knew how to use it.[40]

In 1957, the Bateses' home eventually received formal police protection, but it was not enough. The attacks of rocks, bombs, and dynamite continued. Many believed that the local police took part in or sanctioned the violence. At night, passing vehicles would whiz by and shoot off several rounds, sometimes shattering the windows. Someone burned crosses on their front lawn twice. The Black community gathered around the Bateses and pledged to organize their own security. In a 1959 letter to Thurgood Marshall, then a leading civil rights lawyer, Daisy Bates attested to a Black community of armed resistance. They could take no chances because they were constantly under the threat of violence. She admitted that she and her husband "keep 'Old Betsy' well-oiled and the guards are always on alert"—Old Betsy being her shotgun. Marshall was not surprised by this confession. He had stayed at the Bateses' home just two years earlier when he was litigating the Little Rock School District's attempt to delay court-ordered integration. Marshall remarked that their house was "an armed camp."[41]

It had to be. Though they installed floodlights to see who was coming, nothing deterred white people on a mission to keep the schools segregated. By October 1957, Daisy was fed up. One night she was sleeping in her bed when a crash startled her awake. A man had thrown an object through her window. She bolted out of bed, grabbed her gun, and headed out the front door. She spotted an enraged little man standing in her driveway. He was reaching back to throw another object her way when Daisy pointed her gun in the air and fired it five times in rapid succession. Instantly the man took off running to his car and sped off.[42] Daisy recounted that she had no desire to kill the man even if he was intruding: "I will have to live with myself and I will not let them make a murderer out of me."[43] But had he let loose his arm to send something crashing through another window, the sixth bullet might not have been a warning. Daisy did not wait for her husband or the police to let the man know she was armed. For this and so many other reasons, the community saw Daisy as fearsome and no-nonsense. She knew how to be effective, and she understood the impact guns had in deterring violence.

It was clear the Klan and other white terrorists were frustrated by their inability to scare Daisy away. In July 1958, white supremacists hanged Daisy in effigy in Ouachita County.[44] It sent a message, a reminder really, that the mob was not above lynching a woman. Daisy was unmoved. In fact, with each incident her notoriety around the country grew. She was regularly in the news or being interviewed. Her leadership and persistence made her a symbol of courage and hope in the civil rights movement. In September 1958, *Ebony* magazine dubbed Daisy the "First Lady of Little Rock." The feature story, written by Lerone Bennett Jr., praised her as having "the public-relations know-how of the late Walter White, the ideological nimbleness of the Rev. Martin Luther King and the biting tongue of the late Mary McLeod Bethune."[45] The story identified for its readers the main reason Little Rock Central High School was integrated: "Because Daisy Bates willed it."[46] In another interview, Daisy credited her sex for much of her success. She believed a Black woman leader could "get away with more in the South than a Negro man."[47]

Her reputation for being indefatigable was put to the test again in the fall of 1958. Daisy was driving when a carload of white men rammed into the back of her station wagon. She stopped and got out of her car to survey the damage. Before she could grasp what had happened, the men jumped out of their vehicle and began to taunt her. They threatened to attack her and drag her into the street. Anger was a source of strength for Daisy. "I was so infuriated," she recalled, that she marched back to her car and instinctively "released the lock on the door and simultaneously released the safety catch of my pistol." When the young men saw Daisy with a gun in her hand, their courage shriveled. They rushed back to their car and took off.[48] The interesting thing about force was that many times, the appearance of a gun was a sufficient deterrent from white violence. Warning shots were as good as a shot aimed at a person. What terrified white racists hell-bent on wreaking havoc was not the sight of a gun but the emboldened attitude of a Black person who was unafraid to use it. Daisy knew that most white racists were cowards and easily committed acts of violence when they held a majority or were sanctioned by the state. Operating outside of those conditions made them susceptible to violence as well.

In addition to attempting physical violence, white people from Arkansas wanted to cripple the Bateses economically. Within a few months of its founding, the *Arkansas State Press*'s circulation grew from ten thousand to twenty-two thousand, a number that included both Black and white readers. The Bateses' was the only local newspaper that supported immediate school integration. There were Black and certainly white readers who opposed it and believed the paper was taking a militant stance. On December 13, 1957, an editorial appeared on the front page that argued, "It is the belief of this paper that since the Negro's loyalty to America has forced him to shed blood on foreign battle fields against enemies, to safeguard constitutional rights, he is in no mood to sacrifice these rights for peace and harmony at home."[49] The paper was unapologetic. White advertisers, who had largely been the ones keeping the paper alive, began pulling their ads. The paper required at least $15,000 a year to remain in print. And given that it was the only Black outlet in the state, if it went under there would be virtually no space for Black people to have a voice in Arkansas, nor would there be inspiration for other Black people to start their own newspapers. The Bateses were struggling to make ends meet. Every bit of income that came in went to the newspaper or to paying for guards, or to travel to give talks about integration, or to spread the word about their activism. By 1958, the Bateses' house had been subject to attempted arson more than seven times. They added steel mesh to the windows to keep out rocks and other thrown objects. The Bateses also felt responsible for the care of the Little Rock Nine and their families. These Black students came from hardworking families, but they were not affluent. Every victory came at great cost.

The overall mood of Black Americans across the South was that white violence had to be met with force. The president of the Monroe, North Carolina, branch of the NAACP, Robert F. Williams, publicly declared, "We cannot rely on the law. We can get no justice under the present system. If we feel that injustice is done, we must then be prepared to inflict justice on these people. Since the federal government will not bring a halt to lynching, and since the so-called courts lynch our people legally, if it's necessary to stop lynching with lynching, then we must be willing to resort to that method. We must meet violence with violence."[50] For his comments, the NAACP suspended Williams. Yet Daisy understood this attitude completely and even used her own newspaper to express softer but similar sentiments regarding force. "We do know that at times it is pretty hard to suppress certain feelings, when all around you, you only see hate," wrote the editors. Though the *Arkansas State Press* published widely on nonviolence and self-defense, Daisy and L.C. acknowledged that "nonviolence never saved George Lee in Belzoni, Miss., or Emmett Till, nor Mack Parker at Poplarville, Miss." They also believed that the NAACP's national board of directors should take up such a significant question about mission and tactics as the use of force.[51]

In August 1959, the NAACP did just that. While they voted to uphold self-defense, claiming, "We do not deny, but reaffirm the right of individual and collective self-defense against unlawful assaults," they also voted to approve a measure that would permanently suspend Robert Williams from his position as president for his remarks about violence. Daisy was instrumental in this vote. Roy Wilkins, the executive secretary of the NAACP, knew Daisy was highly celebrated and respected. He needed her support if he wanted to oust Williams and push the organization far away from anything white people would interpret as retaliatory violence. Wilkins put Daisy in a corner. He knew her newspaper was struggling financially. He offered a deal—really, a bribe: if Daisy would vote against Williams, the NAACP would supply $600 a month in financial support through the end of the year. Daisy took it.

Perhaps Daisy felt as if she had no choice. A month before the vote, while Daisy and her husband were home, a bomb was hurled at their front door. Fortunately, it landed in their front yard and not the home itself. She wrote to the United States attorney general that all of the violence had compelled them to hire private guards.[52] The attorney general declined to offer any assistance, on the grounds that her concern was a state issue and not a federal one. When Williams heard about the bomb hurled at the Bateses' home, he wrote a letter to Daisy. "I am sorry to hear that the White racists have decided to step up their campaign of violence against you," he wrote. Then he added, "I deeply regret that you took the position you did on my suspension. It is obvious that if you are to remain in Little Rock you will have to resort to the method I was suspended for advocating."[53]

Just two months after the conference and Williams's gut-punch letter, in October 1959, the *Arkansas State Press* went out of business. After nearly eighteen years of weekly issues, the Bateses no longer had enough money to keep its doors open. And two months after the paper closed, in December, the NAACP made their final payment of $600 to the Bateses. Much had been lost and so little gained. Daisy had learned some of the hardest lessons of her life: in the face of white supremacy, do not back down and do not take the bribe. Civil rights activists worked hard to preserve their lives, but it was equally difficult to preserve their values. With her vote, Daisy likely damaged a friendship with Williams that could have fortified her. The stance that Roy Wilkins was fighting for within the NAACP was never about Black liberation but about appeasing white power structures. Force, like revolution, helps to change a system or circumstance. What might have been different if Daisy had embraced force? Could she have compelled the NAACP to take a more radical stance? What we do know is that efforts to compromise with white supremacy are a dangerous distraction, as a comic strip from the Baltimore *Afro-American* illustrates. The strip features a Black couple discussing what was described as the biggest civil rights story of 1959.

Mary: That "meet violence with violence" remark of an N.C. NAACP official was unfortunate, wasn't it?

John: Yes, but so was his [Williams's] suspension. We have far too many enemies to be wasting time fighting each other.[54]

Daisy might have been the darling of the Black press, but fame did not protect her—force did.

The racial violence in Little Rock continued. In 1960, Carlotta Walls, the youngest of the Little Rock Nine, woke up from an explosion and then screams. White racists had bombed her house. She was sixteen years old. She remembered saying her prayers and getting into bed, and then at some point during the night the bomb exploded.[55] The detonation of two sticks of dynamite could be felt more than two miles away. The windows of her house were shattered, and the beautiful brick bungalow that Carlotta's father, Cartelyou Walls, had remodeled now had a three-foot hole in the foundation. Walls, a World War II veteran, was away from his family when the bomb exploded. He rushed home to find that his wife Juanita and their three daughters had miraculously survived. In an act of defiance, Carlotta showed up to school the next day. Sometimes force was fortitude, because the work of integration could not stop.

For years, Daisy faced relentless attacks. So she did what many people could not afford to do: she left. In 1960, she moved to New York City. She began writing her memoir, *The Long Shadow of Little Rock*, which was published in 1962 with a foreword written by former first lady Eleanor Roosevelt. In August 1963, Daisy was the only woman to speak at the March on Washington. When Daisy arrived at the podium facing hundreds of thousands of people, her remarks were short—142 words, to be exact. Titled "Tribute to Negro Women Fighters for Freedom," she pledged to join hands with all activists who were working for freedom. "We will kneel-in; we will sit-in until we can eat in any corner in the United States. We will walk until we are free, until we can walk to any school and take our children to any school in the United States. And we will sit-in and we will kneel-in and we will lie-in if necessary until every Negro in America can vote. This we pledge to the women of America."[56] Her speech was not a call to arms, but it was still an unwavering commitment to keep forcing freedom, to keep fighting and testing every strategy until something worked. In 1965, Daisy returned to her home state of Arkansas and kept fighting for freedom for decades, until her last breath.

Mabel and Robert F. Williams are perhaps one of the most iconic Black couples of the long freedom struggle. There is a famous photograph of them side by side, in almost-matching white shirts, their pistols pointed outward. They look intimidating, like a Black Bonnie and Clyde. In another image, Robert has a cigar loosely hanging out of the center of his mouth as he teaches Mabel how to use a pistol that was given to him by Fidel Castro. Mabel stands with her arm at a ninety-degree angle, looking determined, undaunted. The pose was practice, and perhaps performative; Mabel knew how to use a gun.

Born on June 1, 1931, Mabel was raised in Monroe, North Carolina. She grew up around guns. "My stepfather always kept his pearl-handled pistol under his pillow," Mabel remembered. "And it was my job to make up his bed every morning. So I would go and get the pearl-handled pistol and put it in the linen closet every morning," she recalled.[57] It was only later that Mabel overheard older folks talking about why the gun was there. Her family had been threatened by the Klan and nightriders. There was always a fear that they might try to do something horrible in the middle of the night. This was not uncommon in the South, particularly during the 1920s and '30s, when the KKK boasted millions of people on their membership rolls. In Union County, where Monroe was located, the Klan was a very large and powerful group.

At one rally nearly five thousand people gathered to march in full regalia. Mabel recalled that at night and on the weekends Klan members would drive out to Black communities and fire off their guns. "You could hear cars screeching and [bullets] flying everywhere!"[58] Resistance to white supremacy began at a young age for Mabel.

She met Robert when she was a teenager. Mabel's older sister was Robert's best friend. Long before Dr. Martin Luther King Jr. was pushing a platform of nonviolence, Mabel believed such tactics would fail. Her grandfather would have never been able to morally persuade the Klan of his humanity or citizenship. One had to use force.

Mabel was not alone in her stance. Mob attacks, riots, and constant death threats compelled journalist Ida B. Wells to value the sword as well as the pen. She, too, owned guns for protection from violent white people. Wells saw the ravages of the Klan firsthand. In 1892, she published *Southern Horrors: Lynch Law in All Its Phases*, which documented southern lynchings, and in 1895, she published a one-hundred-page pamphlet, *The Red Record*, listing all the hidden reasons for white violence and arguing that the remedy for such barbarity was not compassion or reason but armed self-defense. "A Winchester rifle should have a place of honor in every black home," she wrote.[59] Wells's sentiments are both inspirational and a cautionary tale. It is a reminder that in the twentieth century African Americans still did not possess equal protection under the law.

Activist Fannie Lou Hamer once explained, "I keep a shotgun in every corner of my bedroom and the first cracker even look like he wants to throw some dynamite on my porch won't write his mama again."[60] Even Rosa Parks believed in force. Her grandfather always kept a shotgun within reach, and her husband,

Raymond Parks, was also an armed activist. At meetings he conducted, Rosa recalled, her kitchen table was "covered with guns" in case of an emergency. Parks was best friends with Mabel Williams, and when Robert died in 1996, Parks gave his eulogy. In front of a crowded church, Parks rejoiced that her friend had evaded the white supremacist bullets and assassination attempts.[61] Playwright Lorraine Hansberry was deemed radical for the progressive themes of her plays, but her upbringing certainly contributed to her outlook on white violence. When her parents integrated an all-white neighborhood in Chicago, her mother armed herself. When white Chicagoans threatened to attack their home, she made sure they could fight off any intruder.[62]

Mabel understood that segregation and white supremacy were upheld by brute force and needed to be countered with brute force, arguing that "to shout to a raging maniac driven by a passion of hate that one is committed to a nonviolent policy toward him is tantamount to suicide." Mabel suggested that Black activists should "develop situational tactics." Mabel reasoned that Black people had only a few paths to take: "submission, non-violent suicide or violent self-defense." For Mabel, nonviolent tactics could only succeed in a civilized society "that will respect the oppressed's right to protest and seek redress." Thus, Mabel categorically rejected the belief "that a lov[ing] appeal can bring out the latent goodness of an oppressive brute."[63] Brutes were not fought with ethics but with force. For her, nonviolence was a dead end.

Mabel and Robert also learned a valuable lesson from the local Lumbee Tribe. The Lumbee people are a Native American tribe living in and around Robeson County, North Carolina. In 1958, the KKK held a rally on leased land to threaten the Lumbee people, whom they accused of "race-mixing" in a segregated Jim Crow South. The Klan leader, Grand Dragon James W. "Catfish" Cole, promised that thousands of Klansmen would show up and harass the Lumbee people. They planned to occupy a large field and to burn a cross in effigy, as was their standard practice. But on the day of the rally, now known as the Battle of Hayes Pond, only several dozen Klansmen showed up. In response, over five hundred Lumbee people turned up in a counterprotest. They were armed with rifles, pistols, and sticks and led by Lumbee veterans of World War II. The Lumbee surrounded the Klansmen and fired shots in the air that sent the white people scrambling. The battle was over before it started. Cole took off running and even left his wife behind.[64] The KKK gained no footing in the town, and the only arrest was of a Klansman. The *Rocky Mount Sunday Telegram*, the local newspaper, ran this headline on its front page the next day: "Armed Indians Break Up Klan's Rally." A subheading read, "Police Rescue Kluxers from 1,000 Indians." The incident revealed to the Williamses two key insights: the Klan were cowards, and armed defense staved off white supremacist threats, credible or otherwise.

From the moment Williams took office as president of the Monroe NAACP, the couple faced relentless racist attacks and came to the defense of the Black community in major legal cases. In 1958, the Kissing Case put Monroe and its Black leadership on the map. A seven- or eight-year-old white girl named Sissy Marcus kissed two Black boys, nine-year-old James Thompson and seven-year-old David Simpson, on their cheeks. The children were playing. The kisses were impromptu and harmless. However, when Sissy told her mother what she had done, her mother was appalled. She accused the Black boys of rape. The police arrested them and detained them for weeks. They denied James and David visits from their parents and legal counsel. Authorities beat the boys and pushed to get them sentenced to reform school until the age of twenty-one. James stated that each week during his detention, he was sent to a psychologist, "and he'd tell me, 'They should have castrated y'all.'" The case stirred international controversy when the boys' mothers were finally brought in with a reporter to see them. The charges were never dropped, but after a year of protests and international attention, North Carolina governor Luther H. Hodges reluctantly pardoned the boys. They never received an apology for the deep harm inflicted on them and their families.

During that time, the KKK burned crosses on the boys' front lawns and riddled their homes with bullets. After their rallies, the Klan would drive through the Black community in motorcades, honk their horns, and fire pistols from the car windows. In general, the Klan enjoyed tormenting Black people whenever they could outnumber or isolate them. On one occasion, nightriders caught a Black woman on an isolated street corner and made her dance at gunpoint. Tormenting Black people, particularly on the weekends, was how white supremacists had fun. Members of the Thompson family remember sweeping bullet casings off the front porch every morning after the Klan drove through their neighborhood.[65] White supremacy was pervasive. Only twelve thousand people lived in Monroe, but the Klan boasted they could rally over seven thousand men to a meeting that bordered the town.

Black women were not going to let the state violate their children. Mabel ran a day care center in the town, and her sons were nearly the same ages as the boys in the Kissing Case. Nearly everyone knew that their own children could easily end up in the same position through no fault of their own. One of the boys involved in the Kissing Case often accompanied his grandmother when she went to work cleaning white people's homes. This was common during the summer months—Black mothers and grandmothers would regularly bring their children and grand-children to work with them, and the children would even play with white children while their caretaker worked. But after the Kissing Case, few felt it was safe to bring their children any-where near white children. Something had to be done. Something forceful.

The Williamses decided to start a rifle club, a signal of strength and power that played both offense and defense. Robert even ap-plied to the NRA for a charter, and he received one. In a year, their club had sixty members. Being a part of the rifle club was a necessity. "We were all members. I was a member of the rifle club," said Mabel. "We had several of our ladies become members of the rifle club and we started training . . . all for the protection of our homes and ourselves when the Klan and other rabble-rousers decided that they wanted to come in and invade our homes and our neighborhoods." Mentorship was a key part of defense. Adults taught Black youth how to use a gun properly: "The older fel-lows taught them how to shoot but also taught them that they, hopefully, would never have to shoot. They taught them how to use guns safely and what guns are for."[66] Elderly women were es-pecially keen to rise to the occasion. One senior neighbor of the Williamses, Ms. Crowder, had worked as a domestic for decades. She helped hide guns in her home when the men needed places to stockpile arms. "All of these people were Christian, churchgoing people," Mabel noted. "But they were really fed up with the Klan intimidating them all these years."[67] After several attempts to per-suade local, state, and federal authorities to stop the Klan, Black communities took advantage of their Second Amendment right. It was effective. On more than one occasion, Mabel brandished a gun to prevent police officers from invading her home. If the po-lice did not have a valid warrant, they were not coming in.

North Carolina was a hotbed of Black activism. Restaurants, amusement parks, and swimming pools became contested spaces for Black people vying for the ability to enjoy themselves free of harassment and policing by white people. The first order of business among Black community leaders was protecting their families and their children. Black youths were under considerable threat. During the summer months, significant numbers of Black children drowned in dangerous or unsupervised water holes, gravel pits, and ponds because they were denied the right to swim in white-only swimming pools, which had lifeguards, even though these swimming pools were funded by taxes paid by both Black and white families.

For years, the Williamses and the NAACP had been protesting segregated swimming pools. Young people wanted to be involved in pushing for their own rights. Many of them had needlessly lost friends or family members to drowning. To them, access to the pool was about so much more than being able to stay cool during the heat of summer. Mabel and Robert offered the youths protection. In June 1961, the Williamses came to the aid of Black children who were being threatened by an angry mob outside of the swimming pool. Mabel and her best friend, Asa Lee, joined Robert at the pool. Asa clearly remembered seeing Mabel, who was armed, standing next to her husband. Mabel knew that she could not trust the police to defend Black children or Black interests. They would have to serve as their own police force against white mobs. Once again, anger motivates force. Mabel stated, "My feelings then were that if I must die, I'm going to take 'em with me. . . . And so I got my gun in my hand and I determined . . . I was going to kill [the chief of police]."[68] Both Mabel and Robert only utilized gun violence as a protective measure. Mabel recalled, "The powers-that-be were much more threatened by that gun than they were by the nonviolent protests he [Robert] organized. Once they couldn't do violence and be immune to violence, they didn't do as much violence."[69]

When Mabel and Robert's sons wanted to join in varied forms of resistance, Mabel was reluctant to allow them to participate. She knew about the time a little Black boy was beaten up by white men who mistook him for one of the Williamses' sons. Restricting their activities was a form of protection, and Mabel acknowledged that she was "scared to death" for her boys' well-being.[70] But Mabel's son retorted, "I want my civil rights too!"[71] How could she deny such a plea given their activist work? Mabel capitulated, but she refused to be unarmed. When her sons participated in protests at the Monroe Country Club swimming pool, she sat in the car. "I didn't picket," explained Mabel. "I was in the car with guns. . . . We had to protect the kids. . . . At the time, you know, guns were legal as long as they were not concealed in North Carolina. So we had the guns on the seat. [Laughter] They were not concealed."[72] Force enabled her to allow her boys to protest and to ensure that their civil disobedience would not be interrupted.

Mabel lived a long life. While in Monroe, she cofounded and helped maintain *The Crusader,* a weekly newsletter that reached readers in the United States and abroad. She organized the Crusaders' Association for Relief and Enlightenment, a grassroots mutual aid society in Monroe. She also served as an uncredited ghostwriter for much of her husband's book *Negroes with Guns.*[73] Mabel was notable in her effective use of force to counter white supremacy, but she was not alone. As she acknowledged, "Women are pushing harder than the men. . . . That is where our drive is coming from."[74] Indeed, one of the first major moments of armed resistance in North Carolina occurred when the beloved Dr. Albert Perry, vice president of the Monroe NAACP, had been arrested on trumped-up charges. Black women knew he was in danger of being lynched, so a group of them gathered rifles and stormed the jail. With force, they freed him.[75]

Mabel and her family stood their ground until it was no longer possible. Facing increasing threats from the KKK, they fled to Cuba in 1961, where they produced Radio Free Dixie until 1965. They later found refuge in Mao Zedong's China. The Williamses were not radical outliers. They simply believed in self-defense and using force to halt white violence. And Robert was often the face of what Mabel had written or thought. In 1969, they returned to the United States for good and settled in Baldwin, Michigan. Their stance may have put their lives at risk, but force actually extended their lives. Force enabled them to prevent or stop nearly any onslaught of violence. Robert died at the age of seventy-one; Mabel died in April 2014 at the age of eighty-two.

Black women are often left in the shadows of Black men whose activism and celebrity overshadow Black women's contribution by sustaining a narrative that associates Black masculinity with physical force. For example, the best-known of Malcolm X's speeches is "The Ballot or the Bullet," given April 3, 1964, at Cory Methodist Church in Cleveland, Ohio. In a list of the top one hundred speeches of the twentieth century as ranked by scholars and compiled by the University of Wisconsin–Madison and Texas A&M University, this speech was number seven.[76] Put simply, the speech is an ultimatum of force. In an effort to gain voting rights for all people, Malcolm gave his audience two options: equal access to democracy through the ballot or political violence to implement change with the bullet. He declared, "It's time now for you and me to become more politically mature and realize what the ballot is for; what we're supposed to get when we cast a ballot; and that if we don't cast a ballot, it's going to end up in a situation where we're going to have to cast a bullet. It's either a ballot or a bullet."[77] This powerful alliteration was not his formulation but that of civil rights activist Gloria Richardson.

In his biography of Richardson, *The Struggle Is Eternal: Gloria Richardson and Black Liberation*, Joseph Fitzgerald argues that Richardson had a conversation with Malcolm regarding Black voting rights and unmet needs. She claimed in her speeches that she received warnings from her Black community in Cambridge, Maryland, about resorting to violence. She rightly suspected that other Black communities across the country must have felt the same way. Knowing of Malcolm X's major platform and ability to rile his audiences, she encouraged him to include the threat of ballots or bullets. "If it wasn't ballots, then it would be bullets. . . . That was the only fallback position," Richardson reasoned. She persuaded him to incorporate these ideas in his speech.[78] The phrase "the ballot or the bullet" became not only the clarion call but the title of Malcolm's speech. In the spring of 1964, over the course of three weeks, Malcolm gave his famous speech on two separate occasions, first on April 3 and then on April 12. On the twelfth, at King Solomon Baptist Church in Detroit, Malcolm spoke again about Richardson's inspiring ultimatum:

> This is why I say it's the ballot or the bullet. It's liberty or it's death. It's freedom for everybody or freedom for nobody. America today finds herself in a unique situation. Historically, revolutions are

bloody, oh yes they are. They have never had a bloodless revolution. . . . Revolutions overturn systems. Revolutions destroy systems. A revolution is bloody, but America is in a unique position.
She's the only country in history, in the position actually to become involved in a bloodless revolution. . . . But today, this country can become involved in a revolution that won't take bloodshed.
All she's got to do is give the black man in this country everything
that's due him, everything.[79]

Richardson knew well that force was an accelerator of change and
could lead to revolution. For her and Malcolm, force was the ballot and revolution was the bullet, and likely both would be needed
to motivate change among white leaders. Force through the ballot
ensured that a democratic process would uphold unalienable constitutional rights. Revolution is what happens when force is denied
or ignored. Force is not a request; it is a demand. Richardson's options refused compromise. But Richardson is not a household name.
Scholars and society have left her out of this narrative and essentially
erased her from her own idea. But even if Richardson has been forgotten, she was not wrong.

When it comes to force, this is the hard and final truth. As Charles
Cobb explains in his deft work *This Nonviolent Stuff'll Get You
Killed*, "There was no meaningful difference between white responses to armed resistance by blacks and white responses to nonviolent resistance by blacks. Where massive police force or state
power was exercised, as in Birmingham and Selma, Alabama, or
in Jackson, Mississippi, police violence was not a response to either
the use of guns or the practice of nonviolence; rather, it was exercised for the sole purpose of crushing black protest and demands

in any shape."[80] There is no form of protest white supremacy will approve. Whether Black people take a knee or burn down the QuikTrip, the backlash will always be the same. Appeasing white power structures will not work. And when nonviolence is not successful, it is likely because nonviolence is being used as a tool to suppress change. Only by force can freedom be gained. Carrie, Daisy, Mabel, and even my grandmother Reader knew this and recognized that it was better to have a weapon and not need it than to be defenseless. And in a violent white supremacist's world, force is always needed.

Force is, and should be, a remedy of last resort. While white supremacy promotes vengeance, I am always astounded by the levels of restraint in the Black community. In 1993, Toni Morrison appeared on *Charlie Rose*. The occasion was the publication of her novel *Jazz*, but the conversation turned to the eruption of violence in the streets of Los Angeles after the acquittal of three white police officers whose brutal beating of Rodney King had been captured on video. "What struck me the most about the people who were burning down shops and stealing was how long they waited—the restraint. Not the spontaneity, the restraint," Morrison said. She leaned in and stared straight at Charlie Rose. "The moment to be anarchic was when we saw those tapes," she continued. "They waited—how long was it? Nine months? A year? They waited for justice, and it didn't come."[81] Force is what happens when white people fail to live up to the laws of their own creation.

Chapter Four

FLIGHT

A random phone call from my brother-in-law, George, sometimes goes like this:

George: Hey, sis, so what's your exit plan?

Me: My exit plan?

George: Yep. Black folks are talking about leaving, we out. Some people I know are going to Ghana.

Me: Word? Ghana? My friend just built a house in Ghana.

George: Yo, I heard Stevie Wonder has a house in Ghana?

Me: For real, let's do it! And when we leave, we not Ghana come back!

We both burst into laughter. Our conversations are often playful banter, but it also got me thinking about how flight has been a constant refrain or remedy in African American history. Leaving is a form of refusal, and it is something Black people have done in response to white supremacy for centuries.

Flight is one of the most common actions in the history of Black resistance. It can mean quitting a job or place. It can be short term or permanent. During slavery, enslaved people would sometimes take short absences from the place of their enslavement. Maybe running away to the North was not possible, but running away to the swamps, forests, or a neighboring plantation—to withhold labor, perhaps, or visit a loved one—was. It can be argued that the successes of the American Revolution and the American Civil War depended largely not on whether Black folks fought but where they fled: their flight from plantations crippled slaveholders because it robbed them of their labor force. Everything in the South depended on enslaved labor.

In the twentieth century, flight became the Great Migration. From 1890 to 1970 an estimated six to eight million Black southerners left their homes to find new ones in the Midwest and Northeast and on the West Coast. Black folks left en masse, moving from rural areas to urban areas and from the South to the North or West. They left with their families. They left with their labor. They left with their skills, genius, and artistry.[1] Sometimes flight looked like being pushed out. But often it meant being pulled away, drawn to the promise of adventure and pleasure. Flight as a remedy can mean departing for a break or departing for good. A place has to clear a relatively low bar for Black people to move there. Where can Black people go where they will not be exploited or killed? Leaving is about a search for belonging, safety, or a place to just be. Leaving is about creating spaces where Black people can exist.

Leaving is an act of resistance because so many Black people are stuck, unable to leave the ghetto or hood or other place that has suffered from racist neglect and community divestment. During the 1980s, major companies such as steel plants, automobile factories, and other major manufacturers left cities for cheaper labor elsewhere, mainly overseas. When companies left, they took with them jobs and a stable tax base. Because school funding is tethered to property taxes, schools became severely underfunded. Cities were already fragile from white flight: white families that were not interested in integration had left cities for the suburbs decades earlier, in the 1940s and '50s. With no tax base, cities became unlivable. Poor schools, poor sanitation, and food deserts became a norm. Mortgage companies, banks, and realtors created a system of redlining that prevented Black people with means from purchasing homes in white communities. Black homes appreciated at a lower rate, so Black homeowners earned less on their investments. Moreover, the Northeast and Midwest saw a steep decline in the industrial and manufacturing sectors when companies began to outsource their labor to create larger profits.

It should be no surprise that when all the factors of unemployment, underemployment, economic divestment, and failing schools come together, crime is the result. People become compelled to operate outside of the law to provide for their families or survive themselves. The government's solution to Black poverty is policing. Black communities become targets of surveillance and police brutality. Young Black men and women are funneled into the prison system because it appears easier to throw people away than to invest in their success, success that might compete with white people's aspirations. Accordingly, mass incarceration is an entire ecosystem of prisons, jails, courts, parole officers, police officers, investors, and policies, based not on mitigating harm but on punishing crime. And the surest way to dispose of a people is to define Blackness and poverty as synonymous with criminality. The very notion of prison is about an inability to move or have mobility in public spaces.

Moving is often highly restricted because of external conditions. Poverty makes it difficult if not impossible to leave on the precipice of a natural disaster such as a hurricane or fire. Many Black people are chained to their exploitation: during the COVID-19 pandemic, for example, large numbers of white Americans could shelter in place in the comfort of their own homes, but "essential workers," many of them Black and brown low-wage laborers, were still forced to go to work. Confinement—that is to say, restriction and segregation—has made up too much of the Black experience. And these limitations are not organic but constructed. The ghetto is essential to urban planning. Government housing is built with intention—the absence of light, sanitation, safety, and beauty is part of the blueprint. Within these restricted spaces, policing creates an additional layer of surveillance. Any time a person veers off their intended restrictive path and place, they are bombarded with questions such as, Where are you going? What are you doing? Should you be here? White Americans rarely have to consider what it means to be policed or trapped by inhuman conditions and are seldom questioned about whether they have the right to be somewhere.

Even when it comes to vacation travel, most Black people around the world cannot move. There are no African countries whose citizens can enter the United States without a visa. There is no ninety-day tourist exemption that would allow someone from

Botswana to go to Boston or Los Angeles for a holiday without diplomatic hurdles. So much of the Black experience is about isolation—the inability to travel or move from place to place, to be restricted to one town, city, or country. I have thought very deeply about what happens when Black people cannot leave. Many experience not only policing but what it feels to be stuck in a ghetto or the hood. To be trapped in food deserts, failing schools, and crumbling infrastructure and never be able to escape to something better has a demoralizing impact.

The anger and resentment that come with being stuck are best encapsulated in Jamaica Kincaid's classic work *A Small Place*. Kincaid tells the story of her beloved island, Antigua, and writes about the meaningful difference between being a tourist and being a native. She argues that every native of every place is a potential tourist, and every tourist is a native of somewhere, but most natives, most Black and colonized people, will never get to occupy the space of the tourist. She brilliantly lays out the rage and resentment native people have regarding the one who can escape, the tourist. "Every native everywhere lives a life of overwhelming and crushing banality and boredom and desperation and depression, and every deed, good and bad, is an attempt to forget this," Kincaid writes. For her, every native would like to find a way out, a break, a rest, or a tour. But the reality is that most natives in the world cannot go anywhere because they are too poor. Kincaid indicts her readers directly: "They are too poor to escape the reality of their lives; and they are too poor to live properly in the place they live, which is the very place you, the tourist, want to go—so when the natives see you, the tourist, they envy you, they envy your ability to leave your own banality and boredom, they envy your ability to turn their own banality and boredom into a source of pleasure for yourself."[2]

My parents are products of the Great Migration, the movement of millions of Black people from the South to the North. They are the first generation of their families to be born in a northern city—specifically, Detroit. My father's family hailed from Louisiana and my mother's family from Mississippi. When my father traveled from Detroit back south, he never stayed in a hotel. His family slept on the side of the road, as all traveling Black families did. It was the same for my mother. Her family caravanned from Detroit to Mississippi in three or four cars over several days. They all took turns driving, and when it was time to eat, they ate the meals they had packed before they left. When nature called or it was time to sleep, they pulled over to the side of the road. There were no public restaurants they could dine in, or restrooms they could use, or hotels they dared stay in. Segregation was the law and the custom. In fact, my father was well into adulthood before he ever stayed at a hotel. He never forgot the first hotel he stayed in, either—a Days Inn. My mother recalled not even knowing what a hotel was as a child. Why would she know? Nobody in her world could have shared that experience with her until after the passage of the 1964 Civil Rights Act. Even after, it was a while before they could afford to take a vacation. Travel was to see family. If they got a reprieve from childcare or a few days of work, that was the break; that was the vacation.

Flight is about both the collective and the individual. The enslaved left the plantations. Black southerners left the South. Mary Ann Shadd Cary left the United States for Canada. Ida B. Wells left the States for Europe. Black soldiers fighting in world wars left for Europe. For eight years, Paul Robeson tried to leave. James Baldwin left and came back. W. E. B. Du Bois left and could not come back. Josephine Baker left. Mabel and Robert Williams left for Cuba and then China and then came back to settle in Detroit. Some Black Panthers left for Tanzania, Algeria, or Ghana. Some of my family left the South for a better life in the North. And one generation later, they left the North for a better life in the South.

It is not easy to leave home. But in America, as a Black American, what is home? What is an African American safe haven? Home is elusive. Sometimes home is the North and sometimes home is the South. Sometimes home is city and sometimes home is the woods, swamp, or mountains. For some, home is outside of the United States. For someone like Bessie Coleman, the first African American woman aviator, home was in the air. But always, finding home requires leaving somewhere else.

By the 1770s, nearly half a million Black people were living and laboring in what would become the United States. While the transatlantic slave trade was still violently importing hundreds of thousands of Africans to the New World, many were also being born into slavery in the American colonies. Each generation of enslaved people born in America came to have a deeper connection to the land. America was the only "home" many Black people knew. But war, even rumors of war, changed what might be possible for African Americans. War presented them with an opening to pursue freedom during an era of enlightenment and planter absenteeism. When enslavers and plantation owners were off fighting the British, enslaved people made their move. Fighting for one side or the other might foster certain promises or protections, but fleeing removed the hurdle of negotiation.

Initially during the war, General George Washington was adamant about not enlisting Black men to fight. As a slaveholder himself, he could not stomach the idea of Black men taking up arms in a war for freedom, liberty, and equality. In 1775, Washington claimed he was appalled when he found large numbers of Black men fighting against British troops. He feared that the recruitment of Black troops could have devastating effects on the institution of slavery, and he began to outlaw Black enlistment. Permitting the enslaved the right to bear arms and take up defense even against the young nation's enemy was more than Washington could bear. But eventually, the need to win the war superseded his desire to keep enslaved men from fighting.

Knowing that slavery was crucial to the development and empowerment of America, John Murray, the Earl of Dunmore and Virginia's royal governor, sought to undermine patriot efforts by issuing a proclamation. In November 1775, Lord Dunmore threatened to free all enslaved people and set Williamsburg, then the Virginia capital, ablaze if the colonists chose to rebel against British authority. Dunmore's famous proclamation stated, "I do hereby farther declare all *indented servants, Negroes*, or others (appertaining to rebels) *free*, that are able and willing to bear arms, they *joining his Majesty's troops*, as soon as may be, for the more speedily reducing this colony to a proper sense of their duty, to his Majesty's crown and dignity."[3] In other words, if Black people joined the British efforts, freedom was their reward. The proclamation only applied to the colony of Virginia, but it did not matter. Word spread fast that if you were Black and could get to British lines, you could gain your freedom. Dunmore took his strategy one step further by offering to allow Black men to enlist. Within months, Dunmore had over eight hundred Black soldiers in his "Ethiopian regiment." But while many Black men did choose to enlist, more seized the opportunity to flee as far away from their enslavement as possible. Tens of thousands of enslaved people fled their slaveholding colonies for freedom, weakening the institution of slavery itself as they did so.

Wholesale abandonment is the other side to revolutionary violence.[4] Some scholars argue that slave flight was more devastating than rebellion. For example, in South Carolina, over twenty-five thousand enslaved men and women left their plantations. This number represented about a quarter of the enslaved population at the time. Over six thousand abandoned the city of Charleston alone. Roughly fifteen thousand enslaved people fled Georgia, which totaled 75 percent of its enslaved population. Thomas Jefferson believed that Virginia lost thirty thousand enslaved people in one year alone.[5] The enslaved plundered themselves from their owner's coffers. During the Revolution, Black people left their plantations while their enslavers were away fighting the war. Leaving was a vote, a way of casting a ballot in Black interests. To leave the plantation or one's enslaver was to send a clear message about the hypocrisy of American democracy.

By the end of the American Revolution, some scholars estimate, as many as eighty thousand to one hundred thousand enslaved people throughout the thirteen states escaped to the British lines. Though the British lost the American colonies, they kept their word to enslaved people regarding the promise of freedom. Interestingly, this contravened the demands of the Treaty of Paris, which had called for the return of all property, including slaves.[6] Instead, newly freed Black loyalists were sent to Nova Scotia or London. Some were sent to live in free settlements in the West Indies, where slavery was still in operation. They didn't always stay in the place where they initially settled. Some free Black people who had been sent to Nova Scotia, for example, went on to settle in Africa, in the colony of Sierra Leone. While these migrations may have looked like a constant shuffling of

Black bodies, Black people were making conscious and calculated choices about their best opportunities for success. When
they had the chance to leave the United States, they did, and
when Nova Scotia was not all that they had been promised, they
left it, too.

As the United States settled into its new identity as an independent country, leaving became more difficult for Black people.
The war had offered a window of mobility, but by the end of the
eighteenth century that window had closed. For the enslaved who
were trapped in a united, slaveholding South, leaving became all
but impossible. Laws regarding mobility for the enslaved were enforced with stiff penalties. Black codes orchestrated Black life. Enslaved people could not gather in groups larger than three or four.
Curfews were put in place to keep enslaved people from moving
after nine o'clock or nightfall. Slave patrols, which would eventually evolve into police forces, were there to surveil Black behavior.
Nothing could happen without white oversight, not birth or death
or celebrations. All work was monitored. All movement required
passes or special permission.[7]

The 1793 Fugitive Slave Act was passed to provide a way of retrieving property that had stolen themselves away. The law gave
slaveholders congressional authority to obtain their human property and maintain control of any descendants born of enslaved
property. One of the most notable fugitive slaves of this time period was Ona Judge, who escaped her owner, Martha Washington,
wife of President George Washington. On May 21, 1796, while
laboring in Philadelphia, Judge managed to escape with the help
of the abolitionist community. Twice George Washington sent
slave catchers to retrieve her, but to no avail.[8] Judge died virtually
penniless in New Hampshire, and she would have chosen to leave
again knowing the outcome. She had two published interviews

with abolitionist newspapers in her lifetime. When asked whether she regretted leaving the Washingtons, given that her life afterward had been difficult, she replied, "No, I am free, and have, I trust, been made a child of God by the means."[9] Flight was her remedy, and she was satisfied with her solution.

Not everyone could leave and not be caught. Historian Stephanie Camp tells the story of a courageous enslaved woman named Sallie Smith. Sallie's master was a cruel man who forbade his human property to leave the confines of his Louisiana plantation. He promised violent penalties for those who attempted to leave without his express permission. Sallie refused to be trapped, regardless of the consequences. One day she ran, but she was soon caught by authorities. Making good on his promise of violence, Sallie's owner tortured her by placing her inside a barrel that had nails driven through it. Once she was inside, he rolled the barrel. Sallie was cut in every direction, bloodied from head to toe. Her response was astonishing: "I did not stay more than a month before I ran away again. I tell you, I could not stay there."[10] Whatever she was fleeing to, whatever she sought, was more important than what would happen to her if she was caught.

The stories of Ona Judge and Sallie Smith tell us something incredibly valuable about flight. The hope of escape and the act of stealing oneself were more powerful than the prestige of the presidency or the violence of the plantation. No one was promised a better life; in fact, chances were high that flight would fail. And yet, Black women and men left. For enslaved people, leaving—or "stealing away"—robbed the planter of his economic assets and threatened the very foundation of the institution. For free Black Americans, leaving gave them the opportunity to assert their own agency regarding their labor and refuse to live in the subordinated status of northern white supremacist laws and norms. It was better to live a lifetime in poverty than to be enslaved or oppressed for one day.

Flight is about choosing how, when, and where to move. Not all movements of Black Americans fit this definition. During the early nineteenth century, the American Colonization Society (ACS) was founded with the idea of sending Black Americans back to Africa—to the newly established colony of Liberia, in particular. Robert Finley, who founded the organization with other white Americans in 1816, could not make sense of a free Black existence. These men considered themselves abolitionists, but the ACS was not about liberating Black Americans—it was about preserving white supremacy. To the founders of the ACS, free Black people—especially those living in the South—threatened the entire nation's way of life. But flight is about Black people departing on their own terms. The ACS was looking for a way to get rid of Black folks who operated outside of enslavement or subordination. Scholars now understand the ACS as a reactionary response to emancipation and the existence of free Black communities in the United States.[11]

The experiment was also a failure. For starters, despite all of their efforts, the ACS only managed to get about three thousand African Americans to migrate to Africa. The organization never found a base of support among Black communities. Wealthy Black leaders and businessmen such as James Forten were staunchly against the enterprise, and they did not need to work hard to convince other Black Americans to not buy in. By the early nineteenth century, many Black Americans were first-, second-, or even third-generation American born. They had an alliance to the place where they were born and raised. Africa was a foreign place, and many would have struggled to determine their exact country of origin had they wanted to. In any case, the voyage to Africa was perilous and heinously expensive. It cost money to gather Black people, get them to ships, pay for their passage, food, and supplies. Many people died on the long voyage crossing the Atlantic Ocean, and more died from diseases such as malaria in the first few months after their arrival. Nearly 22 percent died within the first year of arriving in Liberia.[12] Some attempted to return once they realized that a new beginning was more difficult than their lives in America. Those who stayed and survived would become the leaders of Liberia. Shockingly, the ACS did not officially dissolve until 1964.

Black leaders who did leave the United States of their own volition left with a mission. Black abolitionist Mary Ann Shadd Cary was born in America. She had what many Black Americans might consider a privileged life. To begin with, she was born to free Black parents in the slaveholding state of Delaware. She was educated in Quaker schools in Pennsylvania, primarily because Delaware did not allow the education of Black children. Despite her freedom and education, as an adult she saw little opportunity for advancement in the North. She had a voice and she wanted to use it. So she left. She joined her brother in the town of Windsor, Ontario, and once she was settled, she got to work. She started her own newspaper, the *Provincial Freeman*, the first publication in North America founded and edited by an African American woman. By leaving America, Shadd Cary could lead on her own terms. She was highly influential in social activism and the Underground Railroad. She used her paper to recruit more Black Americans to Canada and promote Black empowerment.

Shadd Cary's response to most of Black America's problems was to leave, to vote with her feet. A relentless advocate for women's rights, she was particularly interested in directing her message to Black women. She corresponded with many of the community leaders and Black women abolitionists of the day, counseling them to aid their brethren in leaving the United States as soon as possible. Black conventions were being held all across the North. Many of these conventions, which Shadd Cary's father and brother attended, featured a lot of passionate speeches and passed a number of resolutions, but they were not able to implement substantive actions or outcomes—and women who attempted to speak in public at the conventions were shunned. Black women had to find other ways to make their voices heard.

In 1848, Frederick Douglass's newspaper the *North Star* put out a call asking what could be done to uplift the race. Shadd Cary answered. She wrote to the paper declaring, "We should do more and talk less."[13] In 1855, with much controversy, she took the floor of the Black convention. Breaking custom and tradition, she was granted time to make her case regarding emigration to Canada and the fight for abolition. She was charismatic and persuasive. Her audience was spellbound. When her time was up on the floor, the men granted her an additional ten minutes to complete her speech.[14] It may have been the first time many Black people in the audience thought about what it would mean to move on their own terms—not as a political pawn of war or subject of the ACS's white supremacist ploy, but for themselves.

In 1852, Shadd Cary published a pamphlet entitled *A Plea for Emigration; or, Notes of Canada West, in Its Moral, Social and Political Aspect: With Suggestions Respecting Mexico, West Indies and Vancouver's Island for the Information of Colored Emigrants.* The title says it all. The pamphlet examines the benefits of flight, of taking one's labor, talents, and family to a better place, a place where Black people can move beyond surviving and into thriving. During one of the conventions in the 1850s, perhaps Shadd Cary also understood that one could do the work of abolition, but speaking and writing were equally a part of the activism. The pen and sword were required tools to fight new legislation in the 1850s that changed the work and scope of abolitionism.

The 1850 Fugitive Slave Law made it nearly impossible to escape slave catchers or the paranoia of being kidnapped anywhere in the United States. The 1793 law of the same name did not have teeth; it did not fine people for refusing to aid in retrieval or threaten them with six months in prison. The revamped law made the Canadian border the new Mason-Dixon Line. After the 1857 *Dred Scott* decision, which declared that Black people had no rights that a white man was bound to respect, Shadd Cary doubled down on her call for Black people to refuse subjugation and find a new home. In April 1857, a group of Black women abolitionists and community leaders met in Philadelphia to discuss the court's decision. In attendance were Letitia Still, the wife of the Father of the Underground Railroad, William Still; Sarah Parker Remond, a famous orator who often spoke with her equally famous abolitionist brother, Charles Lenox Remond; and Harriet Forten Purvis, daughter of the wealthy sailmaker James Forten and wife of Robert Purvis, the president of the Pennsylvania Antislavery Society. These were women who all accomplished much for themselves, but more importantly, they worked for the benefit of their communities. Shadd Cary knew she could call on her fellow leaders and challenge them to do more.

Shadd Cary wrote to her sisters in the struggle that after the *Dred Scott* decision, more needed to be done: "The resolutions were strong and pointed, but why not go further?" She asked these leaders and others who took part in the April meeting whether they intended to stay in the United States. "If so, the resolutions amount to nothing," Shadd Cary lamented. "Your national ship is rotten [and] sinking, why not leave it, and why not say so boldly, manfully?" Shadd Cary had been living in Canada for several years at this point. She thought that after the Fugitive Slave Law, the solution was clear. In her view, America was never going to grant Black people anything near the kind of rights and privileges they would have in Canada. She argued that it would be better for Black leadership to consider the reality in Canada and emigrate rather than continue to hope and theorize for a better life in America.[15]

Sarah Parker Remond was convinced. In due time, she left for England. While in London, she advocated for the abolitionist cause. She took up studies at Bedford College and used her term breaks to speak on the abolitionist circuit. Once the Civil War began, she did not stop her efforts but urged the British public to support the Union. And when the war ended, she kept advocating for Black people, raising funds to help the newly freed navigate their emancipation. She kept fighting for Black interests, but she never returned home. In 1867, Remond moved from England to Florence, Italy. She trained as a physician and then practiced medicine for almost twenty years. She died in Rome at the age of sixty-eight.

Remond never returned to the United States. She did not trust her country with her talents or her progressive thinking. But Shadd Cary did return, primarily to help recruit Black men to fight in the Civil War. When the war was over, she started a school and taught the formerly enslaved. And in 1883, not satisfied with either her own education or the law, she enrolled at Howard University School of Law and—at the age of sixty—became the second African American woman in the country to earn her law degree. Her new battle would no longer be fighting from a distance, like Remond, but fighting up close. Returning to the United States allowed her to work for change with the law on her side.

Harriet Tubman fought up close as well. After living in Canada for several years, she, too, returned to the United States in 1857. Historian Catherine Clinton argues that the *Dred Scott* decision may have motivated her move. Tubman had also vowed to help John Brown and his raid on Harpers Ferry, though for unknown reasons she was absent during the raid itself. But she was there for the war. For many, the outbreak of the Civil War was the time not to retreat but to return to the United States of one's own volition. Sometimes all people needed was time, a break, a reprieve, after which they could come back and keep the fight going on behalf of those who could not leave their confinement. And Canada was not the only refuge.

In the 1820s, Haiti, the first Black independent nation in the Western Hemisphere, a country that was still seeking diplomatic recognition from the United States, revamped its immigration programs to attract Black Americans. For some, Haiti had never left Black consciousness. The Haitian Revolution was inspirational for those pursuing emancipation and equality. And unlike the failed attempts of the American Colonization Society, emigration to Haiti was a choice of their own.

Black leaders such as Martin Delany, Henry Highland Garnet, H. Ford Douglas, James Theodore Holly, E. P. Walker, J. M. Whitfield, and William C. Monroe were at the forefront of Black American emigration, particularly to the island of Haiti. Such movements dated as far back as the administrations of the Haitian presidents Jean-Jacques Dessalines, Alexandre Pétion, and Jean-Pierre Boyer, all of whom encouraged Black Americans to settle in Haiti in the early 1800s. By the late 1850s, the time was ripe for a resurgence of the notion. Then president of Haiti Fabre-Nicolas Geffrard, who adamantly supported the abolitionist movement and had even held a funeral for John Brown and donated $2,000 to his widow, continued the policy of recruiting Black Americans to leave the United States and come to the island.[16] The Haitian government developed the Haitian Bureau of Emigration, investing over $20,000 and creating more stable employment for Black American leadership than they enjoyed stateside. Central to emigrationist ideology was the potential for economic impact.[17] It is routinely forgotten that during the nineteenth century Haiti was a site of agricultural innovation and economic prosperity and boasted one of the highest standards of living for Black people in the Western Hemisphere.[18]

In 1859, Haitian President Geffard also appointed James Redpath to be his commissioner of emigration in the United States. Redpath felt that Black emigration to the island could help Haiti obtain diplomatic recognition from the US and allow Black Americans to have a better life. The same year, no newspaper endorsed leaving more than the *Weekly Anglo-African*, owned by brothers Thomas and Robert Hamilton. In many ways, the paper became the public relations outlet for the Haitian movement as the Civil War approached. Though it was only in existence from July 1859 until March 1861, during its brief tenure the newspaper developed a reputation for militancy and made sure that readers were aware of the advantages and disadvantages of emigration. James Redpath purchased the newspaper from the Hamilton brothers in 1859, changed its name to the *Pine and Palm*, and used it specifically to advocate for the Haitian emigration movement. I have always thought that the name of the paper stemmed from the notion of trading pine trees for palm trees. When Redpath retired from his paid position as emigration agent of the Haitian emigration movement on May 11, 1861, he turned the paper back over to Robert Hamilton, who changed the paper's name back to the *Anglo-African*. Throughout these changes in the paper's name and ownership, the theme of flight continued to be broadcast in its pages.[19]

As proof that the topic of leaving was becoming unavoidable among Black leaders, those who had previously not favored leaving began to see its utility when the South seceded in 1861. Frederick Douglass and James McCune Smith had previously rejected and ignored the efforts of Martin Delany, the leading emigrationist and Black Nationalist. By 1859, Delany, who had initially focused on emigration to Canada and the Caribbean, was making inroads into West Africa. At the end of 1860, when Delany returned to the United States, Douglass's new empathy toward the emigration movement did not go unnoticed.

Although Douglass had never fully embraced leaving permanently, in the lead-up to the war he came to see it as a practical option because politics had proved useless in attaining Black emancipation and equality. In early 1861, he began to support emigration and to show that support. He even allowed full-page ads recruiting Black Americans to Haiti to run in his newspaper, the *Douglass' Monthly*. In addition, Douglass planned a trip to Haiti himself, with all expenses paid by the Haitian government. As he prepared for his trip, he was informed that South Carolina had fired on Fort Sumter. Without hesitation, he canceled his trip.[20] Though Douglass chose to wait rather than leave for the island just yet, in May 1861, he wrote in his newspaper, "We propose to act in view of the settled fact that many of them [Black Americans] are already resolved to look for homes beyond the boundaries of the United States, and that most of their minds are turned toward Haiti."[21]

During a lecture in Ohio, the abolitionist William J. Watkins explained his position on leaving and the Haitian emigration movement. Watkins saw no hope for gaining equal footing with white Americans. "The social and political disabilities under which we labor crush us to the earth," argued Watkins, adding, "Here in Ohio, our children are not allowed to take their seats in the same school with the whites, but are driven to some nook or corner, in an isolated position, as though they were the special pets of the smallpox. Even the churches refuse the recognition of our equal manhood." Watkins then proceeded to discuss the need to change conditions for African Americans. For Watkins to view America as a place worthy of his continued habitation, he had to be able to answer specific questions in the affirmative: "Will the time ever arrive when the colored man will have *equal rights* with the white man? Will he ever have equal access to the Presidential chair, or occupy seats in the Cabinet, or in the Senate, or on the bench of the Supreme Court?" In sum, Watkins asked, "Will the white man so far forget the black man's complexion that he will consent to be governed by him, or to receive the law from him?" If Black men could not hope for recognition in ways that effectively granted equality, Watkins indicated, he saw no reason to stay in America. He urged his fellows to place themselves in a country where no barriers would oppose the development of their "mental and moral being, but where [their] every faculty [could] proudly sweep the whole circle of human activity."[22]

However, Watkins did not support schemes to leave en masse, such as the colonization efforts in Liberia or Sierra Leone, which he labeled both impossible and impractical.[23] He believed that Haiti and Canada had some of the strongest appeal as destinations. In Haiti, Black Americans could demonstrate their capacity for self-government. Watkins explained that emigrants from Ohio could have their passage to the island paid for by the Haitian government. In addition, each head of household would receive sixteen acres of land, and eight acres would be given to individuals as a payment for their investment in the country. The Haitian government had also promised to provide emigrants with subsistence for up to eight days after their arrival. An Ohio newspaper assured its readers that "much interest will be awakened by this lecture."[24] The land incentives in Haiti were not the only attraction. Black

Americans saw leaving for Haiti as an opportunity to cultivate Black Nationalism. Haiti offered a national identity that was encouraging and elevating to Black Americans after the lamentable *Dred Scott* decision.

Frederick Douglass's and William J. Watkins's decisions to support emigration marked a significant shift in the way Black intellectuals and activists thought about their relationship to America. Even the abolitionist George T. Downing, who was one of the biggest opponents of leaving, had by 1861 shifted his opinion. As the Civil War took hold in America, prominent Black leaders who publicly promoted staying at home at any cost were in the minority. Conditions for Black people in the United States were such that it was difficult not to look favorably on plans to leave. While few went as far as to champion flight as the only true road to progress, it was certainly one road.[25]

Once the country was officially at war, the enslaved made calculated decisions. W. E. B. Du Bois later argued that Black Americans sensed what was about to happen: "All began carefully to watch the unfolding of the situation." Even before the shot at Fort Sumter was fired, movement had begun across the Mason-Dixon Line. Free and enslaved Black Americans were fleeing to the North in unprecedented numbers. Du Bois estimated that roughly two thousand Black Americans left the state of North Carolina alone because of rumors of war.[26] When the war began, it was the enslaved, not Southerners, who mobilized fastest. The enslaved slowed down production and took advantage of absent enslavers. They plotted and even rebelled. But mostly, they left and raced to Union strongholds as soon as they could.

When the Civil War ended, Black Americans connected their newfound citizenship not just to protection under the law but mobility. Newly freed Black people left to find their loved ones and to farm for themselves. African Americans readily understood that the freedom to travel locally, nationally, or internationally was one of the major components of citizenship and, at a deeper level, humanity. Fighting for that mobility was essential. African Americans refused to be banished from trains, steamships, or any mode of transportation that would have required their segregation and subordination. Freedom from discriminatory practices while traveling became a goal in a postemancipation world. Among a long list of grievances that Black Americans faced in the nineteenth century and well into contemporary times was traveling unobstructed. Every trip could be riddled with anxiety regarding the threat of being stopped, confronted, or harmed.[27]

Black travelers regularly contended with verbal assaults and forceful attacks, especially Black women, who could more easily be thrown out of their seats and stiffed the cost of their tickets. In 1866, entrepreneur Mary Ellen Pleasant and two other Black women were thrown off a streetcar in San Francisco. Pleasant was livid and took her fight to the courts. First, she sued the Omnibus Railroad Company, but the suit was withdrawn when the company agreed to change their policy to allow Black people to ride their streetcars without discrimination. Second, she sued the North Beach and Mission Railroad Company. This case went all the way to the California Supreme Court. The railroad company lost, setting a precedent that outlawed segregation for all the city's public transportation.[28] Black mobility had to be enforced by the courts, and even then, laws varied. Discrimination was common across the country.

Restrictions were most prominent in the South. Civil rights activist Ida B. Wells was born into slavery in 1862 near Holly Springs, Mississippi. Her early years were difficult. Though she had been emancipated as a small child, at around the age of sixteen, she lost both of her parents and a sibling to a yellow fever outbreak. She moved to Memphis, Tennessee, and spent the next several years living with relatives. She managed to become educated and worked as a teacher. In 1884, when Wells was twenty-two years old, she purchased a first-class ladies' car ticket on the Chesapeake and Ohio Railway. The conductor of the train ordered her to give up her seat and move to a smoking car, which was unpleasant, hot, and packed with people. Wells refused, and the conductor had two men drag her off the car. Wells, like Pleasant, was humiliated and outraged, and she took her case to the courts. She also wrote about her treatment in a Black weekly newspaper, the *Living Way*. Wells, too, won her case and was awarded $500 by the local circuit court. However, the railroad company appealed. In 1887, her case went to the Tennessee Supreme Court, which reversed the ruling. The court believed it was unjust for a Black woman to seek a "comfortable seat for a short ride."[29] They ordered her to pay court costs.

Wells confessed her deep disappointment with the verdict and with America: "I felt so disappointed because I had hoped such great things from my suit for my people. . . . O God, is there no . . . justice in this land for us?"[30] Just as it had been during slavery, Black mobility was considered suspect, if not criminal. A Black person who was moving around freely had to be up to no good. Surveillance was constant in spaces white people sought to control or monopolize. Accordingly, after emancipation, segregation arose to perpetuate white supremacy. And when Black people could not be stopped from moving freely or from achieving the financial success that would allow them to do so, white people resorted to violence.

Thomas Moss was a beloved and successful grocer in Memphis. His thriving business and his audacity to confront white harassment attracted the attention of white mobs, who lynched him. He used his last breath to send a message: "Tell my people to go west, there is no justice here."[31] Moss's dear friend Ida B. Wells, while heartbroken, took his advice. She, too, encouraged Black people to leave Memphis. In the Black newspaper the *Free Speech and Headlight*, Wells professed, "There is, therefore, only one thing left to do; save our money and leave a town which will neither protect our lives and property, nor give us a fair trial in the courts, but takes us out and murders us in cold blood when accused by white persons."[32] Wells also vowed to speak out and write against such atrocities. She conducted her own investigations into lynchings and published her findings. She revealed that lynchings rarely targeted Black men who had sexually assaulted white women, as was the common justification. Instead, they targeted Black men in consensual interracial relationships, successful Black entrepreneurs who competed with white businesses, and Black people involved in political activity. Wells's editorials and pamphlets enraged white people, who sought to commit unspeakable violence against her. Frederick Douglass wrote Wells a letter praising her efforts and bravery: "Thank you for your faithful paper on the lynch abomination now generally practiced against colored people in the South. There has been no word equal to it in convincing power. I have spoken, but my word is feeble in comparison. . . . Brave woman!"[33]

When the threats of violence began in response to Wells's biting journalism, she was already gone—she had taken a vacation to Harlem in New York. Friends warned her not to return to Memphis, and she stayed in Harlem working for T. Thomas Fortune's Black newspaper, the *New York Age*. Later, Wells traveled extensively throughout Europe, particularly England, Scotland, and Wales. She spoke out against lynching and rejected the label of "tourist."[34] Her travel—her leaving the United States—was about spreading her message to any person or nation that would work to undermine the oppression and violence of the American South. She argued that "we, as a race, cannot get a hearing in the United States," where both "the press and pulpit" are silent about, and thus complicit in, lynch law.[35] Wells was always aware of the utility of leaving, but she was not naive about spaces outside of the United States. She knew they would not be perpetual safe havens. While traveling in Liverpool, she reminded her audiences and readers that the city was the capital of English "slave interests." From the beginning of the slave trade to the British abolition of slavery in 1807, the majority of the slave ships traversing the Black Atlantic were owned and operated by Liverpool merchants. Wells understood that few white people valued Black humanity. Despite all of her travels, Wells never forgot being dragged off a train by men— or the applause of other passengers as they cheered her removal.

Wells eventually settled in Chicago with her husband and four children. She, too, represented the Great Migration. Many left the South to escape racial violence. For example, in 1917, an article in the *Southwestern Christian Advocate*, an African American newspaper, noted, "Some months ago Anthony Crawford, a highly respectable, honest and industrious Negro, with a good farm and holdings estimated to be worth $300,000, was lynched in Abbeville, South Carolina. He was guilty of no crime. He would not be cheated out of his cotton. That was insolence. . . . [The mob] overpowered him and brutally lynched him. Is any one surprised that Negroes are leaving South Carolina by the thousands? The wonder is that any of them remain."[36] With almost every lynching that took place, migrants left the city's violence for any refuge that put enough distance between them and the bloodthirsty mob. For some that meant hundreds of miles; for others it was thousands of miles.

Some Black people left for opportunities, decency, and dignity. A migrant who worked as a carpenter moved to East Chicago,

Indiana, from Hattiesburg, Mississippi. He wrote to his friends back south about his new life: "I was promoted on the first of the month. I should have been here 20 years ago. I just began to feel like a man. My children are going to the same school with the whites and I don't have to umble [*sic*] to no one. I have registered, will vote the next election and there isn't any 'yes sir' and 'no sir'— its all yea and no and Sam and Bill." As a carpenter he was making ninety-five dollars a month during a time when most Black farmers in Mississippi made less than one hundred dollars a year.[37] A man in Philadelphia wrote his friend and former doctor still living in the South, "With the aid of God I am making very good I make $75 per month. I am carrying enough insurance to pay me $20 per week if I am not able to be on Duty. I don't have to work hard. don't have to mister every little white boy comes along I haven't heard a white man call a colored a n— you no now—since I been in the state of Pa. I can ride in the electric street and steam cars any where I get a seat."[38] And yet, the letter writer did not dismiss the South altogether, writing, "I shall ever love the good old South and I am praying that God may give every well wisher a chance to be a man regardless of his color, and if my going to the front [North] would bring about such conditions I am ready any day." He hoped that leaving would remedy the ways of the South or pressure it to cultivate respect for Black people.

But the Great Migration did not cure the South of its racist ways. Nearly thirty years after those letter writers moved, during the 1940s and '50s, Black southern women and men continued to face discrimination and violent oppression. In Montgomery, Alabama, prior to the success of the Montgomery bus boycott, public transportation was precarious. Historian Robin D. G. Kelley laid out the battles Black passengers faced: "The deliberate humiliation of African Americans by operators and other white passengers;

shortchanging; the power of drivers to allocate or limit space for Black passengers; and the practice of forcing blacks to pay at the front door and enter though the center doors. For example, half-empty buses or streetcars often passed up African Americans on the pretext of preserving space for potential white riders. It was not unusual for a black passenger who had paid at the front of the bus to be left standing while she or he attempted to board at the center door."[39]

Initially, Black resistance was about refusing to leave or move on the bus. In 1941 in Montgomery, there were eighty-eight cases of Black people occupying "white seats" and of those, in fifty-five cases Black people refused to give up their seat.[40] One by one, Black women became fed up with their treatment. A Black woman on the College Hills bus line in Montgomery noticed that she had been shortchanged by the driver. At first, she approached the driver respectfully and requested her appropriate change. The driver dismissed her and instructed her to take a seat. According to the official report, "She came up later and began cursing and could not be stopped and a white passenger came and knocked her down. Officers were called and made her show him the money which was .25 short, then asked her where the rest of the money was. She looked in her purse and produced the other quarter. They suspected she was lying. She was taken to jail."[41] In March 1943, a Black woman got into a shoving match with a man on the East Lake–West line. The Black woman was so angered by the white passenger's behavior toward her that she "cursed him all the way to Woodlawn." The driver alerted the police, and when the bus reached Woodlawn the cops were waiting for her. She was "arrested, sentenced to thirty days in jail, and fined fifty dollars."[42]

Many Black people refused to accept the bus company's discriminatory practices by cussing out and even spitting on white drivers and passengers who assaulted them, shoved them, or shortchanged them. In nearly all altercations, police officers were called, and regardless of the harm caused to Black passengers, it was common for them to be arrested, fined, or even given a short jail sentence. On March 2, 1955, Claudette Colvin was just fifteen years old when she refused unfair treatment from a bus driver. She was pulled off the bus while screaming, "It's my constitutional right!"[43] Civil rights activist Rosa Parks is exceptional not just for her refusal to give up her seat but for her composure to refrain from striking out against her offenders.[44] Civil rights leadership had coached her to remain calm. Resistance could also be about refusing to leave, to be moved, and to be oppressed.

Perhaps the most essential element required for flight is grit. There is a story I love to share with my students about a woman named Ever Lee Hairston.[45] Born in 1942, Ever Lee grew up on the Cooleemee plantation in Mocksville, North Carolina, the third of seven children born to Arizona and Clarence Hairston. Her family had lived and worked on the plantation for over one hundred years. Since the days of slavery, Cooleemee had been the home of two large families named Hairston, one Black and one white. The Black Hairstons, who pronounced their name "Hair-stons," were descended from enslaved people, and the white Hairstons, who pronounced their name "Har-stons," were descended from slaveholders.

When Ever Lee was young, the white Hairstons lived in a big white house on the plantation and grew the cotton that the Black Hairstons picked. As sharecroppers, the Black Hairstons never owned any land, and for every dollar they earned, the white Hairstons took seventy cents. The Black Hairstons lived in poverty, their home a tiny log cabin with no running water or plumbing that was more fit to house equipment than people. "My parents and my paternal grandparents, we all lived [in what] some people called . . . just a wood cabin," Ever Lee recalled. "At that time, there were six children, and two sets of parents, and we grew up in this house and didn't have running water."[46]

Ever Lee remembered picking cotton for the Hairston plantation as a child. She hated it. She hated picking cotton. She hated being pulled out of school for nearly two weeks to help her family bring in a harvest for which they made pennies on the dollar. It was hard work, dangerous even. Snakes were everywhere, and some were venomous. It was a life of fear and manufactured shortages. "I looked at sharecropping as another name of slavery," said Ever Lee.[47] But she still had goals and dreams. One of her sisters suffered from a chronic illness, and Ever Lee wanted nothing more than to attend college and study to become a nurse. She wanted to give people the kind of care that her family was often denied—and that she unknowingly needed. Ever Lee had been born with retinitis pigmentosa, a condition that caused poor vision throughout her childhood and led to her complete loss of vision as an adult. As a child she never went to see an eye doctor and kept her struggles with vision a secret.[48]

One day during her senior year of high school, Ever Lee was picking cotton. She traversed rows and rows of cotton with her bag in tow. Like a deer in the woods, Ever Lee was always alert for snakes or anything that might pop out at her while she was picking. "I leaned forward to pick this beautiful cotton out of the cotton boll," she remembered, and "saw a long black snake on the ground." She screamed, "It's a copperhead!" She ran to her siblings, who were also picking cotton, and began to cry. She was shaking. Ever Lee could have been in school—she *should* have been in school—but instead she was tethered to the field and compelled to work to support her family, who, after all their labors, would still not make enough money to meet their needs. In anguish, she wrung her shaking hands and declared out loud, "Oh God, there has to be a better way of life for me."[49]

The usual alternative to picking cotton was working in other people's homes as domestic labor. As a teenager, Ever Lee tried her hand at this: she would take Fridays off school to help her mother clean white folks' houses. The job was labor intensive and always paid less than minimum wage. Ever Lee's specific task was to carefully iron and fold each piece of laundry. But as soon as she thought she might make a dent in the pile of clothing, the woman of the house would bring out another stack of clothes to be ironed. As she walked away, she told Ever Lee, "When it's time to eat you can go out in the garage." Many white employers never wanted to be bothered by the help. Their labor was meant to be invisible. Ever Lee was furious. She thought "I'll show her" and scorched a white blouse with the iron, which she put in the bottom of the basket.[50]

In 1959, after high school, Ever Lee's solution to her unhappiness was simple: she decided she needed to leave. She came up with a plan to move to New York and found a newspaper ad for live-in maids in Hempstead, Long Island. With the wages from a job as a maid in the North, she could save all the money she needed to attend college. She could leave behind the place where she felt stifled and where so many of her family members felt stuck. Two weeks after graduating from high school, Ever Lee traveled to Winston-Salem with her father to catch the bus to New York City by herself. She was seventeen years old. The Greyhound bus ride was sixteen hours long. But Ever Lee was determined to make it on her own, prove her naysayers wrong, and have a better life for herself.

Ever Lee wanted choices. Racism had robbed her of them. But even as Ever Lee's life took many twists and turns, she was determined to never give up. She eventually became blind. She went to college at night and became a drug and addiction counselor. She became an advocate for people struggling with substance abuse and for the visually impaired. Her life was a success story, a story of overcoming. And she was not alone. Her father, Clarence, plotted to leave the plantation as well. He finally amassed enough money to purchase a piece of land in North Carolina, and he built a house on it, one his parents could live in as well. His parents never received a pension or Social Security, but through Clarence's efforts they could finally retire from work. Leaving, for Clarence, was not about moving north but about having something of his own. Owning his own land was, for him, liberation. Labor means something different when every cent of every dollar is yours to claim. By 1972, no Black Hairstons were working for any white Hairstons. It took over one hundred years after emancipation for the Hairstons to be freed from their white employers who exploited their labor. Leaving took time and courage.

In 1996, Ever Lee returned to North Carolina to attend a family reunion of mostly Black Hairstons and some white Hairstons. Her family wanted her to give a talk about her achievements. Not wanting to waste the moment, Ever Lee decided to use her speech to also address the elephant in the room: Judge Peter Hairston. As a white Hairston, the judge owned the land that the Black Hairstons had lived and worked on. Though he saw himself as benevolent, Judge Peter lorded his power over the Black Hairstons. He made a point of attending all of the Hairston family reunions and always seated himself at one of the head tables. He was the man who had paid every Black Hairston thirty cents on the dollar for picking his cotton.

Ever Lee approached the podium and gave a speech on her many accomplishments and successes. And then she told the story of spotting a snake while picking cotton. She recalled her fear and trembling, and then, addressing the judge, she declared, "I thought that there had to be a better way of life for me, Mr. Peter." By calling him out by name, Ever Lee was publicly placing responsibility for her circumstances squarely at Judge Peter's feet. He, and many men like him, were her motivation for leaving. Judge Peter was the real snake, the one who deceitfully exploited the Hairstons and robbed them of wages, land, education, and opportunity. His family had been enslavers for generations. Outside of the reunion, there were stories that one enslaved man was "beaten and placed in a shed without food or water for three days."[51] Another Hairston sharecropper who suffered from a hernia told the story of having to kneel before Judge Peter every time he received his weekly payment.

Later, Ever Lee had another opportunity to confront the judge. He was still upset about her comments, and when Ever Lee spoke of her grandparents, William and Charming, Judge Peter declared, "I treated them quite well." Ever Lee was furious. She vehemently disagreed. They should have had a house with running water and a bathroom. At the very least, Ever Lee wanted "decency" for her grandparents. She told the judge, "They worked for you all of their life. All of their life. What do they have to show for it? Nothing. They don't have anything. Because they gave you their complete life. No pension. No money in the bank. Nothing. I disagree with you." All the judge could say in return was, "They couldn't do any better." Ever Lee's blood boiled at his racist retort. "Perhaps they couldn't," she replied, "but you made them think that they couldn't do any better."[52] The trap of racism, its confinement, is social, political, economic, and emotional. For Ever Lee, leaving was the freedom she needed, a freedom she passed down to her son and daughter-in-law and three grandchildren, who now all live together in a beautiful five-bedroom, custom-built home overlooking the Hollywood Hills. Flight was about proving to the world that she and her family could do better, live better. And they did.

Ever Lee's grit and desire for more reminded me of my father. He told me he left a "good job" working in the automotive industry in Detroit to take a desk job making less money. "Why would you leave a job that paid good money?" I asked. He told me he hated wearing a uniform. He took a new job where he could "wear a suit to work, drink coffee," and—this was really important—where he "didn't have to ask to go to the bathroom." Leaving the automotive industry in Detroit was no small thing. Nearly all Black people saw the Motor City as a way out and up. But having a good job is not just about earning a high salary; it's also about having dignity. It's about being able to wear whatever you want and having the freedom to roam halls, go to the bathroom, or drink coffee. Work should be liberatory. Work should grant economic, social, and political freedom.

My grandfathers, uncles, and aunties all worked for either Ford, Chrysler, or General Motors. They bought homes, drove nice cars, and put their kids through college with their jobs. For tens of thousands of people, if not hundreds of thousands, working in the automotive industry was essential to Black upward mobility and economic security. But my father wanted something different. In a capitalist world, people prioritize money, but whether the job is picking cotton or manufacturing cars, freedom cannot function without choice, decency, and dignity. This looks different for everyone. Flight is less about geography and more about agency. Similarly, freedom for Clarence Hairston was not about leaving but about owning land, being fairly compensated for his labor, and being treated with respect.

By the late 1960s and early 1970s, the South had finally caught up with the economy and industries of the North. The Great Migration had peaked, and what had been an avalanche of Black migrants now flowed like a slow and perhaps seasonal stream. There were still people who left the South, and during the Black Power movement and the height of the Black Panther Party's popularity, some Black leaders left the country. Some fled the government's constant surveillance and the relentless harassment of COINTEL-PRO. Panthers such as Peter and Charlotte O'Neal left for Africa.

In 1971 the O'Neals went into exile. They lived in Algiers with Eldridge Cleaver and other members of the Black Panther Party for about two years before settling in Dar es Salaam, Tanzania. Charlotte filmed a documentary on her life and leaving the United States. She claimed living in Africa finally brought her acceptance: "Everyone looked just like me. I felt immediately at home."[53] She explained how living away from the racial violence in the United States was the first time she was finally able to lay down her guard. Flight was a form of liberation. Interestingly, the bar for new destinations is rather low. Black folks do not necessarily need a utopia or land of milk and honey. They leave to find basic decency, dignity, better opportunities, autonomy, good schools, protection, and joy.

A good friend of mine, Charlene, called to invite me to a gala in Houston. "Sure," I said. "I love any reason to dress up!" She told me the gala was a celebration of Black and women of color pilots. It was called Sisters of the Skies. The evening would be filled with food, fun, dancing, and, most importantly, scholarships. The gala was a big deal. The path to becoming a pilot is challenging. Every pilot has to achieve a certain number of flight hours, certifications, evaluations, and check rides that can take years to accumulate. Training is also costly. Every hour in the plane can cost anywhere from $100 to $250. Pilots need a minimum of 1,500 hours of "pilot in command," which means they have to be in charge of the plane. Many white pilots have family members who were pilots. Young white men can enter aviation spaces bragging about a father or grandfather or uncle who took them flying as a child. Most Black pilots can't claim this inheritance.

A few weeks before the gala, Mattel had just released its latest historical Barbie: the first Black and Native American woman aviator, Bessie Coleman. For every Black woman who has ever considered flying the blue skies, Coleman is a polestar. Born in 1892, Coleman was raised in rural Texas, in a town called Waxahachie. Her family, like most Black families in the town, was poor. Her father, George, who was of African American and Cherokee ancestry, worked as a sharecropper. Her mother, Susan, was African American and a laundress. Coleman was committed to her education, despite having few resources or opportunities. She managed to graduate high school and enroll in the Colored Agricultural and Normal University in Oklahoma, but she had to drop out after only a semester under her belt because she couldn't afford the tuition.

It was around this time that Coleman became obsessed with flying. She began to dream of becoming a pilot. Leaving Texas for better job opportunities in the North was one thing. Leaving to fly a machine made of wood, canvas, and piano wire through the sky was something else. But Coleman's older brothers, Walter and John, had served in the military during World War I, and when they returned home, they filled her head with stories about flight. Coleman moved to Chicago to earn higher wages and save for aviation school. She took a job as a manicurist in a men's barbershop. It was there she met Robert S. Abbott, the publisher of the country's most successful Black newspaper, the *Chicago Defender.* Abbott was one of the wealthiest Black men in the country.

Coleman told Abbott about her dream of becoming a pilot. He supported it and advised her not to stay in the United States but to travel to Europe, where her race and her gender would not be a barrier. No aviation school in the United States would have accepted Coleman as a student. In Coleman's words, "There was no room for blackbirds in the sky over America in the early days of aviation."[54] Abbott never squandered an opportunity to increase his paper's readership. He knew that if he told Coleman's story, people would want to follow along as she pursued her dream. Together with a successful Black banker named Jesse Binga, Abbott subsidized Coleman's trip to France, where she became a student in the Fédération Aéronautique Internationale.[55] She learned to fly alongside French and German pilots. By June 15, 1921, nearly two years before Amelia Earhart, she had earned her international pilot's license, making her the first Black and Native American woman—and the first American—to gain such a credential.

Upon Coleman's return to the United States, Abbott sponsored air shows to showcase her talent. The *Chicago Defender* dubbed her "the world's greatest woman flier."[56] She was an immediate sensation. People traveled from all over to see the Black woman pilot. She was flamboyant, audacious, and highly skilled. She earned the monikers "Queen Bess" and "Brave Bessie." Courage was a requirement for the role; air shows were incredibly dangerous. Many people lost their lives just learning how to fly. In the early days, aviation was nowhere near safe. There were no preflight checklists or superior technology, and Coleman, like all other pilots, flew without safety belts. The Wright brothers had flown their first airplane only eighteen years prior.

In 1923, Coleman was in a plane crash that left her with broken ribs and a broken leg. Family and friends warned her that the profession could take her life, but Coleman was undaunted. She claimed, "The air is the only place free of prejudice."[57] Coleman saw more risk in living her life as a Black woman on the ground than she did in flying thousands of feet in the air in a "fragile 21-foot biplane with a 40-foot wingspan made of wood, wire, steel, aluminum, cloth and pressed cardboard."[58] By 1925, she was back in the cockpit, healed and raring to fly. But her time as a pilot was cut tragically short. On April 30, 1926, just one day before she was scheduled to perform at an air show in Jacksonville, Florida, Coleman was flying a practice run. While in the air, she leaned over to get a better view of the area below. A wrench became lodged in the gears and jammed the plane's mechanics, and Coleman was thrown from the airplane without a parachute. She was killed instantly. The plane itself crashed, killing her copilot, William D. Willis. Onlookers were horrified. In Chicago, thousands of mourners attended her funeral. Her eulogy was given by none other than Ida B. Wells, who deeply valued Coleman's vision and audacity. At age thirty-six, Coleman was gone, along with her dream of opening a flight school where other Black women could learn to fly.

I arrived at the Sisters of the Skies gala excited and slightly intimidated. These Black women were incredible to me—not just because they could fly, but because they had to overcome patriarchal conditions, hostile attitudes, and cultural and financial barriers to do so. There were about five hundred people at the gala in Houston that evening. That was twice as many attendees as there are professional Black women pilots in the entire country. American Airlines currently has the largest number of Black women pilots in their ranks, but of the fifteen thousand pilots they employ, only twenty-eight are Black women. That's 0.00186 percent. But these women were here.

I brought my Bessie Coleman Barbie doll with me, still inside the box. I wanted every Black woman pilot I met to sign it.

I started with Lieutenant Colonel Marcella A. Hayes Ng, who, in 1979, became the first African American woman pilot in the armed forces. She flew helicopters and served twenty-two years in the US Army. When I asked about her postretirement life, she told me that she had traded in her helicopter for another form of transportation: "I fly on my motorcycle." Just above her signature she wrote, "Only by the grace of God." Standing next to Lieutenant Colonel Ng was Dr. Sheila Chamberlain. In 1985, Chamberlain became the first Black woman combat intelligence pilot in the United States Army. She is now the national chair of the Bessie Coleman Aviation All-Stars, an organization that mentors young people interested in aviation. When I asked her to sign my Bessie Coleman doll, she clutched her chest and immediately teared up. She was touched, but the honor was all mine. She made history. Then I saw Theresa Claiborne, the first Black woman to graduate from US Air Force flight training; she flew cargo jets in 1982, the year I was born. She is now a captain at United Airlines. These women are Bessie's legacy.

In August 2022, American Airlines hosted an honorary flight to celebrate the one hundredth anniversary of Bessie Coleman earning her pilot's license. I met and collected signatures from some of the women who made up the first all-Black female flight crew. The plane flew from Dallas–Fort Worth to Phoenix, and every single member of the team was an African American woman. The flight involved thirty-six members—from the flight crew to the load crew, to the cargo team, to the gate agents, to the dispatchers, to the mechanics. All were Black women honoring Coleman's legacy in aviation. On board the flight was also Bessie Coleman's great-niece, Gigi Coleman. These women were busting open doors and working overtime to duplicate themselves, to get more Black women into the field of aviation.

The work Coleman started continues today. Despite the long odds, the expenses involved in training, and the barriers put up by sexism and racism, Black women pilots exist. On that cold February day in Houston, hundreds of Black people gathered together in a ballroom to give each other flowers, scholarships, gratitude, and encouragement. It was the ultimate "I see you, sis!" moment. Veterans and rookies were brought together by their love of the skies. Sometimes leaving is more than just going away. Leaving can be pioneer work. It can be creating a space for those who follow you to find belonging and acceptance, here on earth or beyond.

Today, Black folks still leave the United States. There are travel bloggers and Travel Noire social media groups and countless Instagram photos of Black families, friends, and lovers on their latest excursion. It's beautiful. But I think it is important to return to Jamaica Kincaid's observation: most natives, most Black and colonized people, will never get to occupy the space of the tourist. Many Black people will never get to have their passport stamped or "escape the reality of their lives," as she puts it. Perhaps this is why flight is a remedy, but it is not a cure. It does not change the circumstances that prompt one to leave in the first place. Flight can be a reprieve, a relief, a new shelter, and a new beginning. But flight cannot ensure belonging. Because of racism, Black people will always be intellectually, culturally, and geographically nomadic.

Chapter Five

JOY

The day before Thanksgiving in 2007, I lost my sister Tracie to breast cancer. She was thirty-seven, married, and the mother of three children. I cannot remember what happened the next day. I cannot remember what we ate or even who cooked. Everything is a blur in my memory. About a week later, we held her funeral. My parents had seven children, six daughters and one son, and with family and friends from all over the country pouring into a small church, the funeral was standing room only. It was a sea of red, Tracie's favorite color. As a family, we agreed that though we were racked with grief, her memorial would be a celebration of life.

My only brother, William, spoke at the funeral. Tracie and William were both ministers. As he stood at the podium, he talked about the difference between happiness and joy. "Happiness is fleeting," he said, "but joy is grounded by grief." Joy is birthed from hard places. He shared passages from the Old Testament and reminded us about the trials faced by Job, Joseph, and David. Joy was the antidote to trauma and loss.

I remember feeling empowered when my brother finished speaking. He even managed to make us laugh. He encouraged us. He poured wisdom and assurance down on us as if he were speaking from another era. He was only twenty-seven years old. He had completed his second year of seminary and served three years in the US Army. He was a captain and had spent months serving his country in Iraq. Shortly after Tracie's service, he would deploy again to the Middle East. We all knew that William was special. He was born with sickle cell anemia, a disease that disproportionately affects African Americans. He had faced death many times between his infancy and adolescence. Sickle-shaped red blood cells die off sooner than normal blood cells, which leads to a lack of oxygen in the body—what people who suffer from sickle cell call a crisis. During a crisis he would be in intense pain and often need blood transfusions. He spent days and sometimes weeks in the hospital. His assurance of the promise of joy was a testament to his own life of challenges, delayed victories, and, miraculously, a cure. After my sister's funeral, my parents and siblings flew back to their own homes, still grieving and in shock, but holding on to what my brother said that day.

Days after we laid Tracie to rest, my mother called me. William was being hospitalized. The doctors did not know what was wrong, but he could not breathe. I refused to believe anything bad could happen to him. The world could not be that cruel, that relentless. Within one day, he was on a ventilator, and two days after that, he died. I had not yet unpacked my bags from Tracie's funeral. I collapsed. The grief was so overwhelming, so consuming, so mind-boggling that I do not remember my cousin booking my ticket home. I barely remember flying home. My husband, Nathaniel, was in the Air Force and deployed to the Middle East. He got special permission to return home. Again we all gathered, this time at my parents' house in Houston. We were all like zombies attempting to function as human beings. Two weeks after William's funeral, it was Christmas. Even though we were all together, no one was present. Joy felt impossible, like trying to summit Mount Everest with no oxygen.

My sister's sickness was prolonged. For two years she had battled cancer. Suffering that long made death feel like deliverance. It gave us time to prepare ourselves. But William gave us no warning. He felt ill and then he died. My parents lost two children within two weeks. The doctors had told William he had an infection of pneumococcus, a deadly bacteria that bone marrow transplant recipients, like William, are more susceptible to. William lived over ten years without any sickle cell symptoms. But the bone marrow transplant that cured his sickle cell made him more susceptible to infections, and this one was deadly.

As a Black woman, I never wanted to share information about my siblings' deaths, and when I did, I felt like I had to be quick to qualify it, to explain their diseases for fear of some racialized stigma being placed on them. I often felt that racism hijacked the sympathy of strangers and acquaintances: "You had two siblings die—to what, gang violence? Crime? AIDS? COVID?" I used to feel that I could sense a weird attitude in the people I told about my siblings' deaths. I learned that some deaths are more respectable than others. For many Black people, the *cause of death* dictates how much empathy should be extended to the bereaved. Compassion and condolences are conditional because even our deaths must be respectable. It is ridiculous, but that was how I used to feel, as if I needed to quickly follow up with, "It was breast cancer and pneumococcus."

You may be thinking, "What a way to begin a chapter on joy!" But so much of Black life is filled with compounding grief—loss on top of loss. We are unable to recover from one shooting before there is another death, and another, and another. Tragedy tends to have a domino effect, collapsing life on top of life in what feels like a never-ending cascade of Black bodies falling over into darkness. The irony of joy is that it cannot be understood in isolation or without trials. Joy and oppression often work in tandem.

I have always felt that white people get to be happy while Black people get to have joy. Happiness isn't tethered to anything in the way that joy is tethered to oppression. It just is. This doesn't mean that white people do not also face death, loss, and tragedy. But their trauma is always centered. Their recovery is always prioritized. They do not experience ongoing, oppressive structures that make life difficult on a daily basis because of their race. I see the origin of joy as spiritual: it is a conscious conjuring of pleasure that transcends one's circumstances.

When I think of joy, I think of the Black church. The words of scripture and lyrics of gospel songs remind those who hear them that joy is not stumbled upon. Joy is not an immediate outcome. However, joy is lasting and persists in the midst of hardship. Psalm 30:5 is a constant refrain in the Black church: "Weeping may tarry for the night, but joy comes with the morning." Again, joy is certain, but it is not instant. I remember growing up listening to the Georgia Mass Choir, Dorothy Anderson, and Kirk Franklin bellow out the lyrics:

Joy, joy, God's great joy
Joy, joy, down in my soul
Sweet, beautiful, soul-saving joy
Oh, joy, joy in my soul

Black faith promises joy.[1] Joy is an exhortation. It is dependable during trying times. I'm choosing to end this book with Black joy because I see it as one of the most potent tools of revolutionary work toward liberation. Black joy is the ultimate expression of Black humanity. The joy of laughter, food, dance, dress and adornment, rhetoric, play, and art can be employed to dispel and destroy whiteness as supreme, aspirational, or the norm. Anti-Blackness is the work of white supremacy; it perpetuates beliefs that Black people are subhuman and deficient. Black joy produces the antidote to the degeneration and erosion of Black life. Black joy can be bold or benign. It can involve love, hope, humor, or pleasure. Roller skating, fishing, singing, teasing, sharing, resting, vacationing, getting dressed up, shopping, bathing, working, or quitting—if it compels joy, then it refutes the idea that Black people are subhuman.

The bulk of Black life is made from joy. Joy is not the denial of Black pain, trauma, or death, but the hope that comes with activism, resistance, and refusal. In a love letter to his Black students, Professor Charles McKinney wrote, "We are not solely the history of fighting white folks. That is not who we are. We are double-dutch in summer. We are letting the air out of Big Mama's house. We are Uncle Ray's jokes on top of jokes. We are collards, second lines, and blue lights in the basement. We are swagger in the midst of chaos. We are reunions and step shows. We are the borough and the bayou. We are church till two, and the corner till four. We are a universe of experiences."[2] Black joy is a haven. It cannot be purchased or mimicked. It cannot be stolen because it is intangible.

White supremacy finds satisfaction in treasure, material accumulation, and domination. But Black joy is a collection not of things but of experiences that instill pride, love, and solidarity. The most lasting impact of the Black Power movement was not an increase in the number of Black businesses, Black elected officials, or Black gun clubs, or policy changes affecting Black communities. It was pride. Black pride is a shield against the demoralizing effects of racism. Joy, Black joy, destroys the allure of whiteness.

I understand joy as a remedy on the path to complete healing. If justice is the cure, then joy is the cast or splint, holding a broken bone in place until healing is complete. I return to the story of my great-grandmother Arnesta, who walked with a limp. One of my favorite photographs shows her sitting on her husband's lap. She is wearing a floral dress and beaming. Her smile is as wide as their love. While she was disabled, her limp was not the first thing that you noticed about her. Arnesta's grandmother refused the doctor's brute terms for healing Arnesta's tetanus infection. She insisted on taking Arnesta home and saved her life. This is how I think about Black joy: it marginalizes the pain of oppression. Arnesta had joy. She lived a full life and passed her joy down to my grandfather, my mother, and me. In today's political climate, activists cannot promise the cure that is justice, but we work for it nonetheless, and in the meantime, we use Black joy as treatment, a transfusion, and therapy until complete healing comes.

Black joy can be confusing to white people. In 2020, scholar Imani Perry brilliantly wrote about the meaning of Black joy amid the massive protests sweeping across the country. Protesters would march, chant, shout, and then somewhat organically burst into song and dance. However, Perry rightly argued that no one should be confused by the presence of both pain and performance. Racism is insidious, but resistance to racism is about shaming it and stamping it out. Perry cautioned us that in the past, slaveholders had erroneously claimed the singing or laughter of enslaved people was a sign of their contentment. "No, that laugh—like our music, like our language, like our movement," argued Perry, "was a testimony that refused the terms of our degradation." During the protests, Black people and their allies chanted, danced, and sang, but Perry was emphatic: "Do not misunderstand. This is not an absence of grief or rage, or a distraction. It is insistence."[3]

Nearly every African American could teach a master class in "refusing the terms of our degradation." Some of the most potent examples of Black joy as a refusal have come from slavery. During the Haitian Revolution, contemporary observer Antoine Métral recorded the story of rebel mothers marching to the scaffold to be executed by the French. One Black mother called out to her weeping daughters, "Rejoice! Your wombs will not beget slaves."[4] In another instance, rebel women smiled at their masters before their public execution. Smiling was an act of defiance: enslaved women wanted to ensure slave owners were not *taking* their lives. These Black women were robbing their masters of their own lives and their labor. These warriors refused to be dehumanized.

Joy is not justice, but it is a collective rescue in dire times. It is the reassuring "You're okay, you're okay" whispered by loved ones or even strangers who understand how to triage the blows of unemployment, incarceration, assault, economic stagnation, poverty, humiliation, and death.[5] Black people need reminders that they are not crazy and nothing is wrong with them. Black joy rejects, neglects, and even mocks white feelings of superiority alongside their unearned or ill-gotten gains.

I remember giving an interview on NPR and discussing the topic of slavery. A white listener emailed me after hearing the interview and chided me for "laughing" while discussing the violence of slavery. To be clear, I was not laughing but hemming and hawing as I described historical figures' unbelievable and ridiculous attempts to normalize or even civilize slavery and anti-Blackness. Racism, at face value, is absurd. From the seventeenth century onward, American laws have been designed to empower whiteness and disadvantage Blackness. Beyond the familiar laws segregating schools, transportation, and public accommodation, beyond the bans on interracial marriage, were scores of smaller prohibitions. An 1899 North Carolina law stated, "Books shall not be interchangeable between the White and colored schools but shall continue to be used by the race first using them."[6] In 1914, Louisiana had a law that said, "All circuses, shows and tent exhibitions were required to provide two ticket offices with individual ticket sellers and two entrances to the performance for each race."[7] Birmingham, Alabama, passed laws on utter minutiae: Black people were not to play checkers with white people. When Black people tried to vote in the South before the passage of the 1965 Voting Rights Act, officials would require them to answer impossible questions in a transparent attempt to stop them from voting. The registrar's office in Mississippi would ask, "How many bubbles are in a bar of soap?" In other cases, Black people had to guess how many marbles were in a large mason jar.[8] Many, if not all, Jim Crow segregationist laws were laughable. But the commitment to give credence to such laws knew no bounds.

For some scholars, the concept of race itself is bizarre. Historian Barbara J. Fields argues that "Americans of European descent invented race during the era of the American Revolution as a way of resolving the contradiction between a natural right to freedom and the fact of slavery."[9] Thus, race was born from hypocrisy. Race is not biological. Racism is not a necessary evil, nor is whiteness the default norm for society. During the eighteenth and nineteenth century, scientific racism emerged to give credence to and standards for racial categories. It was believed that Black people were biologically inferior and therefore primed for labor and exploitation. Scientists conducted an array of experiments to try to prove that Europeans were exceptional in their intellectual capacity. But, as Field writes, "no one ventured to ask the most embarrassing question of all, the one that stumped the scientific racists of the late nineteenth and early twentieth centuries: 'How to assign the subjects of the experiments to one "race" or the other without assuming the very racial distinction the experiment is supposed to prove?'"[10] It was impossible to assign racialized categories when the established preference and advantages in society were organized around whiteness. Every experiment perpetuated the empowerment of white people. Accordingly, scientific racism was not about proof but about maintaining power.

More recently, in 1997, renowned Black artist Glenn Ligon conducted an experiment at the Institute of Contemporary Art at the University of Pennsylvania in which he posted side by side two identical life-size, black-and-white photographs of himself. Under one photo was the caption, "Self-Portrait Exaggerating My Black Features"; under the other was the caption "Self-Portrait Exaggerating My White Features." One by one, museum visitors viewed the two photographs and noted his slightly wider nose in the left portrait or his thinner lips in the right portrait. Again, the images were identical, but people convinced themselves they were seeing two different faces. It is comical. But racial ideologies do not need to be plausible or rational to be persuasive to people. Race and racism work well when white people insist on their deficit definitions of others and program society to distort or "make sense of" the things they do and see—routinely and repetitively—on a daily basis.[11] For example, the pervasive myth that "white people commit crimes, but Black people are criminal" enforces the idea that while a white person might steal, that is not who they are, that is not the totality of their identity. But if Black people are criminals in the minds of the public, then it does not matter what they do or say: their very existence is criminal and therefore susceptible to search, seizure, policing, or expulsion. Let me provide an illustration.

On April 29, 2018, a middle-aged white woman named Jennifer Schulte called the police on Kenzie Smith, a Black man who was using a charcoal grill to barbecue in a park with his friends next to Lake Merritt in Oakland, California. Schulte claimed the place where Smith was cooking was not designated for charcoal grilling and his grill was thus not allowed. For nearly three hours, she waited for the cops and refused to stand down, even when confronted by Black and white bystanders about her racist behavior. Smith texted Michelle Snider, his wife at the time, and alerted her to the harassment. Snider, who is white, arrived and began recording the altercation. In a twenty-four-minute video Snider questioned Schulte about why she was calling 911. Finally, Schulte began to walk away and Snider followed her for half a mile, accusing her of harassing Black people. When Schulte approached a police officer at a Quik Stop, she immediately fell apart and began to sob. She morphed from an unrelenting, empowered white woman policing Black people to a quivering victim crying that she was under attack.[12] No one had attacked her. Smith and his friends had gone back to grilling, laughing at Schulte the entire time. No police had shown up in response to her shenanigans. It was a relief. Everyone understood the long history of how the police could be weaponized against Black people. For years the area had been demoralized from the police's constant surveilling of Black people. The City of Oakland had cracked down on festivals, public parties, barbecuing, and drinking near the park. Longtime residents complained that their ability to merely be or belong was repeatedly questioned.[13]

When Snider posted the video on YouTube, it quickly hit over ten million views. Local and national news stations covered the story, and within days a hashtag and viral meme was created. #BBQBecky was fodder for every historical moment or random inaction. The image of Schulte—wearing a navy-blue sweatshirt and dark sunglasses, and holding a turquoise cell phone to her ear—was photoshopped into historical scenes like Dr. Martin Luther King Jr.'s "I Have a Dream" speech and President Obama's first inauguration, and into a battle scene from the Marvel movie *Black Panther*. There were memes of her randomly standing outside of bathrooms and polling places. She was even mocked on *Saturday Night Live*. BBQ Becky could be found trolling any aspect of Black joy.[14] Her image sparked laughter because it reflected the consistent and constant pattern of white women policing Black people purely because of their desire for power. The memes were hysterical and contagious mainly because on this rare occasion, the police did not show up and no one was harmed or killed over trivial, mundane behavior. When white supremacy is not enacting outright violence, the expression of it in interpersonal relationships is foolish. Snider later admitted that the video was hard to watch, but she did not regret recording it.[15]

Collectively, Black people found joy in ridicule. It was a small victory, but it quite effectively revealed the danger and superficialness of white supremacy. Poking fun robs whiteness of its legitimacy. It undermines ideas that routinely and repetitively stunt Black life. In this instance, Black humor served as a remedy from the petty interruptions of racism. Whiteness can be mocked, and when the folly is magnified and defused, it can be ignored. The Black people who gathered at the park that day went back to their barbecue. They ate, and drank, and laughed. Sometimes Black joy is a party to which white people are not invited. The joy can be exclusionary, and that, too, is protective. Black joy reminds us that someone like Schulte should never be taken seriously. Humor undoes the authority of white supremacy. It reveals its irrationality.

But the initial public response to someone like Schulte is anger: "Leave us alone!" In the months after the altercation, a slew of viral incidents of Black surveillance exploded across the country. In May 2018, Lolade Siyonbola, a Black Yale graduate student, had the cops called on her by a white fellow student when she fell asleep while studying in the common room of her dormitory. In June 2018, on a hot summer day, an eight-year-old Black girl had the police called on her in San Francisco for selling bottled water "without a permit." In Cleveland, a twelve-year-old Black boy who had been hired to mow a lawn had the cops called on him when white neighbors complained that he had cut some of the grass on their property.[16] The acts of hostility and policing infuriate African Americans who must remind their peers, neighbors, and strangers that they have a right to be right where they are. Theologian James Cone contends, "Anger and humor are like the left and right arm. They complement each other. Anger empowers the poor to declare their uncompromising opposition to oppression, and humor prevents them from being consumed by their fury."[17] Rage is a natural response. Force, as discussed in Chapter 3, and joy are not incompatible. But rather than physically shove Schulte out of the way, as she alleged, the Black men she confronted mocked her. BBQ Becky is now a joke; her very existence is a punchline.

To be clear, joy does not involve laughing at Black pain. In the 2010s, Americans saw a wave of news coverage posted to You-Tube that was then "meme-ified" to make light of Black trauma and turn it into comedic catchphrases.[18] In 2010, Kelly Dodson was attacked by a man who broke into her bedroom window and attempted to rape her. Her brother, Antoine Dodson, heard the commotion and fought the intruder off. The attacker managed to get away without being caught. The family was distraught and furious. Antoine, the oldest of nine children, was also a victim of sexual assault, and now his sister Kelly had barely escaped sexual assault in her own home. The family was living in the Lincoln Park housing project in Huntsville, Alabama. Their community was outraged and on high alert. Antoine was livid and used his on-camera interview with a journalist to confront his sister's attacker: "Well, obviously we have a rapist in Lincoln Park. He's climbing in your windows, snatching your people up, so hide your wife, hide your kids." Antoine was not laughing. He was livid. He warned the intruder, "We looking for you. We gonna find you. I'm letting you know that. So you can run and tell that. Homeboy!"[19]

However, instead of inspiring viewers to address the trauma of the attack and help find the culprit, Antoine Dodson's rage became a spectacle. Millions flocked to social media to gawk at the clip, laugh, and share with others what they believed was a hilarious character. "Run tell that," like "Ain't nobody got time for that"—a quote from another news interview of a Black person that went viral on YouTube—was in fact Black pain vocalized in Black English, which was then transmuted into slogans, anthems, and auto-tuned songs. This is not Black joy. This is what the negritude writer Aimé Césaire cautions readers against: "Beware, my body and my soul, beware above all of crossing your arms and assuming the sterile attitude of the spectator, for life is not a spectacle, a sea of grievances is not a proscenium, and a man who wails is not a dancing bear."[20] Black joy as humor, as a remedy, is not staged or sponsored by corporations or peddled out for hits. Antoine Dodson was not a dancing bear. The spectacle that became of Dodson and his community was an affront and failed to take seriously the gravity of Black pain. Nor is all Black humor for public consumption. Who gets to laugh and how loud they laugh are important. The consumption of humor across racial lines is not a two-way street. Humor has boundaries. People like Schulte can be punchlines because people with power can sustain the blow.

W. E. B. Du Bois understood the utility of laughter and mockery. In 1942, Du Bois penned an essay for the *Mark Twain Quarterly* called "The Humor of Negroes." He argued that Black people in America and in the West Indies were humorous: "They are filled with laughter and delicious chuckling. They enjoy themselves; they enjoy jokes; they perpetrate them on each other and on white folk." Du Bois reasoned that humor was a defense mechanism or a reaction to tragedy. For Du Bois, humor supplied "those inner pleasures and gratifications which are denied" marginalized people. He also acknowledged Black humor's undercurrent of resentment, anger, and in some ways punishment.[21] Black humor cut white people down to size or revealed their flaws.

Du Bois recalled, "I remember when a celebrated Texas politician was shouting a fervent oration, two undistinguished Negroes listened to him from a distance: 'Who is dat man?' said one.

The other looked on, without smiling: 'I dunno, but he sutin'ly do recommen' hisself mos' high.'" The snarky remark is meant to disarm white supremacy, the joke being, "You're not so supreme or special." Or, even more cutting, "Who dis?" A similar example comes from the actress Keke Palmer taking *Vanity Fair*'s lie detector test in 2019. She was shown a picture of former vice president Dick Cheney and asked to identify him. She was stumped: "I hate to say it. I hope—don't want to sound ridiculous, [but] I don't know who this man is," Keke lamented. "Sorry to this man," she added as she slid his picture back to the interviewer.[22] This playful and even truthful declaration of a Black person who didn't recognize a prominent white person decenters white people and removes them from their pedestal. Du Bois did not quite know what to make of Black humor or what it would become in the future, but he understood this: "To the oppressed and unfortunate, to those who suffer, God mercifully grants the divine gift of laughter." Humor, he believed, allowed all people to face the tragedies of life and make it endurable.[23]

In 2022, C. Brandon Ogbunu wrote about the power of humor on Black Twitter during the pandemic.[24] Black Twitter exists as a nebulous community where the primary weapon of choice is humor. It is also a space where African American vernacular seems to offer its most potent punchlines and gifs during tragedy. As COVID-19 ravaged the Black community, skepticism pervaded Black Twitter discussions about whether or not to get vaccinated. African Americans were among the least-vaccinated groups. When a new variant, Omicron, swept the nation, Black folks on Twitter took to calling the new variant "Omarion" after the popular lead singer of a 2000s Black boy band, B2K. It was a nickname that recalled something familiar, with cultural recognition. I remember Black folks teasing, "You don't want that Omarion, it's spreading like crazy!"

Before "Omarion," nicknames like "Rona" or "Panera" were humorous shorthand for the virus that specialists were still trying to understand. The pandemic, much like the devastating Hurricane Katrina in 2005, revealed racial and economic disparities in public health that were already in place. The pandemic magnified the feeling that Black people were expendable in society. The jokes that played out online lightened the grief, loss, and skepticism that came with anxiety and uncertainty. Levity is a balm.

Black dance has always told a story. It is simultaneously a movement of one's body and *the movement* to foster Black recognition and humanity. Describing his world-renowned dance troupe, the choreographer and dancer Alvin Ailey said that "from his roots as a slave, the American Negro—sometimes sorrowing, sometimes jubilant but always hopeful—has touched, illuminated, and influenced the most remote preserves of world civilisation. I and my dance theater celebrate this trembling beauty."[25] Among the enslaved, dance was movement that evoked sorrow, resistance, love, and joy. Historian Stephanie M. H. Camp tells the story of a formerly enslaved woman named Nancy Williams, who was a young adult when freedom finally came for her at the end of the Civil War. While she was enslaved as a teenager, she would slip away from her Virginia plantation in the middle of the night and travel a few miles into the woods, away from prying ears or eyes. There, in the heart of the forest, she gathered with other enslaved people to dance and to drink the night away.

In African American vernacular, Nancy recalled, "Dem dances was somepin."[26] These dance parties were illicit and illegal during slavery. No enslaved person could be off the plantation without permission, and of course, permission to party would have never been granted. Thus, enslaved people had to carefully plan their soirees and hold them deep in the woods in the middle of the night. Some enslaved people brought musical instruments such as banjos, fiddles, and tambourines. Undoubtedly there were makeshift drums, and just like that, it was a party. Men and women strutted and whooped and hollered with laughter. And Nancy could *dance*. She showed off her skills by balancing a glass of water on her head and dancing without spilling a drop. Three boys bet on her. She reminisced fondly and with humor, "Out dere in de middle o' de flo' jes' a dancing; me an' Jennie and de devil." Dancing was not the only feature of the secret parties. One's outfit mattered as well. Nancy had gone to great lengths to prepare her outfit for the evening. She had dyed her dress yellow and added ruffles. She had even made matching yellow shoes. They were ill-fitting and hurt her feet, but Nancy did not care. She was beautiful and adorned by her own handiwork. Even with painful shoes, Nancy admitted, "Dat ain't stop me f'om dancing." The joy of dancing and being cute superseded her desire to be comfortable or even practical.

When Nancy was asked how she managed to get materials for her yellow dress and matching yellow shoes, she chuckled. "How I get 'em?" She stole them. She stole all she needed to make her outfit, from additional cloth to the paint she used to color her shoes. She was not ashamed—in fact, she was nearly eager to tell her interviewer about her ingenuity. Nancy's joy was about the reclamation of her time, labor, and beauty. Adornment is a form of declaring pride in oneself. Nancy wanted to feel attractive and beautiful. Even her choice of yellow was bold. She wanted to be seen, to be the center of attention, to be the sun personified. Yellow is joy and light. She moved as far away as possible from the muted brown rags of slavery. On that night, she was vibrant and seen, glowing from head to toe in a spectacular, warm, joyful yellow, dancing until her feet hurt.

There is much to love about this story. Nancy had moments during enslavement that she carved out for herself, for her own enjoyment. She knew that if she was caught, the consequences could be dire for all involved, yet she did not care. She prioritized her own joy, even if only for a few hours. Each enslaved person who showed up at the gathering spot engaged in a physical and emotional form of resistance to their enslavement. Camp argues, "Enslaved partygoers had a common commitment to delight and their bodies, to display their physical skill, to master their bodies through competition with others, and to express their creativity. They also had in common the capability of exorcizing discontents violently on one another."[27] They literally pushed past the boundaries of their plantation and their master's will to steal pleasure and even independence for themselves. As an elderly Christian woman, Nancy shied away from approving of her past actions. But it was impossible for her to not look back at her moment of rebellion with a feeling of victory. She was not free, but she did not get caught.

Nancy was not alone in her desire to manufacture joy for herself through theft. Mary Wyatt was enslaved in Virginia, and her mistress owned a dress that Mary "adored."[28] She recalled taking out the dress from time to time and holding it up to herself to pretend she was wearing it. One night, Mary claimed, "de debbil go in me good," and she decided to wear the dress to a plantation frolic during the Christmas season. She took the dress and tied it around her waist, hiding it under her petticoat. In her mind, this was not stealing. Mary had picked the cotton for the dress's fabric and enslaved women like her had processed it. The dress was the fruit of her labor, her hard labor. She enjoyed herself. She too, did not get caught.

Enslavement meant constant surveillance in addition to violence, hard labor, sexual assault, and the severance of Black families. Slaveholders were bent on watching nearly every inter-action among enslaved people. Even dances or parties hosted by slaveholders for the enslaved were attempts at controlling Black pleasure. The white gaze made sure no one drank too much, par-tied too hard, or stayed too long. Everything down to attendance was ordered. At the same time, parties put on by enslaved peo-ple themselves were never spontaneous. The timing, season, and weather had to be perfect. Secrecy was vital. Enslaved people were pushing back on their confinement and against the will of the slaveholder. Dancing at parties was joyous rebellion free from pry-ing eyes. Professor Tara Bynum discusses how scholars and the general public "don't talk enough about what feels good to Black people when there is no white gaze."[29]

Black women domestics in the early twentieth century similarly experienced tremendous joy and even rebellious pleasure when dancing in halls and clubs. Many working-class and middle-class Black people sought a form of play and self-expression that worked to "recuperate their bodies from exploitation."[30] These spaces spurred amusement and controversy. The dance halls allowed Black women who spent their days engaged in long hours of physical labor to be uninhibited. Their sweat came from pleasure instead of work. Dance was an expression of both joy and irrev-erence. It was sensual. Shaking, swaying, skipping, or grinding, it pushed at the boundaries of morality. White people were terri-fied of Black sexuality; thus even dances could be heavily policed. Dance reminded white authorities of Black liberation.[31]

Dance was a central part of Black children's lives, too. The Reverend Solomon Sir Jones was a Baptist minister and amateur filmmaker. In footage that is nearly one hundred years old, Jones documented African American communities in Oklahoma be-tween 1924 and 1928. His silent film captured Black schoolchildren performing choreographed dance moves outside on a sunny day.[32] In the recording, boys and girls are lined up in two rows facing each other. One little girl in a white dress, with white knee-high socks and a big white bow in her hair, exudes excitement. She has her hands on the shoulders of a little boy in front of her, his back to her. She is swaying from side to side, giddy. The film skips, and now boys and girls are holding hands with their partners and with great coordination and timing kick out their right foot, then the left. Their little legs repeat the step, like skipping in place. They spin and laugh and twirl. This scene takes place just forty miles south of Tulsa, only a few years after that city's thriving Black business district was burned to the ground. The film is evidence that not all thriving Black towns in Oklahoma were destroyed.

In jest and in truth, James Brown, the Godfather of Soul, once said, "The one thing that can solve most of our problems is dancing." Dance is a physical expression of joy. It affirms life and beauty. In 1968, Brown recorded one of his most popular songs, "Say It Loud—I'm Black and I'm Proud." The song held the number one spot on the R&B charts for six weeks and was an anthem for the Black Power movement. It not only calls out racism but calls for empowerment. Brown emphasized that being Black was nothing one had to apologize for; in fact, Black people were entitled to justice.

No one could move their legs and cock back their head with the verve and funk that Brown exhibited during his concerts. His signature moves were nearly impossible to mimic, particularly for white people. "Say It Loud" was more than a song; it was a chant—the kind of call and response heard between a Black minister and his church. Brown danced as though he were possessed by a spirit, and his energy was infectious. Joy is pride that can be expressed with swaying hips, stomping feet, and jolts of back-arching dance moves.

Toni Morrison wrote the foreword to *The Black Book*, a collection of images and essays compiled by Middleton A. Harris. *The
Black Book* covered the history of Black culture from 1619 through
the 1940s—everything from Black inventions and genius to Black
folktales and dances. Morrison loved the book. In her 1974 op-ed
published in the *New York Times*, she remarked that reading it
was "like growing up black one more time." What gripped me regarding her description of this book was her essential summation
of Black life. Morrison said, "Finally, in this long trek through
three hundred years of Black life, there was joy, which is what I
mostly remember. The part of our lives that was spent neither on
our knees nor hanging from trees."[33] She relished its seriousness,
humor, irreverence, and humanity. She discussed the idleness and
joy of Black boys doing the hambone, a style of dance that turned
one's body into a drum—the dancer slaps and claps thighs, chests,
and even cheeks to make a sound that mimics music. "Our bodies
in motion at public dances that pulled black people from as far
as 100 miles away," reminisced Morrison, was an example of joy
that could be found when Black folks gathered. For her, dance
was a "glorious freedom of movement in which rites of puberty
were acted out on a dance floor to the sound of brass, strings and
ivory." Dance allowed Black people to find relief and communicate.
Dance was the paradox of controlling one's body and simultaneously letting it go. During Morrison's childhood and all throughout African American history, Black people danced in public and
in private, on porches and in the front yard. "Of course, there was
the music," wrote Morrison. To study the Black past was to behold
a soundtrack: not only the "race records" of the 1950s and '60s, or
the live bands of the '30s and '40s, but the "shout songs and the
remnants of slave jubilees."[34]

In 2022, a video of Black men frolicking went viral on YouTube, Instagram, and Twitter. It showcased numerous Black men in a collage of individual videos exhibiting what they understood "frolicking" to mean. The videos ranged from skipping to all-out sprints. It was hilarious and wonderful to see their interpretations of frivolous joy. Black men were running in fields filled with yellow flowers, skipping with their babies in tow. Black men captured themselves running and then falling and roaring with laughter in a field, a park, or just their yard. Following the hashtags—#frolicking, #blackmenfrolicking, #wefrolicking, and #blackboyjoy—revealed a beautiful array of skin tones and hair types. Black men frolicked with long beards and with long locs bouncing in the air and about their face. Each man defined for himself what it meant or looked like to "play and move about cheerfully, excitedly, or energetically"—the definition of "frolic" according to Encyclopedia.com.[35] One Black man captioned his video, "I ain't never had so much fun."[36]

Dancing is tethered to Black joy. Any wedding, graduation, or celebratory party draws Black people to do the Electric Slide, the Cupid Shuffle, or the Wobble. During much of the pandemic, I found joy watching video after video of the latest dance moves. I hollered with laughter as I practiced and failed to master the latest craze, from the "WAP" dance to "Aye Bay Bay" to Beyoncé's "CUFF IT" challenge. Whether Black people are dancing the choreographed moves of Alvin Ailey, stomping within their fraternities or sororities, or sweating and swaying closely under a blue light in the basement, dance may not solve most of Black problems, as James Brown declared, but it can, for a moment, make us forget.

I often come back to the words of Imani Perry, who reminds us that enslaved and free Black people have "refused the terms of our degradation."[37] Refusal is most prominently seen and understood through labor. When emancipation came, newly freed Black people still had to navigate oppressive restrictions and exploitative labor practices. Throughout the end of the nineteenth century, Black women had few options but to continue the domestic labor of working in white women's homes. By 1880, in big southern cities such as Atlanta, at least 98 percent of all Black women who could earn a wage worked as domestics. This work was long, hard, and dangerous: white households were still a site of violence.[38] Black girls as young as ten could expect to work from sunup to sundown all through their prime years and into their sixties and seventies.[39] A formerly enslaved woman from Nashville recalled waking up long before the sun rose, making fires, and working inside and outside the house. No person did just one task or job. "They hired me to nurse, but I had to nurse, cook, chop in the fields, chop wood, bring water, iron, and in general just do everything," she said. What stunned me about her story was her age: she was just six years old at the time.[40] Some Black teenage girls were paid as little as four or five dollars a month. Slavery denied consent. Saying no was not possible, at least not without violent consequences. In a postemancipation world, Black joy was refusal; it was quitting—similar to flight. When possible, Black women walked off the job. One or two generations out of slavery, quitting was the definitive rejection of one's degradation, and it was filled with joy. Quitting wreaked havoc in the households of white women who wanted to maintain control. One white woman complained, "No matter how important the occasion may be, or how urgent the need for their services, where you have a wedding in the house, or sickness, or whatever you may have, they will just leave the cooking-stove and the housework and everything else and go off on these 'scursions."[41] Quitting was a form of sabotage. It was satisfying to leave without permission.

In a free labor market, quitting also did not require confrontation. Many jobs had to be endured to survive, but whenever possible, Black women reclaimed their time, labor, rest, and enjoyment for themselves. Historian Tera Hunter took the title of her book on southern Black women from a declaration of liberation by a formerly enslaved woman named Julie Tillory. When a white missionary asked Tillory why she would abandon "the comforts of [her] master's plantation," she had her response loaded: "To 'joy my freedom."[42] To enjoy her freedom was paramount. There is no liberation without joy, without the freedom to seek personal pleasure. Tillory's indefatigable spirit was a direct threat to white power in the struggle over Black people's autonomy and labor. Black domestics developed tactics to negotiate the terms of economic, political, and even social contracts.

I think often about the concept of Black joy as refusal when I reflect on my experiences as a teenager in my first job. In 1998, at age sixteen, I worked at McDonald's. It was my first foray into the inner workings of capitalism. I only worked after school and on the weekends, but it was rough. I hated the uniform and I hated how my clothes were saturated with the smell of french fry grease. Customers could be rude and seemed to disdain many of the Black and brown people who worked behind the counter. The position did not pay much above minimum wage. Twenty years earlier, in 1978, scholar Robin D. G. Kelley also worked at McDonald's. His experience was similar to mine; he recalled, "The swing managers, who made slightly more than the rank and file, were constantly on our ass to move fast and smile more frequently. The customers treated us as if we were stupid." His workforce was also made up of 90 percent Black and brown people. He revealed how employees bolstered their compensation by liberating "McDonaldland cookies by the boxful," volunteering to clean the parking lot and lobby only to have an excuse to socialize with friends, and "accidentally" cooking too many Quarter Pounders and apple pies near closing time so they could keep whatever was left over.[43] There was a mischievous pleasure in sticking it to the man. Cooking and consuming McDonald's food was not about generating waste but about creating additional compensation. Small victories could be found in choosing what music to play over the speakers during work hours. As a teenager, I was not thinking hard about wages, time off, or benefits, but I still understood what it meant to work in a place that held few opportunities or aspirations.

Kelley recounted vividly how his fellow workers stylized their work. Uniforms might have flair; caps could be turned up or to the side. Black women would click the register with long, elaborately manicured nails. Menial work, at least among young people, was about creating spaces that fostered Black identity, style, and ease. We pushed back on strict standards of professionalism that whitewashed the customer experience. Yes, it was possible to exhibit being cool on the grill. "Just imagine a young black male 'gangsta limpin' between the toast and the grill, brandishing a spatula like a walking stick or a microphone," Kelley described.[44] I could not hold back my laughter as I read this. Our experiences were nearly twenty years apart yet still the same. We both found ways to "turn work into pleasure." Even I enjoyed testing out my new rap skills while vibing to the latest hit that we insisted be played while we worked. In Texas during the late 1990s, it was screw music and shouting out the lyrics to Lil' Troy's 1998 single, which never got much traction but was the soundtrack of my life during high school: "Wanna be a balla, shot caller / Twenty inch blades on the Impala . . ." The good times I had at McDonald's never involved supplying customers with a fun and fast dining experience, or even taking home a check.

My younger sister Victoria also worked at McDonald's. She quit more times than I can remember. Some days she clocked in and other days she chose to hang out with her friends. Perhaps this was immature, petty, or unprofessional, but it was also a joyous undoing of whiteness, capitalism, and labor. It was a refusal to play by all the rules, particularly rules that perpetuated exploitation, rules our grandparents could not always break. Too often society has dismissed the labor of the Black working class as menial or expendable. But what I and so many other young Black wage workers understood was no different from what our Black ancestors had understood one or two hundred years earlier: that there was no reason to work hard for little to no payoff. African Americans built this country. From the plantations to the White House, from the fields to the railroads, Black labor ushered in American modernity with little compensation, recognition, or gratitude.[45] Slowdowns, sabotage, feigned illness, and petty theft were ways to resist and refuse this oppression, to ensure that no one got the best of Black labor.

Every year as a child my father traveled from Detroit, Michigan, to Monroe, Louisiana, with his parents and brother to spend the summer with his grandparents, aunties, uncles, and countless cousins. One hot summer day when he was ten or eleven, he and his brother went into an ice cream shop in Monroe. The South was still segregated, and while there was only one entrance for both white and Black patrons, the best and fastest service went to white customers. When my dad went to the front counter to order an ice cream cone, the woman behind the counter looked annoyed. She pretended she did not see him and served customers who had come in after my dad and uncle.

When all the white customers had been served, the employee finally decided to take my dad's order. He and my uncle each ordered two ice cream cones, each with a scoop of chocolate and a scoop of vanilla. When the clerk turned to hand my dad the cones, two in each hand, my dad said, "No, thanks, I don't want none!" He and my uncle took off running out the store. They got down the block and around the corner before they stopped, howling with laughter. To see the clerk's rejected and annoyed face was plenty for them. In hindsight, that little stunt could have gotten them into grave trouble, but nothing happened. Even children could refuse subjugation. He wasted her time and perhaps the ice cream that no white patron would touch. Coming from the North, he dared to refuse new terms in a new environment. And as foolish as it was, the act brought him and his brother more joy than ice cream on a hot summer day.

Sometimes Black joy is as simple as seeing yourself reflected in the mirror. Black representation matters and is a constant contributor of joy. If ever there was a film that exuded all of the joy, pleasure, and beauty of Black people, it was *Black Panther*. Anticipation for the film was off the charts in the months before its release. The *teaser*—not even the full trailer—racked up eighty-nine million views in twenty-four hours.[46] After presale tickets were made available, Erik Davis, Fandango's managing editor, announced on Twitter that in the first twenty-four hours, advance ticket sales "exceeded those of any other movie from the Marvel Cinematic Universe."[47] Social media was peddling hashtags like #BlackPantherSoLit and #WelcomeToWakanda. The energy and excitement surrounding the film were insatiable. Journalist Carvell Wallace wrote that announcements of the premiere date—February 16, 2018—caused a frenzy. Fans began posting pictures of themselves on social media wearing kente cloth and what Wallace called

"African-Americana, a kitsch version of an older generation's pride touchstones—kente cloth du-rags, candy-colored nine-button suits, King Jaffe Joffer from *Coming to America* with his lion-hide sash—alongside captions like 'This is how I'm a show up to the *Black Panther* premiere.'"[48] I remember going to the theater opening night in my hometown. My husband and I wore kente cloth shirts in solidarity with the film's theme of African pride. We were ecstatic—and we were not comic book fans. We were not even really fans of the other Marvel films. For us, the excitement was about the representation. We were ready to purchase merchandise just so our son could play as a superhero who looked like him. A Black Panther backpack, check. A Black Panther water bottle, check. A Black Panther lunch box, check, check, check. This kid was ready for school. Representation made us giddy.

Marvel Comics' Black Panther was created in 1966 by Stan Lee and Jack Kirby, two Jewish New Yorkers who wanted to offer Black comic book readers a character to identify with. The hero, Black Panther, whose real name is T'Challa (played in the film by Chadwick Boseman), is the heir to the throne of Wakanda, a fictional nation located in Africa. The tiny country is the sole possessor of vibranium, an extraterrestrial element acquired from a fallen meteor. Vibranium is powerful and fuels their entire economy. It has healing powers and is indestructible.[49] The entire country of Wakanda vows to keep their resources a secret to maintain their autonomy and prevent enemies from taking the vibranium for nefarious purposes. Like all superhero stories, *Black Panther* was action packed and rife with interpersonal conflicts, power struggles, and humor.

One of the most powerful expressions of joy regarding the film came in a viral tweet before its release. In a video, a Black man is holding up his phone and pointing it at a large poster of *Black*

Panther in a theater hallway. The poster features the primarily Black cast looking fierce and ready for battle. The man holding the phone is narrating what he sees: "So we're sitting here looking at this dope ass *Black Panther* poster, and the conclusion that we have come to is [this is] what white people get to feel all the time . . . since the beginning of cinema." His friend is emphatically cosigning the conclusion and interrupts his narration with shouts of "All the time! All the time!" Two other Black men are fawning over the poster. One Black man approaches the poster, opens his arms, and jokingly hugs it. It is empowerment. It is joy. The friend is still repeating himself: "This is what white people get to feel like ALL THE TIME?!" All of the friends are laughing, and the man who is most amazed drops a sobering punchline: "I would love this country, too." It is a gut punch. For Black Americans, patriotism is complicated. White superiority has been cultivated for so long that superheroes—all saviors—are de facto white. The introduction of a Black superhero was a paradigm shift. Crossing one's arms over one's chest and declaring "Wakanda forever!" provided Black audiences the feeling that white Americans must get at the Olympics, chanting "USA, USA, USA!" Representation is joyful. It is the feeling of being seen and feeling seen.

The Black joy found in representation is no small thing. *Black Panther* grossed over $1.3 billion at the box office. It also broke ground by having an African American director and a predominantly Black cast. Critic Jamil Smith wrote, "Hollywood has never produced a blockbuster this splendidly Black."[50] No other superhero film deals with issues of being of African descent and the complexities of the Black Diaspora. The only other media phenomenon that comes close is perhaps the TV miniseries *Roots*.

Roots premiered on January 23, 1977, and was shown over the course of seven consecutive nights on ABC. The story was based on Alex Haley's 1976 book *Roots: The Saga of an American Family*, which put the experiences of enslaved people of African descent at the center rather than the periphery of a family chronicle set in the American South. The book was an instant bestseller. To this day, *Roots* has sold more copies than any other book written by an African American.[51]

The miniseries was just as successful. By the end of the binge-worthy series, more than 130 million people—nearly half of the population of the United States at the time—had seen at least one episode of *Roots*. When the finale aired on January 30, 1977, an estimated ninety million viewers tuned in, making it the most-watched program in television history up to that point. In an era before TV could be easily recorded, Americans canceled meetings and social plans so that they could stay home and participate in this collective cultural event.[52]

Roots opens with scenes of Kunta Kinte's boyhood years in his idyllic eighteenth-century West African village of Juffure (in modern Gambia), where everyone worked together in harmony for the good of the community. Strong and dignified fathers served as role models, wives and mothers cared for home and family, elders dispensed wisdom, and charismatic grandmothers handed out love and discipline in equal parts. It was the first time American audiences saw a realistic, humane portrayal of Africans in mainstream media. Audiences were subsequently horrified when fifteen-year-old Kunta Kinte was kidnapped during a hunting expedition, forcibly marched to the coast, chained, shipped across the Atlantic in the dark hold of a slave ship, auctioned off in Annapolis, Maryland, and finally forced to reckon with his new condition as a chattel slave on a plantation in Virginia. Over the course of the weeklong miniseries, increasing numbers of Americans watched, intrigued by the personal

dramas that characterized Kunta Kinte's resistance, accultura-
tion, and, ultimately, incorporation into the slave community
through his friendship with Fiddler, his marriage to Bell, and,
finally, the birth of their daughter Kizzy. Viewers stayed with
the family saga as generations of Kunta Kinte's progeny grew to
adulthood, sharing in the heartbreak when Kizzy was sold to a
North Carolina planter and later rooting for her son Chicken
George as he saved the winnings he earned as his owner's prize
cockfighting trainer, hoping to someday purchase his and his
mother's freedom. To say that *Roots* was transformative for Black
representation is a clear understatement. Never before had large
American audiences, Black or white, been exposed to portrayals
of the violence and cruelty of slavery, the religious resilience of
Black Muslims praying to Allah, or the brutal separation of enslaved Black families. Seeing these experiences represented on
television could not solve racism. But that was not the point. The
remedy in *Roots* consisted of being seen and heard in new ways.

Before *Roots* appeared, the most iconic popular American stories set in the slaveholding South were *Uncle Tom's Cabin*, *The
Birth of a Nation*, and *Gone with the Wind*. All were first novels
and had wildly popular stage or screen adaptations (or both). The
plots, characters, and iconic scenes from these three sentimental
tales were so deeply woven into the fabric of American culture
that other popular depictions of the pre–Civil War South inevitably contained key stock characters and melodramatic tropes from
them: a pure, virtuous white girl who dies an untimely death, a
Southern belle who becomes the object of a dashing cavalier's af-
fection, and a romance played out against the backdrop of a gra-
cious plantation estate filled with Black "servants" who invariably
loved their kind masters and mistresses more than their own freedom. These scenes were palatable history lessons for American

audiences, easy-to-digest versions of what were then prevailing scholarly arguments about agrarian ideals and the mildness and inefficiency of the "peculiar institution." These celebrations of the antebellum South and its "Lost Cause," as historians like David Blight and film scholars like Linda Williams remind us, performed enormous ideological work, serving as the collective public memory and justifying the nation's pernicious race-based caste system. And they remained extremely popular over the course of the twentieth century. Indeed, just a year before *Roots* debuted, the network broadcast of *Gone with the Wind* "broke all previous records for audience share."[53] Author Nicole Hemmer writes that the emotion most associated with racism is not hatred but pleasure. For some white people, white supremacy is cozy, affirming, romantic, and heroic.

In *Roots'* southern landscape, Black Americans were not happy with their lot as slaves. Enslaved men were not simply cheerful servants of white masters. Black women were not the "mammies" and "jezebels" of popular lore. Rather, enslaved African Americans were mothers, fathers, sisters, brothers, children—members of families and communities who did the best they could under the most repressive circumstances, affirming and protecting their families to the best of their abilities.

The Black joy that *Roots* spawned was as explosive as what *Black Panther* inspired. "*Roots* tracing kits" helped people navigate their family trees and "*Roots* music" flew off the shelves.[54] African Americans began naming their children after characters from *Roots*. In New York City alone, twenty newborns born within days of the program's broadcast were named Kunta Kinte or Kizzy.[55] Haley noted, "I know of at least 12 newborns named for him [Kunta], and in San Francisco the mother of twins named one baby Kunta and the other Kinte."[56] African Americans began placing *Roots* alongside the Bible on the family coffee table. Americans of all backgrounds rushed to their local historical societies to investigate their own heritage.[57]

Though fictional and eventually controversial for allegations of plagiarism and inaccuracies, *Roots* hit at the heart of Black Americans' history of forced migration, violence, and exploitation.[58] *Black Panther* tells of an imagined Black future. It plays with possibility and hope, all the while affirming the beauty, intelligence, and strength of a Black nation. The future is a playground for Black people, a place where it is possible to imagine a world that does not revolve around whiteness or oppression. Both films inspire Black people to remake their worlds and to live their Blackness proudly. Black people must counter death with the same determination that is employed to destroy Black lives. Black joy as representation stunts and defeats the propaganda and lies spread about Black identity as inferior or dysfunctional. Black people can be their own protagonists and heroes. We can save ourselves and others from terrible evil, real or imagined. We can feel joy, all the time.

In 2021, Black America lost the genius bell hooks. I say "Black America" because hooks belonged to us. She was Black Americans' greatest champion. With every word she wrote, she centered Black women and reminded us that we were worthy of love and care. She showed us continuously and fiercely how much she loved us. hooks reminded all her readers that love is powerful, more powerful than happiness. Mourning and grief stem from a rich, all-encompassing love. In her book *All About Love* hooks wrote, "Only love can heal the wounds of the past."[59] The love is how we treat ourselves and how we treat each other.

On the shallow shores of my grief after my siblings' deaths, I wanted happiness, but from the depths, I needed radical healing for those who suffer. I needed "resilience" to not be a bitter word for keeping a stiff upper lip. I needed a world that makes space for grief without qualifications. A world that allows us to ache as a community. I needed a world that also allows me to harness my joy and use it against oppressive systems, warped norms, and despair.

When people ask me how my family got through some of the toughest pain we have ever faced with the deaths of my siblings, my answer is simple: hope, joy, and love. Our church community surrounded us with love and meals for months. Our friends came and stayed with us and rotated visits for months. When I could not recall who cooked or what we ate, it was because so many people loved on us in meaningful ways. We were loved so completely and fully that it healed our hearts and spilled over. Every bit of love we received strengthened us to give it back to others. We gave it back to those who found themselves in similar circumstances or facing other tragedies.

Early on, bell hooks understood that the answer to our grief is love. She also understood that love is devoid of power. In our capitalistic, patriarchal, and hegemonic world, Americans tend to think love is weak and even embarrassing. Because white supremacy is defined by violent power, it can never produce community or compassion. According to hooks, "We cannot know love if we remain unable to surrender our attachment to power." But love makes people vulnerable and thereby connects us to others. Love requires community, and hooks gave us the remedy for pain. She addressed our trauma and prioritized our suffering. She gave her readers language to understand love as a noun, an adjective, and a verb. Healing is a radical communal act.[60] And the greatest expression of love is joy. It is an open mouth, head thrown back, laugh surfacing from deep within.

Wendell Erdman Berry is a writer, farmer, and environmental activist. He argues that when it comes to fixing societal problems, people often want a "solution as large scale as the problem." But rarely can any major problem be solved this way. Instead, he suggested, what is needed are countless small solutions that can chip away at the core issues. But small, interpersonal solutions do not satisfy Americans' need for drama. At a surface level, joy does not feel adequate. At best, it can feel dismissive; at worst, like salt in a wound. But Black joy is not mere optimism. It is hope. We cannot tackle anything, big or small, without first believing change is possible. Some changes will come all at once. Some changes will be incremental. But nothing can be solved without putting our faith into practice.

My five-year-old daughter Josephine has the most delicious and infectious laugh. One day I was looking for my phone and realized she had it. I said, "JoJo, what are you doing?" It turned out that she was recording herself singing along to Disney's *Encanto*, belting her heart out with all the inflection to Mirabel's "Waiting on a Miracle." She handed me the phone but asked to watch the video she had just finished recording. I hit play and together we listened to her rendition. She is offscreen, behind the camera, and the film plays out shakily on my phone. She sings every lyric verbatim, but when it's time for the high note, she misses it by a mile. She is way off but as earnest as she can be in seizing her moment to shine. We both looked at each other, listening to her voice on the recording nearly scream out the note, and we simultaneously burst into laughter. We flung our heads back, opened our mouths wide, and hollered with laughter. It was pure joy and simple pleasure.

What did this moment have to do with white supremacy? Nothing. That is the point. I fight to have these moments make up the bulk of my day. Our laugh was both a remedy and a reminder that Black joy can be anything. I want a revolution, I want to be protected and safe, I want to belong, but mostly I just want to be. I want to be like Zora Neale Hurston, who was "too busy sharpening her oyster knife."[61] I am raising my children to know joy, to allow joy to fortify them and heal them. Then I am teaching them to send joy back out to a hostile world. Black joy is the remedy. Justice is the healing. We can have both.

Finally, I want to conclude where I began. I return to my ancestors Martha, who refused, and Arnesta, who limped. But Arnesta's limp was not the totality of her. This is important. Arnesta lived a vibrant life. Standing just below five feet, at four feet, eleven inches, she was a force. She left Alabama and moved to Michigan. She loved. She actually married five times! She was a fireball, an extrovert, and knew no strangers. Every weekend she hosted elaborate gatherings. Much like myself, she was constantly busy and boasted having ten best friends. Much like my daughter, her laugh was infectious. Arnesta dominated every room she was in. She was a natural and willing leader. She protected her family as best she could. She poured herself into the lives of others and into the life of my mother. She refused. And in her refusal, she created and circulated boundless joy.

DROWNING

A Postscript

When my husband was in high school, he took a summer job as a lifeguard at a local beach. During his training, his instructors discussed what to do if he spotted someone drowning. If the person was panicking, he needed to be careful. A person who was flailing could drown a lifeguard by attempting to jump on them and even push them underwater. If the panicking drowning person was bigger than him, this could be a real problem. The instructors' guidance was simple: let them drown. It's better to rescue a person after they've lost consciousness than to risk being pulled under. Once unconscious, they can be safely rescued and brought to shore, and then a lifeguard or paramedic can resuscitate them. "Let them drown." It seems harsh, but I understand the rationale behind it. A panicked person in the water can be a danger to themselves and others.

I think about this story often when I watch news coverage of the latest racial boogeyman, be it critical race theory, woke culture, or conspiracies regarding stolen elections. It is as though white Americans are lounging in a community pool, propped up by all kinds of floaties because they cannot swim. They fear someone is going to remove a device that allows them to float, so they scream. They splash and kick and lose their balance. White people fear the loss of their superiority, advantage, and safety. They become irrational. They do not need to hoard the floaties; in fact they can just stand up and the water will be at their waist. But they do not trust anyone. The fanatics, white supremacists, and radicalized white parents are kicking and punching and flailing their arms in a panic. In a toxic political environment, I ask myself, how should the public approach these people? Do we let them drown? What does that look like? What would it mean for American racial politics?

I've begun to think that maybe letting someone drown is a refusal to engage a panicked person. Many Black people know what rescue and resuscitation look like in a democracy. It is the work and activism Black women do daily at our jobs, in our communities, and for our families. There is nothing good in America that can be accomplished without the labor and intellect of people of color. When people of color refuse, quit, leave, withhold, strike, boycott, or simply carve out spaces that deny white gazes or do not allow white people entry, institutions must concede. Allowing the drowning is the demand that white people must relinquish their hold on power, violence, and control. The warning before drowning is to call out, "Let go. Stand up. You are not dying."

When America is rescued and resuscitated, then people will also have to answer the hard questions. How do we engage each other as human beings? When Jamaica Kincaid wrote *A Small Place*, regarding her fraught understanding of and relationship with her native home of Antigua, she concluded by writing about Christopher Columbus's "discovery" of the island in 1493. She referred to the European settlers and slaveholders as "rubbish" and all enslaved people as "noble and exalted." In her mind, there was nothing to contest. Men and women who engaged in the practice of slavery were trash and people who were enslaved were honorable and even morally superior. But when slavery collapsed, everyone had to reckon with their own humanity and the humanity of others. Kincaid acknowledged this: "Once you cease to be a master . . . you are no longer human rubbish, you are just a human being, and all the things that adds up to." The same could be said of the enslaved: "Once they are no longer slaves, once they are free, they are no longer noble and exalted; they are just human beings."[1]

Slavery was an institution that deprived white people of their humanity and created a context in which Black people could not be seen as human either. In slavery, there were no humans, white or Black. For people to become human, slavery needed to be abolished. Black people are not afraid to act; they are committed and even willing to trade in their identity as "noble and exalted slaves" to be human. But too many white Americans have settled into their identity as "rubbish" because, as James Baldwin believed, "to act is to be committed, and to be committed is to be in danger. In this case, the danger, in the minds of most white Americans, is the loss of their identity," or in other words, the loss of their manufactured superiority. For too many white Americans, it is better to be hated than to be human. But nothing will change until everyone becomes committed.

Accordingly, in a postemancipation world, everyone's humanity must be reissued and prescribed a meaning that grants everyone enfranchisement. But the only model people have, the only definitions people understand, come from a place of violence and death. Refusal requires redefinition, reparation, and restoration. Justice can only be obtained when people strive to imagine and create a world order that does no harm.

In 1993, science fiction author Octavia Butler published her book *Parable of the Sower*, about an apocalyptic United States that is ravaged by corrupt leadership, deadly plagues, and rampant violence. The first chapter begins with the date Saturday, July 20, 2024. Each chapter opens with an epigraph, a warning of sorts. The epigraph for chapter 6 reads, "Drowning people / Sometimes die / Fighting their rescuers." Black Americans and other people of color cannot risk their lives saving someone who is unwilling to recognize the harm their panic is causing. The wise lifeguard will watch and wait. It can be agonizing, but waiting is not careless. The refusal is not so much a "no" as a "not now." When the hysterical swimmer grows tired and weary and weak and is just on the brink of unconsciousness, then and only then will the lifeguard rescue them from the water.

Black Americans and their comrades serve as the nation's lifeguards. Black people have consistently, from the beginning of this country, blown their whistles and called out the strong tides of the hypocrisy, violence, greed, and absurdity of white supremacy. We can and should continue to rely on revolution, protection, force, flight, and joy. In the chaotic world that Americans live in, Black people can repeatedly pull in the heavy unconscious bodies of extremism or apathy and hope their revival from a near-death experience will be transformative. Or we can let whiteness drown in the violence of its own making. But when we refuse, it is in our power to determine how we can best preserve our lives and the lives of others.

ACKNOWLEDGMENTS

When I was eleven years old, I went on vacation with my family to Disney World. We had a blast. During the trip, my mom was up against a deadline for her book manuscript. My parents went on all the rides with us during the day, but at night, my mom worked and typed for hours. One night we were sitting in our hotel room watching TV while my mother was working. Suddenly, I heard my mother scream, and then scream again and again. Her screams turned into wails. She had lost ninety pages of her book. She was working on an old-school word processor and somehow had erased all that she had written. Ninety pages. Writing is hard. It is energy and thought and care. Good writing is taxing. Even as a child, I knew that this was no small thing. To my mother's relief, when we returned home a technician managed to recover all of her lost pages. Nevertheless, the fear of losing written pages had been instilled in me. I can still hear my mother saying, "Save your stuff. Back it up. Don't play around."

I share this story because *We Refuse* almost never existed. To finish major parts of this book, I went on a writer's retreat and wrote almost one hundred pages of edited and new material, which I saved on an external thumb drive. Not long after, I got word that my grandmother had passed away. My husband and I bought plane tickets to Illinois to attend my grandmother's funeral. In my distracted state, I did not back up my work to a cloud or my computer. It was all on my thumb drive. While at the airport, I pulled out my laptop to work. Even in my grief, I still felt the tyranny of a deadline. Suddenly I heard the announcement that it was time to board. I quickly gathered my things, and then I realized I could not find my thumb drive. I assumed it was buried in my black hole of a purse and boarded the plane. Once we were seated, I began feverishly searching my purse for the missing drive. Nothing. It was nowhere to be found. As the plane pulled away from the gate, I burst into tears and felt the beginnings of a panic attack. If it was lost, there was no question, I would quit working on the manuscript. My husband assured me we would find it. But for now, I needed to be present with my family and bury the last of my grandparents. So I took all my fears and feelings and buried them in the back of my brain. We flew out on a Friday evening and attended the funeral on Saturday morning. On Sunday, we flew back to Boston, arriving at the exact same gate that we had left from on Friday. As I stumbled off the plane, something told me to check the seat I'd been sitting in just three days before. I put my hand in between the two seats, searched the floor, and nearly screamed. Three days later, my thumb drive was right where I'd left it, right where it had fallen on the floor between two seats. My husband's mouth fell open. And then he said, "Save that right now!" I did. And I no longer use thumb drives.

I marvel at what it takes to cultivate an idea and then write a book. I think about how some stories are lost and then recovered. Other stories are lost and never found. Some stories are lost and then written anew. There are people who forge ahead and people who cannot. How these things happen can be inexplicable. I believe some stories must come to life. There are forces that work to ensure nothing can keep a powerful and purposeful message from the printed page. I believe my ancestors needed *We Refuse* in the world. I think my great-great-great-grandmother and her daughter and granddaughter needed this work. I needed this work. We all need to be reminded of the power of refusal in the face of loss, setbacks, or backlash.

Moreover, when something like a book is lost, the stakes are high because others have invested time, energy, and care in the work. I would like to thank all of the people who helped to make *We Refuse* possible. At Basic Books, to Brian Distelberg, Emily Taber, Emma Berry, Kyle Gipson, and Claire Potter, thank you for believing in this project and pushing it through. To Tanya McKinnon, Tamika Franklin, Vanessa Diaz, Dennis Marciuska, Joy Worthy, Jibola Fagbamiye, and Gregory Thomson, you all are a force! In shaping this book, I took part in several writing groups that stretched my thinking. Thank you to Kerri Greenidge, Kendra Field, Heather Curtis, and Abby Cooper. To Mary Frances Phillips, Natalie Leger, and Eziaku Nwokocha, you got me through the pandemic and the hardest parts of *We Refuse*. A special thank-you to Ashley Dennis: you are an iron sharpener.

To my Wellesley colleagues, thank you to Chipo Dendere, Liseli Fitzpatrick, Layli Maparyan, Selwyn Cudjoe, Jenn Chudy, Michelle Lee, Petra Rivera-Rideau, Irene Mata, Baafra Abeberese, Eve Zimmerman, Patricia Birch, Soo Hong, Smitha Radhakrishnan, Sabine Franklin, Patricia Birch, Eric Jarrard, Provost Andy Shennan, and President Paula Johnson. And thanks also go to my phenomenal students, especially Adwoa "Difie" Antwi, Lauren Dines, Izzy Torkornoo, Nia Roberts, Penelope Johnson, Rozey Hill, Mia Maxwell, Madeleine Speagle, Crickett Liebermann, and Bernadette Hargrove.

Thank you to my colleagues, other writers and editors in the field, Tamika Nunley, Elizabeth Hinton, Saida Grundy, Crystal Sanders, Tikia Hamilton, Carol Anderson, Jim Downs, Deirdre Cooper-Owens, Erica Armstrong Dunbar, Eric Foner, Nikki Taylor, Betsy Herbin Triant, Robyn Spencer, Nneka Dennie, Lauren Williams, and Charles McKinney.

To my fellow podcasters, Jody Avirgan, Leah Wright Rigueur, Niki Hemmer, Nina Earnest, Jacob Feldman, Brittani Brown, and all the good people at Radiotopia, thank you for the best conversations. Special thanks to Boston's Museum of African American History and its leadership. Shout out to NPR's *Tiny Desk Concerts* for fueling my writing sessions. Caregivers make nearly all my writing possible. Thank you, Beatriz "Bea" Barreto, Elianah Ogletree, Motsidiso Mofokeng, Sydney Scott, Emebet "Betty" Guerini, and Silvania Alves.

To my incomparable sisterhood known as Boston's Finest, thank you to Kristen Pope, Jocelyn Gates, Kimberly Dickerson Dilday, Essence Souffrant, and Kai Lopes-Stovall. Thank you to the deep friendships that have sustained me, Nafissa Cisse Egbuonye, Nyasha Guramatunhu-Cooper, Mary Lou Fulson, Meghan DeJong, Madelina Young-Smith, Patrice Clark, Megan Lee, Kimberly Muse-Sims, Grace Nieh, Dani Kilgore, Abena Yankah, Regine Jean Charles, Marques Hardin, Ylisse Bess, Richard Pope, Andrea and Ryan Marshall, Asabe Poloma, Sara and Erik Bates, Rebecca Carew, and Tamara McCaw. A special thanks to Michael Lawrence-Riddell, Katiana Victor, and my Highrock family.

I rely heavily on my family for mental, emotional, intellectual, and spiritual support. Thank you to my sisters, Camille Carter, China Jenkins, Crystal Rose, Elizabeth Jackson, Valerie McNeil, Jeanae Jackson, Victoria Jones, and Rachel Anyasi. Thank you to my brothers, Frank Jenkins, Edward Jackson, George Rose, Kevin

Jones, Jamaal McNeil, and Joshua Jackson. Thank you to my nieces and nephews, Benjamin Oberlton, Kingsley-Reine Carter Pissang, Mikayla Oberlton, Edward Oberlton, Jamsin Rose, Andrew Rose, Georgia Rose, Donovan Jenkins, Trace Jenkins, Edward Jackson, Charles Jackson, Mae Jackson, Paul Jackson, Olivia Jones, Morgan McNeil, Kevin Jones, and Vivienne Jones. To Aunt Betty, Aunt Irenner, Aunt Rosa, and Aunt Dorcele, thank you for your calls and reminders of your love. To my parents, William and Norvella Carter and Edward and Cherilyn Jackson, I can never repay all you have poured into me. Nathaniel Jackson, I am nowhere near my best self without you. I am your biggest fan. I cannot believe where our journey has taken us. God is good. To my beautiful children, William, Josephine, and Charlotte, no one loves you more than I do. You are my revolution, my protection, my force, my flight, and my joy.

All that is good, brilliant, and uplifting in this book stems from the invaluable input of a community of scholars, friends, and family. The only exception to this is errors. Should anyone find faults, the failure is mine completely.

NOTES

Preface

1. Throughout this book I have chosen to follow Saida Grundy, Anne Price, Martha Biondi, Ashley Dennis, and other scholars in capitalizing the word "Black." I capitalize "Black" because it is used as often as synonymous with "African American" or people of African descent. It is a proper noun that reflects the self-naming and self-identification of a people whose national and ethnic origins have been obscured by a history of abduction, enslavement, and exploitation. Relatedly, "white" is not capitalized here because historically it has not been used to identify ethnic or national origin; rather, it has indicated social domination, power, and privilege. Anne Price, president of the Insight Center for Community Economic Development, writes, "In an 1878 editorial entitled 'Spell it with a Capital,' Ferdinand Lee Barnett, husband of Ida B. Wells and founder of a Black weekly newspaper, asserted that the failure of white people to capitalize Negro was [a way] to show disrespect to, stigmatize, and 'fasten a badge of inferiority' on Black people. In 1898, sociologist, historian, and civil rights activist W. E. B. Du Bois proclaimed, 'I believe that eight million Americans deserve a capital letter.'" It is with this in mind that I capitalize "Black." See Anne Price, "Spell It with a Capital 'B,'" Insight Center for Community Economic Development, Medium, October 1, 2019, https://insightcced.medium.com /spell-it-with-a-capital-b-9eab112d759a.

2. W. E. B. Du Bois, *Black Reconstruction in America, 1860–1880* (1935; New York: Free Press, 1998), 19.

3. Leo Tolstoy, "What Then Must We Do," in *The World's Classics*, trans. Aylmer Maude ([1942] 1886), 54, https://www.vidyaonline.net/dl/whatthenmustwedo.pdf.

4. Oscar Wilde, "The Soul of Man Under Socialism," in *In Praise of Disobedience: The Soul of Man Under Socialism and Other Works* (London: Verso, 2018), 1–40.

Introduction

1. For more on how racism creates and perpetuates disabilities, see Dennis Tyler's *Disabilities of the Color Line: Redressing Antiblackness from Slavery to the Present* (New York: New York University Press, 2022).

2. Black and Native studies scholars have discussed refusal as a practice and politic for some time now. See in particular Juliet Hooker, *Black Grief/White Grievance: The Politics of Loss* (Princeton, NJ: Princeton University Press, 2023); Tendayi Sithole's *Refiguring in Black* (Hoboken, NJ: Polity Press, 2023); Tina Campt's seminal monographs *Image Matters: Archive, Photography, and the African Diaspora in Europe* (Durham, NC: Duke University Press, 2012) and *Listening to Images* (Durham, NC: Duke University Press, 2017); and Audra Simpson's influential book *Mohawk Interruptus: Political Life Across the Borders of Settler States* (Durham, NC: Duke University Press, 2014).

3. See Vanessa Holden, *Surviving Southampton: African American Women and Resistance in Nat Turner's Community* (Urbana: University of Illinois Press, 2021).

4. Martin Luther King Jr., "Pilgrimage to Nonviolence," chap. 6 in *Stride Toward Freedom: The Montgomery Story* (New York: Harper and Row, 1958), 102; Martin Luther King Jr., *Where Do We Go from Here: Chaos or Community?* (New York: Harper and Row, 1967).

5. King, *Stride Toward Freedom*, 102.

6. Peter Gelderloos, *How Nonviolence Protects the State* (Boston: South End Press, 2007), 35.

7. Angela Davis, interview by Educational Video Group, 1972, shown in *The Black Power Mixtape 1967–1975*, dir. by Göran Hugo Olsson (New York: Sundance Selects, MPI Media Group, 2011). See also "Angela Davis: Interview from Jail," Alexander Street, https://video.alexanderstreet.com/watch /angela-davis-interview-from-jail.

8. Davis, interview.

9. David Leonhardt, "The Right's Violence Problem," The Morning Newsletter, *New York Times*, May 17, 2022, https://www.nytimes.com/2022/05/17 /briefing/right-wing-mass-shootings.html.

10. See Anti-Defamation League, *Murder and Extremism in the United States in 2021*, February 10, 2022, https://www.adl.org/murder-and-extremism -2021.

11. Desmond Tutu, interview by Terry Gross, *Fresh Air*, NPR, May 15, 1984, https://freshairarchive.org/segments/fresh-air-remembers-archbishop-desmond-tutu.

12. Regarding religion in America, I might disagree with Bishop Tutu. Certainly, today's white evangelical church does not see white supremacy as a problem. In fact, in many circles, it has become the clarion call to stir white parishioners to vote, act, or believe in the fantasy of better times (be it slavery or segregation) and long for the religious, cultural, and political subordination of people of color. Dr. Martin Luther King Jr.'s "Letter from a Birmingham Jail" speaks directly to how white moderates and white Christians abandoned their duty to fighting for righteousness and the poor.

13. Tutu, interview.

14. George Jackson to Robert Lester Jackson, April 11, 1968, in *Soledad Brother: The Prison Letters of George Jackson* (New York: Lawrence Hill, 1994), 128, https://www.historyisaweapon.com/defcon1/soledadbro.html.

15. Toni Morrison, "A Humanist View," speech, Portland State University, 1975, https://soundcloud.com/portland-state-library/portland-state-black-studies-1. "The function, the very serious function of racism is distraction. It keeps you from doing your work. It keeps you explaining, over and over again, your reason for being. Somebody says you have no language and you spend twenty years proving that you do. Somebody says your head isn't shaped properly so you have scientists working on the fact that it is. Somebody says you have no art, so you dredge that up. Somebody says you have no kingdoms, so you dredge that up. None of this is necessary. There will always be one more thing."

16. Sandy Alexandre, "Sandy Alexandre (An MIT Community Vigil)," YouTube video, 8:14, posted by Massachusetts Institute of Technology (MIT) on June 11, 2020, https://www.youtube.com/watch?v=tX-IIMsnaEU.

17. Alexandre, "An MIT Community Vigil."

18. While this quote is often attributed to Alexis de Tocqueville, nowhere in his book *Democracy in America* is this sentence or sentiment captured.

19. Audre Lorde, "The Uses of Anger: Women Responding to Racism," in *Sister Outsider: Essays and Speeches* (Berkeley, CA: Crossing Press, 2007), 125–133.

20. Ashley Simpo (@BlackAshley), "Some of us fight racism by raising our Black children to know joy. This matters too.," Twitter, May 29, 2020, 1:56 p.m., https://twitter.com/ashleysimpo/status/1266428248046612489.

21. Imani Perry, "Racism Is Terrible. Blackness Is Not," *The Atlantic*, June 15, 2020, https://www.theatlantic.com/ideas/archive/2020/06/racism-terrible-blackness-not/613039/.

22. See Ashon T. Crawley, *Blackpentecostal Breath: The Aesthetics of Possibility* (New York: Fordham University Press, 2016).

23. Quoted in Aaronette M. White, "All the Men Are Fighting for Freedom, All the Women Are Mourning Their Men, but Some of Us Carried Guns: A Raced-Gendered Analysis of Fanon's Psychological Perspectives on War," *Signs* 32, no. 4 (2007): 857–884, https://doi.org/10.1086/513021.

24. Frederick Douglass, *The Life and Times of Frederick Douglass* (Boston: De Wolfe and Fiske, 1892; Mineola, NY: Dover, 2003), quoted in Shayne Moore and Kimberley McCowen Yim, *Refuse to Do Nothing: Finding Your Power to Abolish Modern-Day Slavery* (Downers Grove, IL: IVP, 2014), 21.

25. Leslie A. Schwalm, *A Hard Fight for We* (Urbana: University of Illinois Press, 1997), 192.

26. Stephanie M. H. Camp, *Closer to Freedom: Enslaved Women and Everyday Resistance in the Plantation South* (Chapel Hill: University of North Carolina Press, 2004), 3.

27. See Mariame Kaba, interview by Josie Duffy Rice and Clint Smith, episode 20, *Justice in America* (podcast), March 20, 2019, https://theappeal.org/justice-in-america-episode-20-mariame-kaba-and-prison-abolition/.

28. Kaba, interview, *Justice in America*.

29. Toni Morrison, "No Place for Self-Pity, No Room for Fear," The Nation, March 23, 2015, https://www.thenation.com/article/archive/no-place-self-pity-no-room-fear/.

Chapter 1: Revolution

1. Vicky Osterweil, *In Defense of Looting: A Riotous History of Uncivil Action* (New York: Bold Type Books, 2020), 245–246.

2. Osterweil, *In Defense of Looting*, 245–246.

3. Franz Fanon, *The Wretched of The Earth*, trans. Constance Farrington, (New York: Grove Press, 1963), 313.

4. See Gerald Horne, *The Dawning of the Apocalypse: The Roots of Slavery, White Supremacy, Settler Colonialism, and Capitalism in the Long Sixteenth Century* (New York: Monthly Review, 2020).

5. Jean Casimir, *The Haitians: A Decolonial History* (Chapel Hill: University of North Carolina Press, 2020), 6.

6. Ella Baker, "The Black Woman in the Civil Rights Struggle," speech, Institute of the Black World, Atlanta, GA, 1969, transcript in Faith Holsaert Papers, Sallie Bingham Center for Women's History and Culture, Duke University, https://repository.duke.edu/dc/holsaertfaith/fhpst05001.

7. Carolyn E. Fick, *The Making of Haiti: The Saint Domingue Revolution from Below* (Knoxville: University of Tennessee Press, 1990), 93.

8. Sylviane Anna Diouf, *Servants of Allah: African Muslims Enslaved in the Americas* (New York: New York University Press, 2013), 152.

9. Laurent Dubois, *Avengers of the New World: The Story of the Haitian Revolution* (Cambridge, MA: Belknap Press of Harvard University Press, 2004), 243–245.

10. Quoted in Madison Smartt Bell, *Toussaint Louverture: A Biography* (New York: Vintage Books, 2008), 265.

11. Dubois, *Avengers of the New World*, 288–289.

12. Quoted in Dubois, *Avengers of the New World*, 292.

13. Quoted in Fick, *Making of Haiti*, 228.

14. C. L. R. James, *The Black Jacobins: Toussaint L'Ouverture and the San Domingo Revolution* (New York: Vintage, 1989), 361.

15. James, *Black Jacobins*, 315.

16. James, *Black Jacobins*, 315.

17. James, *Black Jacobins*, 315.

18. James, *Black Jacobins*, 361.

19. Quoted in Pierre-Louis Roederer, ed., *Oeuvres du Comte P. L. Roederer*, vol. 3 (Paris: Firmin, 1853), 461.

20. Natalie Leger, preface to *Haiti and the Unseen* (Nashville: Vanderbilt University Press, forthcoming).

21. Sibylle Fischer, "Inhabiting Rights," *L'Esprit Créateur* 56, no. 1 (2016): 52.

22. Michael J. Drexler and Ed White, "The Constitution of Toussaint: Another Origin of African American Literature," in *A Companion to African American Literature*, ed. Gene Andrew Jarrett (Oxford, UK: Wiley-Blackwell, 2013), 59.

23. Dubois, *Avengers of the New World*, 304.

24. Eugene Genovese, *Roll, Jordan, Roll: The World Slaves Made* (New York: Vintage, 1974), 592; Mitch Kachun, "Antebellum African Americans, Public Commemoration, and the Haitian Revolution: A Problem of Historical Mythmaking," *Journal of the Early Republic* 26, no. 2 (2006): 252.

25. Althéa de Puech Parham, ed., *My Odyssey: Experiences of a Young Refugee from Two Revolutions by a Creole of Saint Domingue* (Baton Rouge: Louisiana State University Press, 1959), 28; Martin Ros, *Night of Fire: The Black Napoleon and the Battle for Haiti* (New York: Sarpedon, 1994), 5–6. See also *A Particular Account of the Commencement and Progress of the Insurrection of the Negroes in St. Domingo* (London: J. Sewell, 1792), 5–9, which describes the brutal slaughter of white people living on the island.

26. See Brandon R. Byrd, *The Black Republic: African Americans and the Fate of Haiti* (Philadelphia: University of Pennsylvania Press, 2019): Black leadership dispelled the weak myth of white superiority. Over time, the West sought to marginalize the victory of Black revolutionary violence through isolation, erasure, political interventions, and economic exploitation.

27. David P. Geggus, preface to *The Impact of the Haitian Revolution in the Atlantic World*, ed. David P. Geggus (Columbia: University of South Carolina Press, 2002), x–xii; James Sidbury, *Ploughshares into Swords: Race, Rebellion and Identity in Gabriel's Virginia, 1730–1810* (New York: Cambridge University Press, 1998), 39–48; Douglas Egerton, *Gabriel's Rebellion: The Virginia Slave Conspiracies of 1800 and 1802* (Chapel Hill: University of North Carolina Press, 1993); Julius Scott, "The Common Wind: Currents in Afro-American Communication in the Era of the Haitian Revolution" (PhD diss., Duke University, 1986); Elizur Wright, *The Lesson of St. Domingo: How to Make the War Short and the Peace Righteous* (Boston: A. Williams, 1861).

28. Peter M. Beattie, ed., *The Human Tradition in Modern Brazil* (Wilmington, DE: Rowman and Littlefield, 2004), 31.

29. Dubois, *Avengers of the New World*, 305.

30. Alfred Hunt, *Haiti's Influence on Antebellum America: Slumbering Volcano in the Caribbean* (Baton Rouge: Louisiana State University Press, 1988), 190.

31. In 1799, the New York state legislature passed a law for gradual abolition. The law stipulated that the children of slaves born after July 4, 1799, were legally free, pending indentured servitude to the age of twenty-five for women and twenty-eight for men. Similarly, in 1804 New Jersey passed "An Act for the Gradual Abolition of Slavery," which granted freedom to enslaved women upon reaching the age of twenty-one and enslaved men upon turning twenty-five.

32. Robin Blackburn, "The Force of Example," in Geggus, *Impact of the Haitian Revolution*, 17.

33. Much has been written about the relationship between Black Americans and Haitians and the inspiration of the Haitian Revolution. See, e.g., Brandon Byrd, *The Black Republic: African Americans and the Fate of Haiti* (Philadelphia: University of Pennsylvania Press, 2020); Julius Scott, *The Common Wind: Afro-American Currents in the Age of the Haitian Revolution* (New York: Verso, 2018); and Matthew J. Clavin, *Toussaint Louverture and the American Civil War: The Promise and Peril of a Second Haitian Revolution* (Philadelphia: University of Pennsylvania Press, 2011).

34. All 103 issues of *Freedom's Journal* have been digitized by the Wisconsin Historical Society and placed online in two volumes (March 1827–March 1828 and April 1828–March 1829).

35. *Freedom's Journal*, May 4, 1827.

36. *Freedom's Journal*, April 27, 1827.

37. *Freedom's Journal*, October 17, 1828.

38. *Freedom's Journal*, May 4, 1827.

39. Made up of six small islands along a chain of Caribbean isles, Guadeloupe is just north of Dominica and Martinique and south of the smaller islands of Montserrat, Antigua, and Barbuda. Christopher Columbus landed there in 1493 and gave the island its name, though the Indigenous Caribs knew it as "Karukera," which meant "island of beautiful waters."

40. In 1999, artist Jacky Poulier designed and sculpted the statue of La Mulâtresse Solitude. It stands in the middle of the Héros aux Abymes Boulevard in Guadeloupe.

41. Sowande' M. Mustakeem, *Slavery at Sea: Terror, Sex, and Sickness in the Middle Passage* (Urbana: University of Illinois Press, 2016). See also Stephanie Smallwood, *Saltwater Slavery: A Middle Passage from Africa to American Diaspora* (Cambridge, MA: Harvard University Press, 2008).

42. Mustakeem, *Slavery at Sea*, 3–16.

43. Antoine Métral, *Histoire de l'insurrection des esclaves dans le nord de Saint-Domingue* (Paris: F. Sceref, 1818), 60; Bernard Moitt, *Women and Slavery in the French Antilles, 1635–1848* (Bloomington: Indiana University Press, 2001), 127.

44. Moitt, *Women and Slavery*, 127.

45. Moitt, *Women and Slavery*, 128; Auguste Lacour, *Histoire de la Guadeloupe* (Basse-Terre: Éditions de diffusion de la culture antillaise, 1976), 3:311.

46. Lacour, *Histoire de la Gaudeloupe*, 3:311.

47. Laurent Dubois, "Solitude's Statue: Confronting the Past in the French Caribbean," *Outre-mers* 93, nos. 350–351 (2006): 33.

48. Moitt, *Women and Slavery*, 128.

49. Moitt, *Women and Slavery*, 130.

50. Lacour, *Histoire de la Gaudeloupe*, vol. 3, chap. 4–7. See also Dubois, "Solitude's Statue."

51. Yarimar Bonilla, "The Past Is Made by Walking: Labor Activism and Historical Production in Postcolonial Guadeloupe," *Cultural Anthropology* 26, no. 3 (2011): 321–322.

52. Casimir, *Haitians*, 6.

53. Jonathan Dusenbury, "Slavery and the Revolutionary Histories of 1848," Age of Revolutions (website), October 10, 2016, https://ageofrevolutions.com/2016/10/10/slavery-and-the-revolutionary-histories-of-1848/.

54. John Adams, "Humphrey Ploughjogger to the *Boston Gazette*," *Boston Gazette*, October 14, 1765, in *Papers of John Adams*, ed. Robert J. Taylor, Mary-Jo Kline, and Gregg L. Lint, vol. 1, *September 1755–October 1773* (Cambridge, MA: Belknap Press of Harvard University Press, 1977), http://www.masshist.org/publications/adams-papers/index.php/view/PJA01d077.

55. Caesar Sarter, "Essay on Slavery," *Essex Journal and Merrimack Packet* (Newburyport, MA), August 17, 1774, http://rethinkingschools.org/wp-content/uploads/2020/06/ROC2-EssayOnSlavery.pdf.

56. Sarter, "Essay on Slavery."

57. Sarter, "Essay on Slavery." Bible verse is from Exodus 21:16.

58. Quoted in Manisha Sinha, *The Slave's Cause: A History of Abolition* (New Haven, CT: Yale University Press, 2016), 44. For more on this topic, see Christopher Cameron, *To Plead Our Own Cause: African Americans in Massachusetts and the Making of the Antislavery Movement* (Kent, OH: Kent State University Press, 2014).

59. Sinha, *Slave's Cause*, 44.

60. Sinha, *Slave's Cause*, 44.

61. William Brown, ad for return of Crispus Attucks, *Boston Gazette*, October 2, 1750, https://revolutionaryspaces.org/explore/exhibits/reflecting-attucks/reflecting-attucks-man-many-worlds/reflecting-attucks-putting-pieces-together/.

62. Brown, ad for return of Crispus Attucks.

63. See Jared Ross Hardesty, *Unfreedom: Slavery and Dependence in Eighteenth-Century Boston* (New York: New York University Press, 2016).

64. Patrick J. Kiger, "8 Things We Know About Crispus Attucks," History.com, February 3, 2020, https://www.history.com/news/crispus-attucks-american-revolution-boston-massacre. For more on Attucks, see Douglas R. Egerton, *Death or Liberty: African Americans and Revolutionary America* (New York: Oxford University Press, 2009).

65. Howard Zinn, *A People's History of the United States* (New York: Harper Collins, 2015), 67.

66. Kiger, "8 Things We Know." See also Egerton, *Death or Liberty*.

67. Kiger, "8 Things We Know."

68. Founded in 1660, Granary Burying Ground is Boston's third-oldest cemetery and serves as the final resting place for Revolutionary War patriots such as Paul Revere, Samuel Adams, and John Hancock.

69. John Adams, "Adams' Argument for the Defense: 3–4 December 1770," Founders Online, National Archives, https://founders.archives.gov/documents/Adams/05-03-02-0001-0004-0016.

70. For more on ideas and words associated with Black criminality in the eighteenth century, see Hardesty, *Unfreedom*; and John Garrison Marks, *Black Freedom in the Age of Slavery: Race, Status, and Identity in the Urban Americas* (Columbia: University of South Carolina Press, 2020).

71. Adams, "Argument for the Defense."

72. Adams, "Argument for the Defense."

73. See Nell Irvin Painter, *The History of White People* (New York: W. W. Norton, 2010).

74. Eric Hinderaker, *Boston's Massacre* (Cambridge, MA: Belknap Press of Harvard University Press, 2019).

75. Wendell Phillips, "Crispus Attucks," speech, Faneuil Hall, Boston, March 5, 1858, in Wendell Phillips, *Speeches, Lectures and Letters*, ed. Theodore C. Pease (Boston: Lee and Shepard, 1891), 69–70.

76. Martin Luther King Jr., *Why We Can't Wait* (New York: Signet Classics, 2000), ix, quoted in Mitch Kachun, *First Martyr of Liberty: Crispus Attucks in American Memory* (New York: Oxford University Press, 2017), 169.

77. Stokely Carmichael, "African American Involvement in the Vietnam War," speech, Garfield High School, Seattle, WA, April 19, 1967, quoted in Kachun, *First Martyr of Liberty*, 169.

78. Kachun, *First Martyr of Liberty*, 226–238.

79. Sinha, *Slave's Cause*, 49.

80. Frederick Douglass, "What to the Slave Is the Fourth of July?," speech, Rochester, NY, July 5, 1852, abridged version at https://masshumanities.org /files/programs/douglass/speech_abridged_med.pdf.

81. Frederick Douglass, "Lecture on Haiti," speech, Haitian Pavilion, World's Fair, Chicago, January 2, 1893, transcript at http://faculty.webster .edu/corbetre/haiti/history/1844-1915/douglass.htm.

82. Douglass, "What to the Slave."

83. "Civil Rights Act of 1875," African American Civil Rights Movement (website), University of Massachusetts History Club, accessed November 27, 2023, http://www.african-american-civil-rights.org/civil-rights-act-of-1875/.

84. Quoted in Ta-Nehisi Coates, *We Were Eight Years in Power* (New York: One World Publishing, 2017), xiii. See also "Sept. 10, 1895: South Carolina Constitutional Convention Convened," Zinn Education Project (website), accessed November 27, 2023, https://www.zinnedproject.org/news/tdih /sc-constitutional-convention.

Chapter 2: Protection

1. A note on the meaning of violence is important. I am examining the utility of violence in the broadest definition possible; thus violence is not merely physical but also rhetorical, emotional, and destructive. In my own work, *Force and Freedom: Black Abolitionists and the Politics of Violence*, I define violence as a political language, a way of communicating to oppressive forces when traditional avenues for reform, such as the ballot, are not available. See also Ella Forbes, "'By My Own Right Arm': Redemptive Violence and the 1851 Christiana, Pennsylvania Resistance," *Journal of Negro History* 83, no. 3 (1998):

159–167. Forbes rightly argues that "the use of a rhetoric of redemptive violence was designed to exhort African-Americans to resist oppression but more importantly, it sought to establish the African's right to resist" (163).

2. Zoé Samudzi and William C. Anderson, *As Black as Resistance: Finding the Conditions for Liberation* (Edinburgh: AK Press, 2018), 78.

3. Ellen N. Lawson, "Lucy Stanton: Life on the Cutting Edge," *Western Reserve Magazine*, January–February 1993, 9.

4. Kellie Carter Jackson, *Force and Freedom: Black Abolitionists and the Politics of Violence* (Philadelphia: University of Pennsylvania Press, 2019), 50–51.

5. *Chicago Journal*, June 13, 1851, reprinted in the *Liberator*, July 11, 1851.

6. Frederick Douglass, "Capt. John Brown Not Insane," *Douglass' Monthly* (Rochester, NY), November 1859, https://heinonline.org/HOL/Page?collection =slavery&handle=hein.slavery/dougmo0001&id=151&men_tab=srchresultsn.

7. Lucy Stanton, "A Plea for the Oppressed," in *The Three Sarahs: Documents of Antebellum Black College Women*, ed. Ellen NicKenzie Lawson and Marlene D. Merrill (New York: Edwin Mellen, 1984), 203–208.

8. Stanton, "Plea for the Oppressed," 203–208.

9. Stanton, "Plea for the Oppressed," 203.

10. Stanton, "Plea for the Oppressed," 203.

11. Benjamin Quarles, *Black Abolitionists* (New York: Oxford University Press, 1969), 204–205; Nina Moore Tiffany, *Samuel E. Sewall: A Memoir* (Boston: Houghton Mifflin, 1898), 63; Leonard W. Levy, "The 'Abolition Riot': Boston's First Slave Rescue," *New England Quarterly* 25, no. 1 (1952): 85–92.

12. Julie Roy Jeffrey, *The Great Silent Army of Abolitionism: Ordinary Women in the Antislavery Movement* (Chapel Hill: University of North Carolina Press, 1998), 179; Joan E. Cashin, "Black Families in the Old Northwest," *Journal of the Early Republic* 15, no. 3 (1995): 474; Dorothy Sterling, *We Are Your Sisters: Black Women in the Nineteenth Century* (New York: W. W. Norton, 1991), 222.

13. Lawson and Merrill, *Three Sarahs*, 284; Jeffrey, *Great Silent Army*, 177–178.

14. William Parker, "The Freedman's Story," *Atlantic Monthly*, February 1866.

15. J. D. B. DeBow, *Statistical View of the United States* [. . .] *a Compendium of the Seventh Census* [. . .] (Washington, DC: Beverley Tucker, Senate Printer, 1854), 63–65.

16. For more on Eliza and William Parker, see Stanley W. Campbell, *The Slave Catchers: Enforcement of the Fugitive Slave Law, 1850–1860* (Chapel Hill: University of North Carolina Press, 1970); and John Hope Franklin and Loren Schweninger, *Runaway Slaves: Rebels on the Plantation* (New York: Oxford University Press, 1999).

17. Parker, "Freedman's Story," 161.

18. Parker, "Freedman's Story," 283.

19. Parker, "Freedman's Story," 160, 163, 165, 286; Thomas P. Slaughter, *Bloody Dawn: The Christiana Riot and Racial Violence in the Antebellum North* (New York: Oxford University Press, 1991), 57–61.

20. Parker, "Freedman's Story," 284.

21. *Frederick Douglass' Paper*, September 25, 1851; Forbes, "'By My Own Right Arm.'"

22. Parker, "Freedman's Story," 288.

23. Parker, "Freedman's Story," 289–292.

24. Frederick Douglass, *The Life and Times of Frederick Douglass* (Boston: De Wolfe and Fiske, 1892; Mineola, NY: Dover, 2003), 334.

25. Slaughter, *Bloody Dawn*, 57.

26. Slaughter, *Bloody Dawn*, 78–79.

27. Parker, "Freedman's Story," 292.

28. Parker, "Freedman's Story," 292.

29. Slaughter, *Bloody Dawn*, 96–97; *Pennsylvania Freeman*, September 1851, reprinted from the *New York Independent*.

30. Slaughter, *Bloody Dawn*, 97–99.

31. Slaughter, *Bloody Dawn*, 97–99. The 1847 antikidnapping act worked to severely limit local efforts to assist in the recapture of fugitive slaves. Governor Johnston was known to be a Free-Soiler, and in 1847 he switched from the Democratic Party to the Whig Party in order to run for the Pennsylvania Senate. After the Christiana Resistance, Johnston lost his reelection bid.

32. Slaughter, *Bloody Dawn*, 97–99.

33. Slaughter, *Bloody Dawn*, 96–97.

34. Slaughter, *Bloody Dawn*, 182.

35. Jeffrey, *Great Silent Army*, 183.

36. *Liberator*, December 12, 1845; George DeBaptiste to Douglass, November 5, 1854, in *Frederick Douglass' Paper*, November 17, 1854; *Provincial Freeman*, May 31, 1856; *Frederick Douglass' Paper*, January 26, 1855; Quarles, *Black Abolitionists*, 153.

37. Jeffrey, *Great Silent Army*, 182.

38. While some might argue that David Ruggles was the father of the Underground Railroad, Still maintains this title in popular culture, not because he was the first conductor but because he was responsible for shepherding so many people and he kept extensive records regarding enslaved runaways, published in his self-published book *The Underground Railroad Records*. Ruggles and Still each assisted one of the greatest abolitionists: Ruggles, Frederick Douglass; and Still, Harriet Tubman. Ruggles was plagued by poor health and died rather young at the age of thirty-nine, while Still

lived to be eighty years old. For more on Ruggles, see Graham Russell Gao Hodges, *David Ruggles: A Radical Black Abolitionist and the Underground Railroad in New York City* (Chapel Hill: University of North Carolina Press, 2010).

39. Nikki Taylor, interview by Henry Louis Gates Jr., *The African Americans: Many Rivers to Cross, with Henry Louis Gates Jr.*, "The Age of Slavery," episode 2, season 1, aired October 29, 2013, on PBS. See also Nikki M. Taylor, *Driven Toward Madness: The Fugitive Slave Margaret Garner and Tragedy on the Ohio* (Athens: Ohio University Press, 2016).

40. American Anti-Slavery Society, Annual Report (New York), May 7, 1856, p. 46; also quoted in Julius Yanuck, "The Garner Fugitive Slave Case," *The Mississippi Valley Historical Review* 40, no. 1 (1953): 65, https://doi.org /10.2307/1897542.

41. Stanton, "Plea for the Oppressed."

42. Catherine Clinton, *Harriet Tubman: The Road to Freedom* (New York: Little, Brown, 2004), 90–91.

43. Kate Clifford Larson, *Bound for the Promised Land: Harriet Tubman, Portrait of an American Hero* (New York: Ballantine, 2004), 157.

44. Jean M. Humez, *Harriet Tubman: The Life and the Life Stories* (Madison: University of Wisconsin Press, 2003), 34.

45. Clinton, *Harriet Tubman*, 132.

46. Abraham Lincoln, First Inaugural Address, March 4, 1861, *Chicago Tribune*, pamphlet, Gilder Lehrman Institute of American History, https://www.gilderlehrman.org/history-resources/spotlight-primary-source /president-lincoln%E2%80%99s-first-inaugural-address-1861.

47. Alice George, "Why Harriet Tubman's Heroic Military Career Is Now Easier to Envision," *Smithsonian Magazine*, June 8, 2020, https:// www.smithsonianmag.com/smithsonian-institution/why-harriet-tubmans -heroic-military-career-now-easier-envision-180975038/.

48. George, "Why Harriet Tubman's."

49. George, "Why Harriet Tubman's."

50. Franklin B. Sanborn, *Commonwealth* (Boston, MA), July 10, 1863. See also Earl Conrad, "General Tubman," HarrietTubman.com, accessed October 10, 2023, http://www.harriettubman.com/tubman2.html.

51. George, "Why Harriet Tubman's."

52. Thavolia Glymph, "Rose's War and the Gendered Politics of a Slave Insurgency in the Civil War," *Journal of the Civil War Era* 3, no. 4 (2013): 501–532.

53. Glymph, "Rose's War," 522.

54. John R. McKivigan, Joseph R. McElrath, and Jesse S. Crisler eds., *The Frederick Douglass Papers, Series II: Autobiographical Writings, Volume III:*

Life and Times of Frederick Douglass (New Haven, CT: Yale University Press, 2012), 367.

55. Bruce E. Baker, *This Mob Will Surely Take My Life: Lynchings in the Carolinas, 1871–1947* (London: Continuum, 2008), 71–92.

56. Baker, *This Mob Will Surely*, 71–92.

57. Quoted in Mary King, *Freedom Song: A Personal Story of the 1960s Civil Rights Movement* (New York: William Morrow, 1987), 318.

58. Charles E. Cobb Jr., *This Nonviolent Stuff'll Get You Killed: How Guns Made the Civil Rights Movement Possible* (Durham, NC: Duke University Press, 2014), 3. See also Hasan Kwame Jeffries, *Bloody Lowndes: Civil Rights and Black Power in Alabama's Black Belt* (New York: New York University Press, 2010).

59. See Lance Hill, *The Deacons for Defense: Armed Resistance and the Civil Rights Movement* (Chapel Hill: University of North Carolina Press, 2005).

60. Black Panther Party, "The Black Panther Party Ten-Point Program," October 15, 1966, BlackPast.org, https://www.blackpast.org/african-american -history/primary-documents-african-american-history/black-panther-party-ten -point-program-1966/. See also Huey P. Newton, "War Against the Panthers: A Study of Repression in America" (PhD diss., University of California, Santa Cruz, 1980).

61. For more, see Curtis J. Austin, *Up Against the Wall: Violence in the Making and Unmaking of the Black Panther Party* (Fayetteville: University of Arkansas Press, 2006).

62. Robyn C. Spencer, *The Revolution Has Come: Black Power, Gender, and the Black Panther Party in Oakland* (Durham, NC: Duke University Press, 2016), 59.

63. David Hilliard, ed., *The Black Panther Party: Service to the People Programs* (Albuquerque: University of New Mexico Press, 2008).

64. Alondra Nelson, *Body and Soul: The Black Panther Party and the Fight Against Medical Discrimination* (Minneapolis: University of Minnesota Press, 2011).

65. Hilliard, *Black Panther Party*.

66. Jisha Joseph, "90-Year-Old Grandmother Steps in Front of Black Grandson to Defend Him from Gun-Wielding Policemen," Upworthy.com, June 1, 2020, https://scoop.upworthy.com/90-year-old-grandmother-tries-defend -Black-grandson-gun-wielding-cops.

67. "90-Yr-Old Grandmother Steps in Front of Cops to Protect Grandson," *Tribune* (India), May 28, 2020, https://www.tribuneindia.com/news/world /90-yr-old-grandmother-steps-in-front-of-cops-to-protect-grandson-92084.

68. For more information on lynching in Texas, see the Lynching in Texas website, hosted by Sam Houston State University, https://lynchingintexas.org/.

69. In Midland, the local high school, which opened in 1961, was named after Robert E. Lee until October 2020, when the school board voted to change its name to Legacy High School. Mitch Borden, "After 59 Years, Midland ISD Agrees to Change the Name of Robert E. Lee High," *Texas Standard*, August 3, 2020; Shelby Webb, "Fight over Whether to Change Name of Robert E. Lee High School Leaves Scars in Baytown," *Houston Chronicle*, March 24, 2021.

Chapter 3: Force

1. For more on Black violence, see Kellie Carter Jackson, *Force and Freedom: Black Abolitionists and the Politics of Violence* (Philadelphia: University of Pennsylvania Press, 2019); Bruce E. Baker, *This Mob Will Surely Take My Life: Lynchings in the Carolinas, 1871–1947* (London: Continuum, 2008), 71–92 (regarding the lynching of Manse Waldrop); Lance Hill, *The Deacons for Defense: Armed Resistance and the Civil Rights Movement* (Chapel Hill: University of North Carolina Press, 2005); Carol Anderson, *The Second: Race and Guns in a Fatally Unequal America* (New York: Bloomsbury, 2021); Nicholas Johnson, *Negroes and the Gun: The Black Tradition of Arms* (New York: Prometheus, 2014); Akinyele Omowale Umoja, *We Will Shoot Back: Armed Resistance in the Mississippi Freedom Movement* (New York: New York University Press, 2014); David F. Krugler, *1919, the Year of Racial Violence: How African Americans Fought Back* (New York: Cambridge University Press, 2014); Charles E. Cobb Jr., *This Nonviolent Stuff'll Get You Killed: How Guns Made the Civil Rights Movement Possible* (Durham, NC: Duke University Press, 2014); and Elizabeth Hinton, *America on Fire: The Untold History of Police Violence and Black Rebellion Since the 1960s* (New York: Liveright, 2021).

2. Anderson, *The Second*.

3. United States Supreme Court, Roger Brooke Taney, John H. Van Evrie, and Samuel. A Cartwright, *The Dred Scott Decision: Opinion of Chief Justice Taney* (New York: Van Evrie, Horton & Co., 1860), https://www.loc.gov/item/17001543/.

4. Frederick Douglass, "Men of Color, to Arms!," *Douglass' Monthly*, March 21, 1863, https://www.americanantiquarian.org/Manuscripts/menofcolor.html.

5. Douglass, "Men of Color, to Arms!"

6. Douglass, "Men of Color, to Arms!"

7. Abraham Lincoln, speech, Richmond, Virginia, April 4, 1865, in *Recollected Words of Abraham Lincoln*, ed. Don Edward Fehrenbacher and Virginia Fehrenbacher (Stanford, CA: Stanford University Press, 1996), 257.

8. Nicholas J. Johnson, "A Considered African American Philosophy and Practice of Arms," *Journal of African American History* 107, no. 2 (2022): 164–166.

9. Carol Anderson, *White Rage: The Unspoken Truth of Our Racial Divide* (New York: Bloomsbury, 2016), 3.

10. W. E. B. Du Bois, "Returning Soldiers," *The Crisis*, May 1919, 13.

11. Krugler, *1919*, 5.

12. Ursula Wolfe-Rocca, "Remembering Red Summer—Which Textbooks Seem Eager to Forget," Zinn Education Project (website), September 17, 2020, https://www.zinnedproject.org/if-we-knew-our-history/remembering-red-summer.

13. Carter G. Woodson, *The Negro in Our History* (Washington, DC: Associated Publishers, 1922), 326–328.

14. It is important to note that the homes in this neighborhood no longer exist because of changes in city planning over time.

15. Krugler, *1919*, 85.

16. "Mobs in Race Clash Surge Through Streets," *Washington Evening Star*, July 22, 1919, 2.

17. Patrick Sauer, "One Hundred Years Ago, a Four-Day Race Riot Engulfed Washington, D.C.," *Smithsonian Magazine*, July 17, 2019, https://www.smithsonianmag.com/history/one-hundred-years-ago-four-day-race-riot-engulfed-washington-dc-180972666/.

18. Delia Mellis, "'Literally Devoured': Washington, D.C., 1919," *Studies in the Literary Imagination* 40, no. 2 (2007): 1–24.

19. "Girl to Be Tried in Murder," January 11, 1921; "Girl Faces Murder Charge," July 9, 1921; "Girl Is Convicted in Wilson's Death," January 14, 1921; "Girl Gets New Trial," June 4, 1921; all in *Washington Post*.

20. "They Started It," *Washington Bee*, July 36, 1919.

21. Mellis, "'Literally Devoured.'"

22. Quoted in Sauer, "One Hundred Years Ago."

23. Quoted in Sauer, "One Hundred Years Ago."

24. Martina Simms, "Washington Riot," *Afro-American*, August 15, 1919, https://www.flickr.com/photos/washington_area_spark/8449563264.

25. Quoted in Mellis, "'Literally Devoured.'"

26. Quoted in Jefferson Morley, "The D.C. Race War of 1919: And the Forgotten Story of One African American Girl Accused of Murdering a Police Officer," *Washington Post*, July 17, 2019, https://www.washingtonpost.com/news/magazine/wp/2019/07/17/feature/the-d-c-race-war-of-1919-and-the-forgotten-story-of-one-african-american-girl-accused-of-murder/.

27. Morley, "D.C. Race War of 1919."

28. Krugler, *1919*, 226–227.

29. Krugler, *1919*, 226–227.

30. Morley, "D.C. Race War of 1919."

31. Teresa Krug, "A Rural Town Confronts Its Buried History of Mass Killings of Black Americans," *The Guardian*, August 18, 2019, https://www .theguardian.com/us-news/2019/aug/18/a-rural-town-confronts-its-buried -history-of-mass-killings-of-black-americans.

32. Linda Reed, "The Legacy of Daisy Bates," *Arkansas Historical Quarterly* 26, no. 5 (1996): 616–628.

33. Daisy Bates, *The Long Shadow of Little Rock* (New York: David McKay, 1962), 22; Linda A. Reed, "The Legacy of Daisy Bates," *Arkansas Historical Quarterly* 59, no. 1 (2000): 76–83.

34. Quoted in Carolyn Calloway-Thomas and Thurmon Garner, "Daisy Bates and the Little Rock School Crisis: Forging the Way," *Journal of Black Studies* 26, no. 5 (1996): 616–628.

35. Bates, *Long Shadow of Little Rock*, 111.

36. Quoted in Bates, *Long Shadow of Little Rock*, 111.

37. United States Department of the Interior, National Park Service, National Historic Landmark Nomination, Bates, Daisy, House, https://npgallery. nps.gov/NRHP/GetAsset/NHLS/01000072_text.

38. Timothy B. Tyson, *Radio Free Dixie: Robert F. Williams and the Roots of Black Power* (Chapel Hill: University of North Carolina Press, 2001), 159.

39. Tyson, *Radio Free Dixie*, 159.

40. Tyson, *Radio Free Dixie*, 159.

41. Daisy Bates to Thurgood Marshall, August 3, 1959, box 2, Daisy Bates Papers (State Historical Society of Wisconsin); Marshall on Bates, Grif Stockley, *Daisy Bates: Civil Rights Crusader from Arkansas* (Jackson: University of Mississippi Press, 2005), 132.

42. Bates, *Long Shadow of Little Rock*, 96, 158–159, 174; Stockley, *Daisy Bates*, 186.

43. Stockley, *Daisy Bates*, 187; *Afro-American*, October 18, 1958.

44. "National Historic Landmark Nomination for Daisy Bates House," National Park Service.

45. Lerone Bennett Jr., "First Lady of Little Rock," *Ebony*, September 1958, 17–18.

46. Bennett, "First Lady of Little Rock," 17.

47. Bennett, "First Lady of Little Rock," 22.

48. Bates, *Long Shadow of Little Rock*, 96, 158–159, 174; Stockley, *Daisy Bates*, 186.

49. Editorial, *Arkansas State Press*, December 13, 1957, quoted in Grif Stockley, "Arkansas State Press," Encyclopedia of Arkansas, Butler Center for Arkansas Studies, July 11, 2023, https://encyclopediaofarkansas.net/entries /arkansas-state-press-592/.

50. Quoted in "The Robert Williams Case," *The Crisis*, June–July 1959, 327–329; see also quoted in Timothy B. Tyson, "Robert F. Williams, NAACP Warrior and Rebel," *Crisis*, December/January 1998, 17.

51. Editorial, *Arkansas State Press*, May 23, 1959.

52. Quoted in Tyson, *Radio Free Dixie*, 165.

53. Robert F. Williams to Daisy Bates, August 17, 1959, box 2, Bates Papers, State Historical Society of Wisconsin, Madison, WI; Tyson, *Radio Free Dixie*, 165.

54. *Baltimore Afro-American*, May 23, 1959.

55. *Jet*, February 25, 1960.

56. Daisy Bates, "Tribute to Negro Women Fighters for Freedom," speech, March on Washington, Washington, DC, August 28, 1963, transcript at "Daisy Bates Speaks at the 1963 March on Washington," blog post, AnnaJuliaCooper.com, 2012, http://cooperproject.org/daisy-bates -speaks-at-the-1963-march-on-washington/.

57. Pero Gaglo Dagbovie, "'God Has Spared Me to Tell My Story': Mabel Robinson Williams and the Civil Rights–Black Power Movement," *Black Scholar* 43, nos. 1–2 (2013): 70.

58. Mabel Williams, interview by David Cecelski, interview K-0266, Listening for a Change, Southern Oral History Program, University of North Carolina at Chapel Hill, August 20, 1999, transcript excerpt in David Cecelski, "Mabel Williams: Standing Up to the Klan," Listening to History, *News and Observer* (Raleigh, NC), November 14, 1999.

59. Ida B. Wells, "Southern Horrors: Lynch Law in All Its Phases" (1892), https://www.digitalhistory.uh.edu/disp_textbook.cfm?smtid=3&psid=3614.

60. Quoted in Charles M. Payne, *I've Got the Light of Freedom: The Organizing Tradition and the Mississippi Freedom Struggle* (Berkeley: University of California Press, 1995), 233.

61. Tyson, *Radio Free Dixie*, 307; Rosa Parks, eulogy for Robert F. Williams, Central Methodist Church, Monroe, NC, November 22, 1996, description from notes by Timothy B. Tyson, who was in attendance.

62. Ron Grossman, "Flashback: A Chicago Family Defied a Racist Real Estate Covenant. The Backlash and Legal Fight Inspired 'A Raisin in the Sun,'" *Chicago Tribune*, July 10, 2020, https://www.chicagotribune.com/history /ct-opinion-flashback-hansberry-house-restrictive-convenant-20200710 -dslzaju35ngmpghgwazpcodosq-story.html.

63. Mabel Williams, "Liberty and the Choice of Weapons," *The Crusader*, June 25, 1960, 52 edition; Jasmin A. Young, "Strapped: A Historical Analysis of Black Women and Armed Resistance, 1959–1979" (PhD diss., Rutgers University, 2018), 98.

64. Cole's wife's car was stuck in a ditch. The Lumbee people helped get her out of the ditch and back on the road. Within a year of the battle, she filed for divorce. Brandon Weber, "The Battle of Hayes Pond: How Indian Country Defeated the KKK," *Native America Today*, accessed November 27, 2023, https://nativeamericatoday.com/the-battle-of-hayes-pond/.

65. "'The Kissing Case' and the Lives It Shattered," *Morning Edition*, NPR, April 29, 2011, https://www.npr.org/2011/04/29/135815465/the-kissing-case-and-the-lives-it-shattered.

66. Williams, interview by Cecelski.

67. Williams, interview by Cecelski.

68. Young, "Strapped," 105.

69. Williams, interview by Cecelski.

70. Williams, interview by Cecelski.

71. Pero Gaglo Dagbovie, "'God Has Spared Me to Tell My Story': Mabel Robinson Williams and the Civil Rights–Black Power Movement." *The Black Scholar* 43, no. 1–2 (2013): 78, https://doi.org/10.5816/blackscholar.43.1-2.0069.

72. Dagbovie, "'God Has Spared Me,'" 78.

73. Dagbovie, "'God Has Spared Me,'" 73.

74. Quoted in Vicky Osterweil, *In Defense of Looting: A History of Uncivil Action* (New York: Bold Type Books, 2020), 172.

75. Osterweil, *In Defense of Looting*, 172.

76. University of Wisconsin–Madison and Texas A&M University, "Top 100 American Speeches of the 20th Century," accessed October 22, 2023, https://news.wisc.edu/archive/misc/speeches/.

77. Malcolm X, "The Ballot or the Bullet," speech, April 3, 1964, Cory Methodist Church, Cleveland, OH, transcript at SoJust: Social Justice Speeches, EdChange, accessed November 27, 2023, http://www.edchange.org/multicultural/speeches/malcolm_x_ballot.html.

78. Joseph R. Fitzgerald, *The Struggle Is Eternal: Gloria Richardson and Black Liberation* (Lexington: University Press of Kentucky, 2018), 183.

79. Malcolm X, "The Ballot or the Bullet," speech, April 12, 1964, King Solomon Baptist Church, Detroit, MI, transcript at American RadioWorks, American Public Media, accessed November 27, 2023, https://americanradioworks.publicradio.org/features/blackspeech/mx.html.

80. Cobb, *This Nonviolent Stuff'll*, 241.

81. Toni Morrison, interview by Charlie Rose, *Charlie Rose*, PBS, May 7, 1993.

Chapter 4: Flight

1. On the Great Migration, see, e.g., Isabel Wilkerson, *The Warmth of Other Suns: The Epic Story of America's Great Migration* (New York: Vintage, 2011).

2. Jamaica Kincaid, *A Small Place* (New York: Farrar, Straus and Giroux, 1988), 18–19.

3. Dunmore's Proclamation, *Pennsylvania Journal and Weekly Advertiser*, December 6, 1775, Gilder Lehrman Institute of American History, GLC01706, https://www.gilderlehrman.org/history-resources/spotlight-primary-source /lord-dunmores-proclamation-1775.

4. For more on the flight of the enslaved, see Cassandra Pybus, *Epic Journeys of Freedom: Runaway Slaves of the American Revolution and Their Global Quest for Liberty* (Boston: Beacon, 2007); and W. E. B. Du Bois, *Black Reconstruction in America, 1860–1880* (New York: Harcourt, Brace, 1935).

5. Toni-Lee Maitland, "Slavery and Revolution: Henry Laurens and the Problem of Freedom" (undergraduate honors thesis, University of Florida, 2014), 33, http://ufdc.ufl.edu/AA00057636/00001; S. Max Edelson, *Plantation Enterprise in Colonial South Carolina* (Cambridge, MA: Harvard University Press, 2011), 244.

6. See Graham Russell Hodges, ed., *The Black Loyalist Directory: African Americans in Exile After the American Revolution* (New York: Garland, 1995).

7. Elizabeth Stordeur Pryor, *Colored Travelers: Mobility and the Fight for Citizenship Before the Civil War* (Chapel Hill: University of North Carolina Press, 2016), 47.

8. See Erica Armstrong Dunbar, *Never Caught: The Washingtons' Relentless Pursuit of Their Runaway Slave, Ona Judge* (New York: 37 Ink, 2017).

9. Adams, T. H., Rev., "Washington's Runaway Slave," The Granite Freeman, May 22, 1845, https://karinwulf.com/wp-content/uploads/2017/11 /KW-Never-Caught-Source-Reader.pdf.

10. Quoted in Stephanie M. H. Camp, "'I Could Not Stay There': Enslaved Women, Truancy and the Geography of Everyday Forms of Resistance in the Antebellum Plantation South," *Slavery and Abolition* 23, no. 3 (2002): 1–20, http://dx.doi.org/10.1080/714005245.

11. See William Lloyd Garrison, *Thoughts on African Colonization, or an Impartial Exhibition of the Doctrines, Principles and Purposes of the American Colonization Society* [. . .] (Boston: Garrison and Knapp, 1832); and Eric Burin, *Slavery and the Peculiar Solution: A History of the American Colonization Society* (Gainesville: University of Florida, 2008).

12. Zephaniah Kingsley, "A Treatise on the Patriarchal, or Co-operative System of Society (1828–1[8]34)," in Daniel Stowell, ed., *Balancing Evils Judiciously: The Proslavery Writings of Zephaniah Kingsley* (Gainesville: University Press of Florida, 2000), 39–75.

13. Quoted in Megan Special, "Overlooked No More: How One Woman Shook Up the Abolitionist Movement," *New York Times*, June 7, 2018.

14. Colored National Labor Convention, Proceedings of the Colored National Labor Convention, Washington, DC., December 6–10, 1869, Colored Conventions Project Digital Records, https://coloredconventions.org/mary-ann-shadd-cary/shadd-cary-and-the-conventions/1869-labor-convention/.

15. *Provincial Freeman*, April 8, 1857; Kellie Carter Jackson, *Force and Freedom: Black Abolitionists and the Politics of Violence* (Philadelphia: University of Pennsylvania Press, 2019), 102–103.

16. Laurent Dubois, *Haiti: The Aftershocks of History* (New York: Henry Holt, 2012), 135; Manisha Sinha, *The Slave's Cause: A History of Abolition* (New Haven, CT: Yale University Press, 2016), 563.

17. *Weekly Anglo-African*, April 20, 1860; Chris Dixon, "An Ambivalent Black Nationalism: Haiti, Africa, and Antebellum African-American Emigrationism," *Australasian Journal of American Studies* 10, no. 2 (1991): 14.

18. Laurent Dubois and Deborah Jenson, "Haiti Can Be Rich Again," *New York Times*, January 8, 2012. The island did not limit its support to Black Americans. In fact, during the Civil War, Haiti was one of the few Caribbean islands that welcomed the US Navy and helped to maintain the Union blockade in the Florida Straits—a strategically important point during the war (Dubois, *Haiti*, 153). It was also during this time that the United States gave diplomatic recognition to Haiti for its efforts. Haiti also filled a gap left by the American South by exporting cotton to the United States until the war was over. Given this favorable atmosphere, by 1861 the Black abolitionist James Theodore Holly, who later became the first Black Episcopal missionary bishop of Haiti, had succeeded in settling a group of Black Americans east of Croix-des-Bouquets. See James Theodore Holly, *A Vindication of the Capacity of the Negro Race for Self-Government and Civilized Progress, as Demonstrated by Historical Events of the Haytian Revolution* [. . .] (New Haven, CT: W. H. Stanley, 1857). See also Maurice Jackson and Jacqueline Bacon, eds., *African Americans and the Haitian Revolution: Selected Essays and Historical Documents* (New York: Routledge, 2010).

19. I. Garland Penn, *The Afro-American Press and Its Editors* (Springfield, MA: Willey, 1891), 86–88; C. Peter Ripley, *The Black Abolitionist Papers: Vol. V: The United States, 1859–1865* (Chapel Hill: University of North Carolina Press, 2015), 28–29.

20. Benjamin Quarles, *Black Abolitionists* (New York: Oxford University Press, 1969), 222; Jackson, *Force and Freedom*, 152–153.

21. Frederick Douglass, *Douglass' Monthly*, May 1861, vol. 3, no. 1, 449–450, https://edan.si.edu/transcription/pdf_files/12961.pdf; Howard Holman Bell, *A Survey of the Negro Convention Movement, 1830–1861* (New York: Arno Press, 1969), 221; see also David P. Geggus, preface to *The Impact of the Haitian*

Revolution in the Atlantic World, ed. David P. Geggus (Columbia: University of South Carolina Press, 2002), xvi.

22. William J. Watkins, speech, Ohio, transcript in *Pine and Palm*, November 23, 1861, Black Abolitionist Archives, doc. no. 24731, University of Detroit Mercy.

23. Watkins, speech, 1861.

24. Watkins, speech, 1861. The Ohio newspaper's article was reprinted in the *Pine and Palm*, but researchers believe it was originally printed in the *Toledo* (OH) *Daily*.

25. See Brandon Byrd, *The Black Republic: African Americans and the Fate of Haiti* (Philadelphia: University of Pennsylvania Press, 2019); Leslie Alexander, *Fear of a Black Republic: Haiti and the Birth of Black Internationalism* (Urbana: University of Illinois Press, 2022); Dixon, "Ambivalent Black Nationalism," 14; and Chris Dixon, *African America and Haiti: Emigration and Black Nationalism in the Nineteenth Century* (Westport, CT: Greenwood, 2000).

26. Du Bois, *Black Reconstruction in America*, 59.

27. For more, see Pryor, *Colored Travelers*.

28. Lynn Maria Hudson, *The Making of "Mammy Pleasant": A Black Entrepreneur in Nineteenth-Century San Francisco* (Urbana: University of Illinois Press, 2002); Jason B. Johnson, "A Day for 'Mother of Civil Rights': Entrepreneur Sued to Desegregate Streetcars in 1860s," *San Francisco Chronicle*, February 10, 2005.

29. "Chesapeake, Ohio & Southwestern Railroad Company v. Ida B. Wells, (Supreme Court of Tennessee; April Term, 1887)," *Southwestern Reporter* (St. Paul: West Publishing Company, 1886), 5.

30. Ida B. Wells, *Crusade for Justice: The Autobiography of Ida B. Wells*, ed. Alfreda M. Duster (Chicago: University of Chicago Press, 1970), xviii, quoted in Mia Bay, *To Tell the Truth Freely: The Life of Ida B. Wells* (New York: Hill and Wang, 2009), 67.

31. Paula Giddings, *Ida: A Sword Among Lions: Ida B. Wells and the Campaign Against Lynching* (New York: Amistad Press, 2008), 207.

32. Quoted in Giddings, *Ida*, 178–180, 183, 207.

33. Frederick Douglass to Ida B. Wells, October 25, 1892, in *African American Classics in Criminology and Criminal Justice*, ed. Shaun L. Gabbidon, Helen Taylor Greene, and Vernetta Diane Young (New York: Sage, 2002), 25.

34. Gary Totten, "Embodying Segregation: Ida B. Wells and the Cultural Work of Travel," *African American Review* 42, no. 1 (2008): 47–60.

35. Quoted in Totten, "Embodying Segregation," 48.

36. *Southwestern Christian Advocate*, April 26, 1917.

37. Anonymous to Dr. ––, letter, East Chicago, IN, June 10, 1917, in "Letters from South to Friends North and from North to Friends South,"

Journal of Negro History 4, no. 3 (1919): 464, https://www.gutenberg.org/files/21093/21093-h/21093-h.htm.

38. Anonymous, letter, Philadelphia, PA, October 7, 1917, in "Letters from South to Friends North and from North to Friends South," *Journal of Negro History* 4, no. 3 (1919): 461–462, https://www.gutenberg.org/files/21093/21093-h/21093-h.htm.

39. Robin D. G. Kelley, "'We Are Not What We Seem': Rethinking Black Working-Class Opposition in the Jim Crow South," *Journal of American History* 80, no. 1 (1993): 103.

40. Kelley, "'We Are Not What We Seem,'" 104.

41. Quoted in Kelley, "'We Are Not What We Seem,'" 104.

42. Quoted in Kelley, "'We Are Not What We Seem,'" 105.

43. Amanda Dawkins, "'Unsung Hero' of Boycott Paved Way for Parks," *Huntsville Times*, February 7, 2005, 6B.

44. Kelley, "'We Are Not What We Seem,'" 103–105.

45. Ever Lee's story is told in Henry Wiencek, *The Hairstons: An American Family in Black and White* (New York: St. Martin's, 1999). See also Brittany Luse and Eric Giddings, "The Best of the Nod: The Hairstons," *The Nod* (podcast), August 6, 2018, https://gimletmedia.com/shows/the-nod/v4hbvo.

46. Luse and Giddings, "The Hairstons."

47. Luse and Giddings, "The Hairstons."

48. Wiencek, *Hairstons*.

49. "How Ever Lee Hairston Overcame Racism, Poverty and Disability to Realize Her Dream," KCAL News, February 26, 2021, CBSNews.com, https://www.cbsnews.com/losangeles/news/how-ever-lee-hairston-overcame-racism-poverty-and-disability-to-realize-her-dream/.

50. Luse and Giddings, "The Hairstons."

51. Luse and Giddings, "The Hairstons."

52. Luse and Giddings, "The Hairstons."

53. Joanne Hershfield, dir., *Mama C: Urban Warrior in the African Bush* (Perennial Films, 2013).

54. "A Highflying Groundbreaker," *Chicago Tribune*, December 30, 1990, p. 19; quoted in Kim Creasman, "Black Birds in the Sky: The Legacies of Bessie Coleman and Dr. Mae Jemison," *The Journal of Negro History* 82, no. 1 (1997): 158.

55. Philip Hart, *Flying Free: America's First Black Aviators* (Minneapolis, MN: Lerner, 1992), 14–17.

56. Tammy Gibson, "O'Hare Airport Honors Bessie Coleman," *The Chicago Defender*, August 11, 2021, https://chicagodefender.com/ohare-airport-honors-bessie-coleman/.

57. Maria Lynn Toth, "Daredevil of the Sky: The Bessie Coleman Story," *Los Angeles Times*, February 10, 2001.

58. Toth, "Daredevil of the Sky."

Chapter 5: Joy

1. Tara A. Bynum, *Reading Pleasures: Everyday Black Living in Early America* (Urbana: University of Illinois Press, 2023), 3.

2. Charles McKinney, "We are not solely the history of fighting…" June 12, 2020, https://www.facebook.com/charles.mckinney.353/posts/pfbid0t FRQPtusQ5smCFaoD7GfKDn8jakGsoNZUPBuANgXpUbDUtHs bUjzoPty5dqHoPBDl; see also quoted in Kellie Carter Jackson, "Black Joy—Not Corporate Acknowledgment—Is the Heart of Juneteenth," June 19, 2020, The Atlantic, https://www.theatlantic.com/culture/archive/2020/06 /juneteenth-has-always-been-worthy-celebration/613270/?fbclid=IwAR3WO rNAhQOh9xr-y4fsMYsyrguyst92fYgOYs-s5HzLB00965AEzyjKq6s.

3. Imani Perry, "Racism Is Terrible. Blackness Is Not," *The Atlantic*, June 15, 2020, https://www.theatlantic.com/ideas/archive/2020/06/racism -terrible-Blackness-not/613039/.

4. Antoine Métral, *Histoire de l'insurrection des esclaves dans le nord de Saint-Domingue* (Paris: F. Sceref, 1818).

5. The phrase "You OK, sis?" became a campaign to combat street harassment and intervene when strangers became aggressive in publicly taunting women. See Amanda Rosa, "You OK, Sis?," *Affinity*, November 14, 2015, https://affinitymagazine.us/2015/11/14/20151207you-ok-sis/.

6. North Carolina Department of Public Instruction, "Biennial Report of the Superintendent of Public Instruction of North Carolina for the Scholastic Years 1933–1934 and 1935–1936," https://archive.org/stream/biennialreportof 19341936nort/biennialreportof19341936nort_djvu.txt.

7. See American Public Media, "Jim Crow Laws," https://americanradioworks .publicradio.org/features/remembering/laws.html.

8. See Carol Anderson, *One Person, No Vote: How Voter Suppression Is Destroying Our Democracy* (London: Bloomsbury, 2018).

9. Barbara Jeanne Fields, "Slavery, Race and Ideology in the United States of America," *New Left Review*, May/June 1990, 110.

10. Fields, "Slavery, Race and Ideology," 97n3.

11. Fields, "Slavery, Race and Ideology," 110.

12. Shomik Mukherjee, "Five Years Ago, Oakland's Infamous 'BBQ Becky' Confrontation Gave Racism a New Name," *Times-Herald* (Vallejo, CA), July 4, 2023, https://www.timesheraldonline.com/2023/07/04/five-years -ago-oaklands-infamous-bbq-becky-confrontation-gave-racism-a-new-name-2/.

13. Mukherjee, "Gave Racism a New Name."

14. Antonia Noori Farzan, "BBQ Becky, Permit Patty and Cornerstore Caroline: Too 'Cutesy' for Those White Women Calling Police on Black People?," *Washington Post*, October 19, 2018, https://www.washingtonpost.com /news/morning-mix/wp/2018/10/19/bbq-becky-permit-patty-and-cornerstore -caroline-too-cutesy-for-those-White-women-calling-cops-on-Blacks/; "BBQ Becky: Woman Photoshopped into Black History After Barbecue Complaint," BBC.com, May 18, 2018, https://www.bbc.com/news/newsbeat-44167760; "Listen: 'BBQ Becky's' Viral 911 Call Made Public," YouTube video, 12:40, posted by KTVU FOX 2 San Francisco on August 31, 2018, https://www .youtube.com/watch?v=LgaU1h0QiLo.

15. Mukherjee, "Gave Racism a New Name."

16. Mukherjee, "Gave Racism a New Name." See also Brandon Griggs, "A Black Yale Graduate Student Took a Nap in Her Dorm's Common Room. So a White Student Called Police," CNN.com, May 12, 2018, https://www.cnn .com/2018/05/09/us/yale-student-napping-black-trnd/index.html.

17. James Cone, *Malcolm and Martin in America: A Dream or a Nightmare* (New York: Orbis, 1991), 333.

18. See, e.g., Kimberly "Sweet Brown" Wilkins being interviewed after escaping a fire in an apartment complex, which aired on April 8, 2012, on Oklahoma City NBC affiliate KFOR-TV and then went viral on YouTube.

19. Paul Gallagher, "Antoine Dodson: From Local News Item to Internet Sensation," *The Guardian*, August 15, 2010; "Antoine Dodson: Riding YouTube Out of the 'Hood,'" *Tell Me More*, NPR, August 23, 2010.

20. Aimé Césaire, *Notebook of a Return to the Native Land* (Middletown, CT: Wesleyan University Press, 2001), 45.

21. W. E. B. Du Bois, "The Humor of Negroes," *Mark Twain Quarterly*, Fall–Winter 1942, reprinted in *Mark Twain Journal*, Spring 1998, p. 8.

22. "Keke Palmer Takes a Lie Detector Test," YouTube video, 11:43, posted by Vanity Fair on September 11, 2019, https://www.youtube.com /watch?v=YBwAAAOa9Kk&t=216s.

23. Du Bois, "Humor of Negroes."

24. C. Brandon Ogbunu, "Go Ahead, Joke About the Pandemic: The Public Health Power of Humor on Black Twitter," *The Atlantic*, November 12, 2022.

25. Miles Orvell, ed., "Alvin Ailey," in *Encyclopedia of American Studies* (Baltimore: Johns Hopkins University Press, 2011), https://eas-ref.press.jhu .edu/ailey_alvin.html.

26. Stephanie M. H. Camp, *Closer to Freedom: Enslaved Women and Everyday Resistance in the Planation South* (Chapel Hill: University of North Carolina Press, 2004), 60.

27. Camp, *Closer to Freedom*, 61.

28. Camp, *Closer to Freedom*, 85.

29. Bynum, *Reading Pleasures*, 1.

30. Tera W. Hunter, *To 'Joy My Freedom: Southern Black Women's Lives and Labors After the Civil War* (Cambridge, MA: Harvard University Press, 1997), 169.

31. Hunter, *To 'Joy My Freedom*, 185; John Fiske, *Understanding Popular Culture* (Boston: Unwin Hyman, 1989), 49–95.

32. "Reverend S S Jones Rare Footage of All Black Towns of Oklahoma," YouTube video, 5:49, posted by NMAAHC [National Museum of African American History and Culture, Smithsonian] on May 30, 2021, https://www.youtube.com/watch?app=desktop&v=GU5yKtp76HY.

33. Toni Morrison, "It Is Like Growing Up Black One More Time," *New York Times*, August 11, 1974.

34. Morrison, "Like Growing Up Black."

35. Encyclopedia.com, s.v. "frolic," accessed October 26, 2023, https://www.encyclopedia.com/social-sciences-and-law/law/law/frolic.

36. Tomas Kassahun, "Black Men Are Frolicking and Bringing Some Much-Needed Joy to the Internet," Blavity, May 25, 2022, https://blavity.com/black-men-are-frolicking-and-bringing-some-much-needed-joy-to-the-internet.

37. Perry, "Racism Is Terrible."

38. See Thavolia Glymph, *Out of the House of Bondage: The Transformation of the Plantation Household* (New York: Cambridge University Press, 2008); Hunter, *To 'Joy My Freedom*, 59–61.

39. Hunter, *To 'Joy My Freedom*, 50.

40. Hunter, *To 'Joy My Freedom*, 12; "Sixty-Five Years a 'Washer & Ironer,'" in *God Struck Me Dead: Religious Conversion Experiences and Autobiographies of Negro Ex-Slaves*, ed. A. P. Watson, Paul Radin, and Charles S. Johnson (Westport, CT: Greenwood, 1972), 186. See also Emma J. S. Prescott, "Reminiscences of the War," typescript, p. 53, Atlanta History Center, Atlanta, GA.

41. Testimony of Mrs. Ward, November 15, 1883, *Report of the Committee of the Senate upon the Relations Between Labor and Capital* (Washington, DC: US Government Printing Office, 1885), 4: 328, quoted in Hunter, *To 'Joy My Freedom*, 60.

42. Hunter, *To 'Joy My Freedom*, 1–2.

43. Robin D. G. Kelley, *Race Rebels: Culture, Politics, and the Black Working Class* (New York: Free Press, 1996), 1–3.

44. Kelley, *Race Rebels*, 1–3.

45. See Blair LM Kelley, *Black Folk: The Roots of the Black Working Class* (New York: Liveright, 2023).

46. Carvell Wallace, "Why 'Black Panther' Is a Defining Moment for Black America," *New York Times Magazine*, February 12, 2018, https://www.nytimes

.com/2018/02/12/magazine/why-black-panther-is-a-defining-moment-for
-black-america.html.

47. Wallace, "Why 'Black Panther.'"

48. Wallace, "Why 'Black Panther.'"

49. Wallace, "Why 'Black Panther.'"

50. Jamil Smith, "The Revolutionary Power of Black Panther," *Time*, February 19, 2018, https://time.com/Black-panther/.

51. Donald R. Wright, "The Effect of Alex Haley's 'Roots' on How Gambians Remember the Atlantic Slave Trade," *History in Africa* 38 (2011): 300.

52. Erica L. Ball and Kellie Carter Jackson, introduction to *Reconsidering Roots: Race, Politics, and Memory*, ed. Erica L. Ball and Kellie Carter Jackson (Athens: University of Georgia Press, 2017).

53. Linda Williams, *Playing the Race Card: Melodramas of Black and White from Uncle Tom to O.J. Simpson* (Princeton, NJ: Princeton University Press, 2001), 239.

54. William L. Van Deburg, *Slavery and Race in American Popular Culture* (Madison: University of Wisconsin Press, 1984), 155.

55. Robert J. Norrell, *Alex Haley and the Books That Changed a Nation* (New York: St. Martin's, 2015), 168.

56. Haley, "What Roots Means to Me," *Reader's Digest*, 110 (May 1977), 73–76.

57. Michelle Hudson, "The Effect of *Roots* and the Bicentennial on Genealogical Interest Among Patrons of the Mississippi Department of Archives and History," *Journal of Mississippi History* 53, no. 4 (1991): 321–336.

58. For more on Alex Haley and his controversy regarding plagiarism and authenticity, see Ball and Jackson, *Reconsidering Roots*; and Matthew Delmont, *Making of Roots: A Nation Captivated* (Oakland: University of California Press, 2016).

59. bell hooks, *All About Love: New Visions* (New York: William Morrow, 2000).

60. hooks, *All About Love*. See also Kellie Carter Jackson, "Grief Is Evidence of Love," *The Atlantic*, December 20, 2021, https://www.theatlantic.com/culture/archive/2021/12/bell-hooks-you-cant-get-through-grief-alone/621051/.

61. Zora Neale Hurston, "How It Feels to Be Colored Me," in *You Don't Know Us Negroes and Other Essays*, ed. Henry Louis Gates Jr. and Genevieve West (New York: Amistad, 2022), 187.

Drowning: A Postscript

1. Jamaica Kincaid, *A Small Place* (New York: Farrar, Straus and Giroux, 1988), 80–81.

INDEX

Kellie Carter Jackson is the Michael and Denise Kellen '68 Associate Professor of Africana Studies at Wellesley College. Her book *Force and Freedom* was a finalist for the Frederick Douglass Book Prize and the Museum of African American History Stone Book Award. She lives outside of Boston.